John Gilbert

Documents Relating to Ireland, 1795-1804

John Gilbert

Documents Relating to Ireland, 1795-1804

ISBN/EAN: 9783337322236

Printed in Europe, USA, Canada, Australia, Japan

Cover: Foto ©ninafisch / pixelio.de

More available books at **www.hansebooks.com**

DOCUMENTS

RELATING TO

IRELAND, 1795–1804:

OFFICIAL ACCOUNT OF SECRET SERVICE MONEY.
GOVERNMENTAL CORRESPONDENCE AND PAPERS.
NOTICE OF FRENCH SOLDIERY AT KILLALA.
STATEMENTS BY UNITED IRISHMEN.
LETTERS ON LEGISLATIVE UNION WITH GREAT BRITAIN, Etc.

EDITED BY

JOHN T. GILBERT, LL.D., F.S.A., M.R.I.A.,

LATE SECRETARY OF THE PUBLIC RECORD OFFICE OF IRELAND;
AUTHOR OF "A HISTORY OF THE CITY OF DUBLIN;" "HISTORY OF VICEROYS OF IRELAND;"
"CALENDARS OF ANCIENT RECORDS OF DUBLIN;"
EDITOR OF "FACSIMILES OF NATIONAL MSS. OF IRELAND;" CHARTULARIES OF CISTERCIAN INSTITUTIONS IN IRELAND;
"CONTEMPORARY HISTORY OF IRELAND, 1641-1652;" "HISTORY OF THE IRISH CONFEDERATION AND WAR;"
REGISTER OF ABBEY OF ST. THOMAS, DUBLIN; MSS. OF JAMES, FIRST EARL OF CHARLEMONT;
JACOBITE NARRATIVE OF WAR IN IRELAND, 1688-1691, ETC.

ILLUSTRATED WITH PORTRAITS AND FACSIMILES.

DUBLIN:
PRINTED FOR THE EDITOR BY
JOSEPH DOLLARD, WELLINGTON-QUAY.
1893.

[*All rights reserved.*]

PREFACE.

The contents of this volume illustrate portions of the history of a period of high interest and importance.

Methods and views of administrators of the Government in Ireland at the time are disclosed in some of the documents here printed, while others of them furnish authentic details in connection with the movements of the "United Irishmen," who projected the establishment of a republic in Ireland.

The Secret Service money, in relation to which an original record is reproduced in the following pages, was issued under the tenth section of an act[1] passed by the parliament in Ireland in 1793. By it the High Treasurer, Vice-Treasurer, Vice-Treasurers, or other authorized persons, were empowered to make payments to the principal secretary of the Lord Lieutenant, or other chief governor of Ireland for the time being, for secret service in detecting, preventing or defeating treasonable or other dangerous conspiracies against the State in any place in the kingdom of Ireland.

The original manuscript account of Secret Service money here printed is of small quarto size, bound in plain green vellum. The contents are written in a minute and occasionally indistinct style, in

---

[1] "An act for the support of the honour and dignity of his majesty's crown in Ireland, and for granting to his majesty a civil list establishment under certain provisions and regulations."—33 George III., cap. 34. The tenth section concludes as follows:—"And that it shall be sufficient to acquit and discharge such secretary to whom such secret service hath been paid, to make oath before one of the barons of the exchequer in the form following:—I, A.B., do swear that the money paid to me for secret service for the purposes of detecting, preventing, or defeating treasonable or other dangerous conspiracies against the State, has been bona fide applied to such purposes and no other. So help me God."—"Statutes passed in the parliaments held in Ireland," vol. ix., p. 730, Dublin: 1799.

black and red inks, somewhat faded and occasionally illegible. The total number of leaves in the book is eighty-six. On the left-hand pages are entered the monies received from the Treasury and the statements of the balances carried forward. The sums registered as received, with the respective dates, are printed on page 3 of the present volume, and amount in all to fifty-four thousand five hundred pounds.

The payments commence on 21 August, 1797, and terminate on 31 March, 1804. These entries are in order of date on the right-hand pages of the book, and are here printed line for line, as they stand in the original.

The "Principal Secretaries" to the Lords Lieutenant, referred to in the accounts as having sanctioned payments, were Thomas Pelham, Robert Stewart, Viscount Castlereagh, and William Wickham.

From August, 1797, to 1801 the payments were, according to memoranda[1] in the book, vouched by affidavit of Edward Cooke, Under-Secretary of the Civil Department of the Government in Ireland. Cooke, on his resignation in 1801, was succeeded as Under-Secretary at Dublin Castle by Alexander Marsden, who was in office in 1804, in March of which year the entries in the book terminate.

The manuscript, about the year 1840, came by purchase into the hands of a bookseller in Dublin.[2] It was subsequently acquired by Charles Haliday, a Dublin merchant, director of the Bank of Ireland, and member of the Royal Irish Academy. After the death of Haliday in 1866, the volume, with his collection of books and manuscripts, was presented by his representative to the Royal Irish Academy, in the library of which institution it has been carefully preserved, and its contents are now for the first time printed in full.

The accounts contain numerous entries of payments made to individuals who furnished private information to the Government of

---

[1] *See* pp. 2, 62.

[2] Under the heading of "Items extracted from an original official document," several entries from the book were published by R. R. Madden, M.D., in his work on the "United Irishmen," 1842, 1858.

the day, and some of whom appeared as witnesses on behalf of the Crown against associates to whom they had been pledged by solemn engagements. The highest aggregate amount here entered as paid to any one of this class, for himself, is six thousand pounds to Thomas Reynolds. Lord Castlereagh considered that Reynolds rendered "truly important services" to the country. Curran,[1] in an address at the bar of the House of Commons, in Dublin, averred that Reynolds, "by his own confession, was an informer and a bribed informer. A man, whom," he continued, "seven respectable witnesses had sworn, in a court of justice upon their oaths, not to be credible on his oath— a man upon whose single testimony no jury ever did nor ever ought to pronounce a verdict of guilty; a kind of man to whom the law resorts with abhorrence and from necessity, in order to set the criminal against the crime; but who is made use of by the law upon the same reason that the most noxious poisons are resorted to in medicine."

Among the Crown witnesses named in the accounts before us as paid at lower rates, and either by occasional sums or periodical allowances, were William Lawler, alias Wright, who gave evidence against the "Defenders" in 1796; James Feris, an ex-attorney of ill-repute;[2] and Hugh Wheatley, an intemperate Scotch "Fencible," who swore against William Orr,[3] in 1797.

Some of the "informers" were domiciled in a tower of the Castle of Dublin, near apartments in which Governmental deliberations were held. To this class of "informers" and their localization Curran referred as follows in 1797:—

"I speak not now of the public proclamations for informers with a promise of secrecy and extravagant reward. I speak not of those unfortunate wretches who have been so often transferred from the table to the dock and from the dock to the pillory. I speak of what your own eyes have seen, day after day, during the course of this commission while you attended this court:—the number of horrid miscreants who acknowledged

---

[1] Speeches of J. P. Curran, Dublin: 1805, p. 242.
[2] Trials of James Dunn and Patrick Carty for conspiring to murder the Earl of Carhampton, Dublin, 1797.
[3] Trial of William Orr, of Farranshane, in the county of Antrim. Dublin: 1797.

upon their oaths that they had come from the seat of Government—from the very chambers of the Castle [of Dublin], where they had been worked upon by the fear of death and the hopes of compensation to give evidence against their fellows; that the mild, the wholesome and virtuous councils of this Government are holden over those catacombs of living death, where the wretch that is buried a *man* lies till his heart has time to fester and dissolve, and then is dug up an *Informer*.

Is this a picture created by a hag-ridden fancy or is it fact? Have you not seen him after his resurrection from that tomb, make his appearance upon your table, the living image of life and death, and the supreme arbiter of both? Have you not marked when he entered, how the stormy wave of the multitude retired at his approach? Have you not seen how the human heart bowed to the awful supremacy of his power in the undissembled homage of deferential horror? How his glance, like the lightning of heaven, seemed to rive the body of the accused and mark it for the grave, while his voice warned the devoted wretch of woe and death—a death which no innocence can escape, no art elude, no force resist, no antidote prevent? There was an antidote—a juror's oath. But even that adamantine chain, which bound the integrity of man to the throne of eternal justice, is solved and molten by the breath which issues from the mouth of the informer; conscience swings from her moorings, the appalled and affrighted juror speaks what his soul abhors, and consults his own safety in the surrender of the victim."[1]

Several of the prisoners and Crown witnesses were for a time in the charge of James O'Brien, to whom many payments appear in the accounts before us. His evidence on oath was discredited by a Dublin jury in the case of Patrick Finney, tried in 1798, before Justice Chamberlain and Baron Smith. O'Brien acted under Henry Charles Sirr, deputy town major of Dublin, till found guilty of a murder, for which he was executed in 1800. Continuous payments are entered to Sirr and men on "his list," or actively employed by him. He, according to Curran, was invested by the Government at Dublin, "with all the real powers of the most absolute authority."

Lord Castlereagh, in a letter[2] from Dublin Castle, in November, 1798, stated that he felt it an incumbent duty on him to bear testimony in the strongest terms to the merits of Sirr, who had been constantly

---

[1] "Report of the trial of Peter Finerty upon an indictment for a libel." By William Ridgeway, Barrister-at-law. Dublin, 1798, p. 83.
[2] Memoirs and correspondence of Viscount Castlereagh, 1850, i., 428.

employed confidentially by the Government. In an official note[1] to Castlereagh towards the close of 1800, Cooke the Under-Secretary, wrote:—" I think it might be right to get rid of many of our little pensioners, and major Sirr's gang, by sums of money instead of pensions. Marsden will be kind enough to confer with Sirr upon the several cases, and see which can be got rid of by a sum of money [and] which require stipends."

Disbursements made in accordance with this suggestion appear in the accounts, where they are entered as settlements "in full of claims on Government for services."

Some entries of the payments to and in connection with Edward John Newell tend to confirm statements in a publication issued under his name, in 1798, as a confession of his penitence for having acted as an informer to Government. Newell, an unskilful miniature painter of dissolute character, born in Downpatrick, was engaged by Governmental officials to supply evidence on oath in relation to treasonable designs of United Irishmen, of whose Society he was a member. Disguised as a light horseman, with blackened face, he traversed at night the streets of Belfast, accompanied by a guard of soldiers, who, under his orders, arrested and carried to prison such persons as he indicated. Newell subsequently described the proceedings of himself and his associates under official protection as a series of acts of perjury and imposture, alternated with luxurious debauchery, maintained by lavish expenditure of funds derived from Governmental sources.[2]

Among the various recipients of Secret Service money were the following: the Protestant bishops of Derry and Killaloe, the Rev. Mr. Nelligan, of Ballina, the parish priests of Mallow and Middleton, and the Rev. George Lambart. Payments of considerable sums appear to others, as one thousand pounds to Richard Jones; seven hundred pounds to J. Magin or Maguan; five hundred pounds to Dr. Harding, from Cork; five hundred pounds to George Clibborn; one hundred

---

[1] Cornwallis Correspondence, 1859, iii., 320.
[2] For further notice of Newell, see p. xiv.

pounds to Lord Boyle; and periodical instalments to Henry St. George Cole. Francis Magan, called to the bar at Dublin in 1796, is here set down for sums amounting to nine hundred pounds, of which five hundred were paid by direction of William Wickham, Chief Secretary.

James Mac Guckin, attorney of Belfast, agent and legal adviser to United Irishmen in Ulster, also received large sums as well as a pension, for the valuable and correct information in relation to their movements which he supplied to Government. He had been described officially as " a most active, mischievous rebel, and a most dangerous man." John Pollock, attorney, registrar to William Downes, justice of the King's bench, Dublin, was an acute agent under the secret service arrangements. Pollock, in addition to the many payments here entered to him, obtained the appointment of Clerk of the Crown for the Leinster circuit. Cooke, in a letter[1] to Lord Castlereagh, urged Pollock's claim to a pension on the ground that he had "done much," and had secured for Government the services of Leonard Mac Nally and James Mac Guckin.

In some instances initial letters only for the recipients of the money are entered in the accounts—occasionally with brief mention of the special objects in view, or reference to the persons by whom the amounts were transmitted, or by whose sanction the disbursements were made.

The highest single sum entered under initials is that on 20 June, 1798 :—" F. H., discovery of L. E. F., £1,000." This is believed to indicate payment to Francis Higgins for information which led to the capture of Lord Edward Fitzgerald on the 18th of the preceding month. The amount thus paid was offered by proclamation on 11 May, 1798, for the apprehension of Lord Edward.

Among the payments here recorded under initials are the following : B., £100; F., £100; G. M. J., £50, £50, £100; K., £50, £100; N., £30; W. A. H., £68 5s.

Sums entered to L. M., M. N., and T. W., or J. W., are assignable

---

[1] Cornwallis Correspondence, 1859, iii., 320.

to Leonard Mac Nally, a member of the bar both in England and Ireland, dramatic author and compiler of law books. The initials " McG " indicate James Mac Guckin, already mentioned.[1]

Out of the Secret Service fund payments were made for guards, conveyances, subsistence and medical attendance for prisoners, prosecutions, executions and miscellaneous objects. Disbursements are entered in connection with the arrests of the delegates of the United Irish Society, in Dublin, in March, 1798, and of Lord Edward Fitzgerald in May of the same year.

Payments appear to major Swan, who assisted in arresting Lord Edward, and to the widow of Captain Daniel Ryan, who died from wounds received in the struggle. There are also entries for medical attendance on Lord Edward in prison, and while he was "in a delirium."

Expenses are entered in relation to the removal to Dublin of Theobald Wolfe Tone, from Derry, and of his brother, Matthew, taken prisoner at Ballinamuck. A charge also appears for horses from Naas, with John Esmonde, M.D., who, after trial by court-martial, was hanged on Carlisle bridge, Dublin.

In the accounts is a disbursement for the "Beauties of the Press." This was the title of a volume containing reprints of articles from Arthur O'Connor's Dublin newspaper styled the "Press," which was suppressed by Government in 1798.

From an entry in the accounts we learn that a report of the trial of Henry and John Sheares, at Dublin in 1798, was printed at London, under the direction of Lord Castlereagh, and paid for out of the Secret Service fund. Reports of Curran's defences of Sheares and of other political prisoners at the same period are stated to have been suppressed.[2] It appears from an entry at page 38 that the Government

---

[1] Details on these and correlative matters will be found in works of W. E. H. Lecky, W. J. Fitzpatrick and the late R. R. Madden, M.D. The subject of Secret Service payments in England, during the administrations of Lords North and Shelburne, is at present under investigation by Mr. B. F. Stevens, Editor of "Facsimiles of Manuscripts in European Archives relating to America," London: 1892.

[2] Life of J. P. Curran, by his son. Edinburgh: 1822, vol. ii., pp. 3, 64.

officials defrayed from the Secret Service funds the cost of a pamphlet issued at Dublin in 1798, with the object of impressing on Roman Catholics in Ireland that domination by French "Jacobins and Atheists" would be fatal to them. The title-page of this publication was as follows :—" The Fall of Underwald, one of the Catholic cantons of Switzerland.[1] By a native of Araw, its capital, who was an eye-witness. Translated from the German."

To notice other matters of interest recorded in these Secret Service accounts would exceed our present limits, but to facilitate reference a copious index has been appended.

The letters and documents in the second part of the present volume extend from 1795 to 1799. Many of them are from the hitherto unpublished papers of Thomas Pelham, Chief Secretary to the Lord Lieutenant of Ireland,[2] from 1795 to 1798, and subsequently Earl of Chichester. Sir Jonah Barrington mentioned that Pelham, without great talents, had "good sense, good manners, a frank address, with humane, honourable and just intentions."

---

[1] The following is from pages 13, 14 of the "Fall of Underwald":—"Every one knows the cruelty of the French Republicans, and how many defenceless creatures have on every occasion been sacrificed in cold blood, as victims of their uncontrolled barbarity; their conduct is but too familiar to all Europe, their plunder of all property, their violation of everything that is esteemed most sacred, their confiscations, their sacrilege, and their massacres; but never was their inhuman rage more strongly exemplified than on this day, so fatal to my gallant countrymen. Our priests, our nuns, our old men, our wives and children, were indiscriminately butchered even at the altar. Churches, houses, the property of the unoffending and defenceless inhabitants, the little fortunes which the unremitted labours of a century had accumulated, were all given as a prey to the flames. Standztaadt, Bucks, Beckened, and every house as far as Ennemos, are burnt to ashes. The ground is everywhere strewed with bodies and covered with blood, and the smoke still ascending from the ruins of our once peaceable and happy dwellings, spreads itself over the whole atmosphere, and adds to the horror of the scene. Such are the glories of France! Such the triumphs of Jacobins and Atheists."

[2] Pelham at the same time sat as member for Armagh in the House of Commons, Ireland. He had been Chief Secretary in Ireland in 1783-4; member for Carrick; Privy Councillor in Ireland and Great Britain. Pelham was summoned to Parliament as Baron Pelham in 1801; he held the office of Secretary of State for the Home Department, 1801-3, was Chancellor of the Duchy of Lancaster in 1803; and Post-Master General, 1807 till 1826, in which year he died.

In addition to letters written by Thomas Pelham, there will be found here communications from Earl Camden and Marquis Cornwallis, viceroys of Ireland; Luttrell, Earl of Carhampton; Viscounts Carleton and Castlereagh; Edward Cooke; General Dalrymple; William Elliot, Richard Griffith, Frederick Augustus Hervey, Earl of Bristol and Bishop of Derry, General Gerard Lake, Robert Marshall, Francis Moylan, Roman Catholic Bishop of Cork; the Duke of Portland; Sir George Shee; and Matthew Young, Protestant Bishop of Clonfert.

The communications relate to contemporary public affairs in England and Ireland, and the writers, for the most part, apparently intended them to be regarded as of a private and confidential character.

Among the papers here printed[1] for the first time, is a private report made in 1795 to the Duke of York by Henry Lawes Luttrell, Earl of Carhampton, Lieutenant-General of the army in Ireland, on the defenceless state of Dublin in case of a coup de main. "There is," wrote Carhampton, "no part of the king's dominions so much exposed to the attempts of the enemy in this war as Ireland. It is high time to understand its situation, to take measures for its safety, and no longer to delay, because its infatuated inhabitants seem lulled into a fatal security."

"It must be clear to demonstration to those who have consider'd the subject, and know its relative situation to the ports of Brest, port L'Orient and Rochefort, that a body of 3,000 men and a few field pieces might be equipped, unknown to us, from either of those ports, be landed in the vicinity of Dublin, and possess it before the inhabitants were well aware of the attempt. In the space of twenty-four hours a million of money, at least, might be raised in contribution, the city handed over to a municipality formed of the dregs of the people, who, armed with pikes and whiskey, would probably plunder and burn the town, and the whole kingdom then be undone for a century to come. I do assert that an attempt of this nature could not fail of success at this very hour: a wind from west to south, including the eight intermediate points, lasting three days, would serve to bring over and disembark a body of troops sufficient for the attempt; two days more to effect their purpose and re-embark; and were it then to blow from another quarter, they could escape from superior force, by Belfast, without a probability of being overtaken."

---

[1] Pages 91-99.

Killiney bay, where frigates might anchor in five fathoms of water, was, according to Carhampton, "the place best calculated for disembarkation, a firm, sandy, dry beach, where fifteen hundred men at least, together with field pieces in proportion, might be landed at once in any time of tide, not up to their knees in water, and possession of the heights overlooking Dublin taken before eight hundred soldiers of the garrison could be disentangled from the town, or thrown into any position even half-way between the enemy and Dublin."

With considerable detail, Carhampton set out the measures which in his view would be most effective for the protection of the metropolis, and concluded with recommendations in relation to the defence of Cork and Belfast.

Many characteristic details appear (pp. 104-116) in the private memoranda made by Thomas Pelham in relation to the evidence of witnesses before the Secret Committee of the House of Commons at Dublin, in 1797. The first of these witnesses was Edward John Newell, already mentioned at page ix. Of his proceedings at this time, Newell's subsequent statements in his "Apology" were as follow:

"We left Belfast about four o'clock, the 30th of April [1797], and at twelve the next day arrived in Dublin, having travelled in chaises and four which were carefully ready at every inn; an express went before for the purpose. We were accompanied by little Atkinson, Lieutenant Elison and Major Fox, who bore the expense of the journey, and had also a strong escort. The guards made the people believe us to be prisoners; and when we stopped at an inn, numbers flocked round the carriages commiserating our suffering, and requesting to know how they might assist us. I own my heart bled at their generous treatment. I then first lamented what I had done, really repented my deserting a cause which could produce such friendly sentiments. I must in particular gratefully mention the behaviour of a Miss Shaw of Dundalk. This lady, in the most delicate manner, offered every civility; which treatment hurt me then more than the most scurrilous abuse the public papers have since bestowed on me, or even the manner in which I found myself shunned by honest men.

"When we arrived in Dublin we waited on messieurs Cooke [Under Secretary] and Pelham [Chief Secretary], who, after questioning us on the good effects produced by what had been done, and a determination of prosecuting the scheme of terror further, informed me, that on Tuesday I should be before the Committee of the House of Commons, and, on my going away, gave me ten guineas, to take care of myself until a place was provided for me in the Castle. This was in one fortnight £36 8s. I had received; a very promising appearance on the first commencement of the business, but, as the sequel will show, falls far short of the manner [in which] I was afterwards treated.

"During two or three days I dined with Mr. Fox, and shall only give, as a proof of his generous treatment and the allowance of Government, that I have seen him, for one dinner and wine, for six persons, pay above seven pounds. The remainder of that week, and part of the next, I slept at Mr. Cooke's, in the Castle [of Dublin], and breakfasted with himself. Murdoch[1] and I dined and supped in the Castle Tavern, at the rate of three guineas a day, which Mr. Cooke cheerfully accounted for.

"On the 3rd of May I attended in the Speaker's chamber at the Parliament House [Dublin]; and at two o'clock, was admitted to the room where the Secret Committee of the Commons were then sitting. After the usual formalities, I was with great ceremony placed in a high chair, for the benefit of being better heard.

"I went through the subject of the examinations, improving largely on the hints and instructions Cooke had given me; propagating circumstances which never had, nor, I suppose, ever will happen; increased the number of United Irishmen, their quantity of arms and ammunition; fabricated stories which helped to terrify them, and raised me high in their estimation as a man whose perfect knowledge of this business made his information of highest importance. I told them of laws framed to govern the republic, when they had overthrown the present Government; many of which they approved of highly, though they had no foundation but the effusions of my own brain. I embellished largely the dangers that royalty and its friends were liable to, from the machinations of the United men, who, I informed them, were regularly disciplined, and constantly improving themselves in military tactics; assured them there were men of the first rank and abilities connected with this business; that the French were hourly expected; they were to land at Galway, not at Bantry, as they supposed; that the people looked with eagerness for their arrival; and that Government should not trust the people of the south, who had formerly pretended to rise in their defence, their loyalty being only 'finesse,' the readier to join the French on their landing; that I was confident, from the disposition of the people, they would in a few weeks, even if they did not arrive, attempt an insurrection, in which they were sure of succeeding, on account of their numbers, the justice of their cause, and their hopes from the soldiery.

"They seemed dreadfully terrified at my information, and instantly became incapable of asking me any more questions relative to this business. Will it be believed that a boy, even one of the swinish multitude of the north, filled with consternation and terror

---

[1] Payments to Murdock, hearth-money collector, Belfast, and Newell, are entered in the Secret Service accounts, *see* pp. 5, 6, 11.

the leaders of the army and the senate!—they who are to face the conquerors of Italy could he make tremble, by relating scenes of imaginary terrors!

" The Attorney-General [Toler], after a long discourse upon the nature and danger of what he had heard, thought it would be advisable to try to conciliate the people, by granting them some of their wishes, until Government should be better prepared to resist; if granting would have the desired effect. He then addressed me: 'Mr. Newell, you must now consider that we are a select committee of the parliament of Ireland; that that parliament is to be guided by these gentlemen, and that these gentlemen are to be guided in their proceedings by you: weigh well, then, the situation in which you now sit, and its consequences, and tell me, would a reform of parliament please the people, and put an end to disturbances?' 'Sir, from my knowledge, nothing but the overthrow of Government and establishing a republic would now satisfy the people.'

" Major Fox, Lieutenant Ellison and little Atkinson were then called to identify the papers which had been seized with the societies taken in Alexander's, according to my information; and for which so many of our countrymen are now sustaining the loathsome sufferings of a pestilent tender. We were then dismissed, with many thanks for our attention, and with every encouragement for our continuance in loyalty. I should have mentioned that Mr. Toler, the Solicitor-General, during my discourse assured the committee they might place the greatest confidence in whatever I advanced, as he had long known me; and, until I went to Belfast, he was sure I was a most honourable lad.

" As the committee of the Lords was only a routine of the same business, it is unnecessary here to mention it, except that for the four hours I was with them, by my artifices, I raised in the breast of these hereditary wisdoms the same surprise and fear that I had before in that of the Commons, magnifying every report to enhance my own importance. In consequence of which, they agreed to the Report and Address from the Committee of Secrecy of the House of Lords, of the 12th of May, 1797."

Newell, on relinquishing the office of "informer," averred that his operations in that capacity during upwards of ten months had cost the Government upwards of two thousand pounds, that he had caused the imprisonment of 227 innocent men, and the flight of three hundred persons.

A full-length figure of Newell, from a drawing by himself, was issued in 1798, and of this a reproduction appears in the present volume.

The chief subjects treated of in most of the letters and documents here printed from the Pelham papers, are indicated in the annexed table of contents. In several of them references appear to the possible separation of Ireland from England, the courage displayed by the Irish in arms, and the formidable character of their hostile movements. "Rely upon it," wrote Castlereagh, "there never was in any country so formidable an effort on the part of the people." "They fought," he added, "with determined bravery." Cooke, the Under-Secretary, in a letter to Pelham, mentioned that the situation was "critical," and expressed his doubts as to what might be the result if parts of the south should "burst forth." In connection with the French soldiery at Killala, a facsimile will be found at page 191 of a passport issued by Charost, the officer in command of them in September of that year.

Of the views and movements of the United Irishmen, expositions appear in the statement made by three of their leaders, Thomas Addis Emmet,[1] Arthur O'Connor,[2] and William James Mac Neven,[3] M.D., in August, 1798, while incarcerated at Dublin as State prisoners. Further information on this subject is supplied by the examinations of Mac Neven and Emmet before the Secret Committees of the Houses of Lords and Commons at Dublin in the same year. We have also here an account by Mac Neven of the treaty between the imprisoned United Irishmen and the Government at Dublin in 1798.

In connection with the negotiations with the State prisoners, some particulars additional to those in the second part of this volume, are given in an unpublished letter addressed to Thomas Pelham on 26th July, 1798, by Henry Alexander, representative of Derry in the parliament at Dublin, and a member of the Secret Committee. Of John M'Cann and Michael William Byrne, who were executed in July, 1798, Alexander stated that the first died "with a firm and manly courage; the other plunged into the abyss of eternity with a constitutional indifference as to existence, and an ambition of being esteemed firm to his cause." Alexander, in continuation, wrote as follows:

"Ninety-two of the State prisoners signed a new kind of round-robin not likely to be extensively adopted, offering all evidence in their power as to arms, foreign

---

[1] Died at New York, in 1827.   [2] Died at Bignon, France, in 1852.
[3] Died at New York, in 1841.

correspondence, schemes of rebellion, plans of warfare, and to give security to leave this kingdom and to reside wherever pointed out by the minister, in Europe, with any State at peace with Great Britain. His excellency consulted such gentlemen as are in his confidence, and it was declined yesterday.

"This morning Oliver Bond, who is my relation, sent for me. I waited on him, and never conceived that in the plenitude of French conceit any man could value higher his means of being useful or formidable. He desired me to state that he would not move out of the ranks to save his own life (this was within a few hours of his execution), but that he would act with those men now State prisoners, and that he conceived I ought to inform our administration that an opportunity might be lost not regainable if he was executed; and that he conceived nothing could more tend to the tranquillity of the State than the communications and exertions of him and his associates; that his mind was reconciled to death, and that he would not solicit life except as a man acting with a class of men anxious to save him. He added, he and they could give the only informations capable of saving this country from an aggravated civil war. He proposed to Government banishment for some, emigration for all, discoveries of the depots of arms, of all foreign and English correspondences, all schemes of warfare, the organization, and, he added a word of his own, the ramifications of this conspiracy.

"He was to-day respited from one to four, and from four to Monday next. Nothing has been decided. My part in the negotiation has ceased, and Cooke [Under-Secretary] has gone to him as a man of more penetration and habits of investigation than I possess. . . Cooke is to have a conversation with Mac Neven, the O'Connors, etc., as to their Continental visits prior to the decision of Bond's fate. His reprieve has excited much clamour and much terror, and is disapproved of by many very loyal men. At the same time, the offers, if sincere, are very great . . .

"Oliver Bond's reprieve and Buonaparte's reported capture [are] the general theme. I forgot to tell you the overtures of the rebels were intended to be sent through Lord Charlemont to Government. He declined to carry them, and thus they devolved upon me. I thought it my duty to state them, but Government has the responsibility of judging."

In a letter dated from the Lower Castle-yard, Dublin, Monday, 4 August, 1798, Alexander wrote again as follows to Pelham:

"His excellency's[1] reception has augmented the sense I feel of your kindness. I waited on him last Friday, and as I was the last in the levée, I barely sent in my name that I attended his excellency, but had no particular reason to solicit the honour of an audience, as I understood from his aide-de-camp he proposed an immediate ride.

---

[1] Marquis Cornwallis, Lord Lieutenant of Ireland.

He admitted me, and his manner of reception convinced me how much I owe you. We talked over the affairs of this country generally (notwithstanding frequent attempts on my side to shorten the conversation) for an hour, and the result was a wish on his side that I should wait on him after, and that he would treat me without ceremony in seeing or dismissing me, as circumstances rendered convenient.

"The publick papers carry you the outlines of the negotiation between the State and its prisoners, and I have no doubt your confidential friends have written you a detail I have not avenues to. As to such circumstances as may throw light upon what you know that have come to my knowledge, I shall risk your loss of time by a recital.

"I wrote to you in my last that, unwilling in some degree to risk my reputation, but much more from a doubt of my capacity, I left the negotiation, after having marked out its objects, in the hands of Mr. Cooke and the administration. [Arthur] Dobbs, Lord Charlemont's friend, carried to the prisoners the round-robin for signatures, and from an enthusiastic warmth of temper possibly effected more than a guarded man could have done. Whether he exceeded or not the right he had of giving hopes, I know not, although it may, where so many individuals are concerned, become a mixed question hereafter. In my own opinion, some will act candidly with Government, others will not, and that an arrangement for each herring to hang by its own head may become impracticable. I wrote to you Bond was reprieved, although within twenty minutes of death, and that he did not appear to lay great stress upon what was within his immediate knowledge, but said in a most decided tone, where he stepped forward no man of the party dare keep back. Your friend [Samuel] Neilson, on the contrary, stretching out his arm, with his hand clenched, said : ' I hold in my hand every muscle, sinew, nay, fibre of the internal organization—nay, every ramification of the United Irishmen ;' and, gradually opening his hand, ' I will make it as plain as the palm of my hand if our terms are complied with.'

"I use his words and describe his action as nearly as I can. You know the man ; and although he may not have heard logic and rhetoric compared to the shut and opened hand, the vivacity and earnestness of his manner struck me, not with an opinion of his sincerity, but of the impressive habit he seems to have acquired. I thought I read in his looks great fear of death, but shading itself under a pretended anxiety to save Bond, who appeared next to indifferent about his fate. The examination has taken place before the Chancellor [Lord Clare] of some of their leaders, and the confidence reposed by the public in his sagacity and firmness has in some degree allayed, although by no means extinguished, a clamour excited at Bond's reprieve and the circulated reports of a general pardon. Reports of bribery, of a change of measures, a change of men, angry threats and silly suspicions pervaded Dublin from Friday, the day of reprieve, to the following Monday. The yeomen who have acted so meritoriously, had amongst them men who canvassed strongly that if the execution was further delayed they might lay down their arms."

A communication to Pelham from Alexander, dated five days after the preceding letter, contained the following additional details:

"The negotiation to save Bond's life has been the theme of wonder, of discontent, of panegyric. The fact is this—several of the State prisoners, upon Byrne's and Bond's conviction, felt tottering; many had a high regard for Bond; efforts to prevent his conviction having failed, the next effort was to save his life. Some friends of Bond's were admitted to him; they wanted him to give information, when some casual proposition occurred, that all the State prisoners should offer to give all the information in their power without mentioning and implicating persons, and emigrate for life, Byrne and Bond to be included.

"This proposition was signed by almost all the State prisoners, through the medium of Lord Charlemont's member, Dobbs, and presented to Government. Lord Cornwallis thought it a proposition to be acceded to, so did Lord Castlereagh; my own ideas were strongly in favour of it. The law servants, Lord Carleton, Lord Kilwarden, attorney, solicitor-general and prime sergeant were consulted. They were against it upon legal grounds, saying that if persons so convicted were pardoned, judges and juries might be chagrined, and that the public might be disgusted. The proposition was not accepted—Byrne was executed. The next day the proposition was renewed. Lord Cornwallis felt his opinion confirmed. The same persons were again consulted; they relented a little. Bond was respited.

"Let me state the case. There were between seventy and eighty State prisoners. There had been four capital trials and convictions and executions, the treason in its extent was proved most completely and satisfactorily. Justice was restored. Example was made. It was to be feared that many executions would raise criminals into martyrs. A loophole was to be opened for United Irishmen to creep through. They wanted a pretext for returning to loyalty. Clemency was the fairest pretext. It was impossible to have seventy-four trials at bar, supposing our proofs complete. If our proofs failed in any case, and they were likely to fail in Neilson's, the rebels gained a triumph. But what was the justification to Government when all the capital traitors, Emmet, O'Connor, Mac Neven, etc., were to come forward, confess themselves conspirators and traitors, and engaged for above two years in a correspondence with France? What an overthrow would such a confession be to all the Lord Moiras,[1] Mr. Foxes, Duke of Bedford, Judge Buller, Maidstone juries, etc.!

"Such being the case, could a respite have been refused? During the agitation of the subject, the Chancellor [Lord Clare] was in the country. The Speaker [Foster]

---

[1] The Earl of Moira, C. J. Fox and Lord John Russell were witnesses at the trial at Maidstone, for high treason, of Arthur O'Connor and others, before Sir Francis Buller and special Commissioners.

was frantic against it; the popular cry of Dublin loud against it. The yeomen were to lay down their arms; all the loyalists felt themselves deserted. Luckily, so soon as the Chancellor arrived he expressed himself most warmly in favour of the measure, first in private, then in parliament, and said that the Government would have been inexcusable if they had not entertained it. Public confidence revived.

"What is the consequence? O'Connor, Emmet and Mac Neven have prepared a memoir,[1] in which they detail the treason from 1791, state the views of separation of the United Irishmen and their correspondence with France. This memoir, being political and justificatory, is not admitted by Government, upon which they have consented to be examined on oath before the committee of the lords. Mac Neven and O'Connor have already appeared and given the amplest evidence, admitting their correspondence with France in all its extent."

In relation to ecclesiastical arrangements at this time in Ireland, there will be found here a characteristic communication from Hervey, the noted bishop of Derry, and papers in connection with projected Governmental provision for the Roman Catholic clergy.

Contemporary letters are also included on the parliamentary debates at Dublin, in 1799, on the proposed Union between Great Britain and Ireland, from which, and other papers here printed, may be gathered some of the views then prevalent on that measure

The portrait of Lord Edward Fitzgerald, prefixed to this volume, has, by the kind permission of the Duke of Leinster, been copied from the original in his Grace's collection at Carton.

JOHN T. GILBERT.

VILLA NOVA, BLACKROCK,
    Dublin, 1st December, 1892.

---

[1] See pp. 144, 147, 222,

CONTENTS.

	PAGE

I.—ACCOUNT OF SECRET SERVICE MONEY, IRELAND, 1797—1804.

Memorandum on receipts and payments 2
Advances received from Treasury 3
Payments: 1797,—page 4.—1798,—p. 8.—1799,—p. 24.—
1800,—p. 38.—1801,—p. 51.—1802,—p. 65.—1803,—p. 73.
1804,—p. 84.

II.—LETTERS, DOCUMENTS, ETC.

1. 1795.—DEFENCELESS STATE OF DUBLIN:

Report by Lieutenant-General the Earl of Carhampton to the
Duke of York, on the state of Dublin in case of a coup-
de-main 91

2. 1795.—IRISHMEN IN THE ARMY AND NAVY:

To Duke of York from Thomas Pelham, Chief Secretary to the
Lord Lieutenant of Ireland 99

3. 1797.—STATE OF IRELAND:

i. ii.—To Duke of York from T. Pelham 101

4. 1797—POLITICAL MOVEMENTS IN IRELAND.—STATEMENTS TO SECRET COMMITTEE OF HOUSE OF COMMONS, DUBLIN:

Private memoranda by T. Pelham 104

5. 1797—MILITARY EXECUTION:

General Gerard Lake to T. Pelham 117

CONTENTS.

	PAGE
6. 1797.—Transmission of Public Money: George Rose to T. Pelham	117
7. 1797—Rewards for discoveries in Ireland: T. Pelham to Lieutenant-General Dalrymple	118
8. 1797.—Apprehended movements in Ireland:	
i.—To T. Pelham from Edward Cooke, Under-Secretary, Civil Department, Ireland	119
ii.—To T. Pelham from Earl Camden, Lord Lieutenant of Ireland	119
iii.—Edward Cooke to T. Pelham	120
9. 1798.—Tithes and Clergy in Ireland.—Suggested regulations: To T. Pelham from Frederick Hervey, Bishop of Derry	121
10. 1798.—Affairs in Dublin, Wexford, etc.: Robert Marshall to T. Pelham	124
11. 1798.—Orange Associations.—Movements in Leinster.—Death of Lord Edward Fitzgerald: To T. Pelham from Hon. William Elliot, Under-Secretary, Military Department, Ireland	125
12. 1798.—War in Wexford.—Death of Colonel Walpole.—Probability of general revolt in Ireland: Viscount Castlereagh to Thomas Pelham	127
13. 1798.—Possible loss of Ireland.—Demand for more troops from England: To T. Pelham from Earl Camden, Lord Lieutenant of Ireland	128
14. 1798.—Affairs in Wexford and Ulster.—Formidable character of the Irish movement: Viscount Castlereagh to T. Pelham	130

CONTENTS. [3]

PAGE

15. 1798.—Danger of Ireland being lost to Great Britain:
Earl Camden to T. Pelham ... 132

16. 1798.—Wexford.—Ulster.—Militia arrangements:
Viscount Castlereagh to T. Pelham 133

17. 1798.—Apprehensions of the French.—Consideration of measures for pacification in Ireland:
Edward Cooke to T. Pelham 135

18. 1798.—Determined bravery of the Irish.—Ulster, Wexford.—Arrangement of British troops:
Castlereagh to William Elliot 135

19. 1798.—Letters from Earl Camden, Lord Lieutenant of Ireland:
i.—To William Elliot, London 137
ii.—To T. Pelham, ib. 138

20. 1798.—Ulster.—Wexford.—Kildare.—Earl Camden.—Protection of Dublin:
Castlereagh to T. Pelham, London 139

21. 1798.—Changes of Viceroy of Ireland and Chief Secretary:
Edward Cooke to T. Pelham 141

22. 1798.—Lord Cornwallis, Viceroy.—Retirement of Earl Camden:
Camden to T. Pelham ... 141

23. 1798.—Lord Cornwallis and his Chief Secretary.—Trials.—Parliament in Ireland:
Edward Cooke to T. Pelham ... - ... 142

24. 1793.—Reduction of insurgents.—Trials.—Thomas Reynolds.—State Prisoners.—Execution.—Attainders.—Union with England.—Cornwallis.—Castlereagh.—Chief Secretaryship in Ireland:
William Elliot to T. Pelham 143

CONTENTS.

PAGE

25. 1798.—Origin and progress of "United Irish" movements:
Memoir or detailed statement of the origin and progress of the Irish Union. Delivered to the Irish Government by Thomas Addis Emmet, Arthur O'Connor and William James Mac Neven, M.D., 4 August, 1798 147

26. 1798.—Negotiations with prisoners.—Secret Committee.—Movements in Carlow.—Orange Societies.—Wicklow:
William Elliot to T. Pelham 162

27. 1798.—Examination of William James Mac Neven, M.D., before the Secret Committee of the House of Lords, Dublin, 7 August, 1798 163

28. 1798.—Examination of William James Mac Neven, M.D., before the Secret Committee of the House of Commons, Dublin, 8 August, 1798 168

29. 1798.—Substance of Thomas Addis Emmet's examination before the Secret Committee of the House of Lords, Dublin, 10 August, 1798 176

30. 1798.—The examination of Thomas Addis Emmet before the Secret Committee of the House of Commons, 14 August, 1798 183

31. 1798.—French soldiery at Killala:
i.—Memorandum by John Knox of Bartera 190
ii.—Passport from Commandant Charost 191

32. 1798.—Viceroyalty of Marquis Cornwallis.—Project of provisional government for England in Ireland.—Pelham.—Lord Clare:
Duke of Portland to Pelham 191

33. 1798.—Bishopric of Clonfert.—State of Ireland.—Union.—Measure for permanent tranquillity:
Marquis Cornwallis to T. Pelham ... ...

34. 1798.—George III.—Duke of Portland.—Pelham.—Protestant bishoprics in Ireland:
Duke of Portland to T. Pelham 193

CONTENTS.

		PAGE
35.	1799.—To T. PELHAM FROM FRANCIS MOYLAN, D.D., ROMAN CATHOLIC BISHOP OF CORK	194
36.	1799.—SUGGESTIONS BY ROMAN CATHOLIC PRELATES IN IRELAND FOR GOVERNMENTAL PROVISION	195
37.	1799.—LETTERS TO T. PELHAM ON DEBATE IN PARLIAMENT, AT DUBLIN, ON LEGISLATIVE UNION WITH GREAT BRITAIN:	

i.—From Henry Alexander, M.P., for Londonderry ... 197
ii.— ,, Richard Griffith 198
iii.— ,, Hugh Viscount Carleton, Chief Justice Common Pleas 201
iv.— ,, Sir George Shee, M.P. for Knocktopher 202

88. 1799.—VIEWS ON LEGISLATIVE UNION OF IRELAND WITH GREAT BRITAIN:
To T. Pelham from Matthew Young, Protestant Bishop of Clonfert 203

39. 1799.—CONSIDERATION IN RELATION TO LEGISLATIVE UNION OF IRELAND WITH GREAT BRITAIN.—GOVERNMENTAL ARRANGEMENTS SUGGESTED FOR ROMAN CATHOLIC CLERGY IN IRELAND:

To T. Pelham from Francis Moylan, D.D., Roman Catholic Bishop of Cork 205

40. 1799.—IDEAS AS TO ARRANGEMENTS BETWEEN ENGLISH GOVERNMENT AND ROMAN CATHOLIC CLERGY IN IRELAND:

Duke of Portland to T. Pelham 207

41. ACCOUNT OF THE TREATY BETWEEN THE UNITED IRISHMEN AND THE ANGLO-IRISH GOVERNMENT IN 1798.—BY WILLIAM J. MAC NEVEN ... 208

TABLE OF REFERENCES TO LETTERS, DOCUMENTS, ETC. ... 233

INDEX TO ACCOUNT OF SECRET SERVICE MONEY 235

INDEX TO LETTERS, DOCUMENTS, ETC. 244

LIST OF ILLUSTRATIONS.

No.
I. Portrait of Lord Edward Fitzgerald: born 1763; died 1798. Original by Horace Hone, in collection of His Grace the Duke of Leinster, Carton, Ireland.
            To face title page

II. Facsimile of portrait of Edward John Newell, as issued in 1798 ... ... Page 104

III. Portrait of Arthur O'Connor, a leader of the United Irishmen, State prisoner, 1798: inscribed—" Arthur O'Connor, Esquire, late member of the Irish Parliament for the borough of Philipstown. Painted by J. Dowling, engraved by W. Ward" ... Page 147

IV. Passport from M. Charost, French commander at Killala. Original in collection of the Editor. Page 191

[IRELAND.]

ACCOUNT
OF
SECRET SERVICE MONEY,

APPLIED IN DETECTING TREASONABLE CONSPIRACIES, ETC.,
PURSUANT TO THE PROVISIONS OF THE CIVIL LIST ACT, 1793:
FROM 21 AUGUST, 1797, [TO 28 MARCH, 1804.]

[Memorandum on page 2 of the Ms.]

For former receipts and payments on this head, see General Account of Secret Service in book with marbled paper cover, viz. :—

	£	s.	d.
From April, 1795 (the commencement of Earl Camden's administration), to 12th January, 1796,—per affidavit by Mr. Hamilton	445	7	6
From 12 January, 1796,—per affidavit by Mr. Pelham	2,673	9	10
„ 18 May, [17]96, to 19 August, 1797,—per affidavit by Mr. Cooke	5,921	1	9
	£9,039	19	1
From 20 August, 1797, to 30 September, 1801, per this account and affidavit of Mr. Cooke	£38,419	8	0

ACCOUNT OF SECRET SERVICE MONEY, IRELAND, 1797-1804.

Received per advances from the Treasury by letters.

1797	£			1800	£		
September 2	...	1000		January 22	...	1000	
October 14	...	1000		February 21	...	1000	
December 14	...	1000		May 25	...	1000	
December 20	...	1000	[£4,000]	July 18	...	1000	
				November 14	...	1500	
				December 3	...	1500	
1798	£			„ 24	...	1500	[£8,500]
February 3	...	1000		1801	£		
March 14	...	1000		April 4	...	1000	
„ 23	...	1000		May 30	...	1500	
April 21	...	1000		June 27	...	1500	[£4,000]
May 12	...	1000					
June 12	...	2000		1802	£		
July 25	...	1000		January 13	...	1500	
August 16	...	1500		March 5	...	1500	
September 13	...	1000		May 29	...	1000	
„ 28	...	1500		July 30	...	1000	
December 15	...	1500	[£13,500]	December 15	...	1500	[£6,500]
				1803	£		
				April 9	...	1000	
1799	£			June 13	...	1000	
January 8	...	1500		August 5	...	1500	
„ 24	...	1500		November 5	...	1500	
February 13	...	1500		December 2	...	1000	[£6,000]
March 23	...	1000					
May 3	...	1000		1804	£		
June 14	...	1000		January 21	...	1500	
August 9	...	1000		February 16	...	1000	[£2,500]
December 14	...	1000	[£9,500]				
			[£27,000]				[£27,500]

[Total amount received in above period, £54,500.]

ACCOUNT OF SECRET SERVICE MONEY, IRELAND, 1797.

1797.		PAID	£	s.	d.
August	21.	E. Cooke for M.	50	0	0
,,	22.	Newell, per Mr. Dawes, junior ...	11	7	6
,,	,,	Mr. Cooke, for Darcy Mahon, esq.	20	0	0
,,	26.	Mitchell, 1 g.; Grey, 5 gs.			
,,	28.	Mr. Cooke, for Magowan, 1 g.	7	19	3
,,	29.	Lord Castlereagh's bill to Wm. Jolly, dated 18th August	56	17	6
Sept.	1.	Mr. Cooke, for M.	10	0	0
,,	2.	Mitchell, 1 g.; Lowry, 4 Aug., 4 gs. and 6th Sept., 4 gs.	10	4	9
,,	,,	Mr. Cooke, for D. Mahon	20	0	0
,,	5.	Captain Sterling, account of subsistence for R. Hamilton and John Kervan, Barracks, James'-street	11	7	6
,,	6.	Mitchell, 3 gs.; Mr. Cooke, for Boyle, 5 gs.	9	2	0
,,	7.	Mr. Dawes (Messenger), for diet and lodging of Mr. Smith and wife, 9 Sept. to 23 Nov.,'96, and Mrs. Smith, 1 to 13 May,'97	77	17	10
,,	,,	Do., for 10 pair sheets and earthen ware for prisoners, per R.	15	10	6
,,	,,	Jeremiah Hassett, keeper of the Tower (this makes 29 gs.)	5	13	9
,,	9.	Mitchell, 1 g.; Grey's wife, 1 g.; Mr. Cooke, for B., £10	12	5	6
,,	11.	Sir G. F. Hill, per receipt	100	0	0
,,	12.	Mr. Cooke, for M.	100	0	0
,,	13.	Mitchell, to buy coat and hat, 2 gs.; 16th, Grey, 1 g.; Mitchell's wife, 1 g. ...	4	11	0
,,	15.	Edward Joyce, by direction of Mr. Cooke	5	13	9
,,	16.	J. Bell, esq., expenses in search of offenders, per Mr. Sirr	45	10	0
,,	19.	Mr. Dawes, for Smith	20	0	0
,,	,,	Lowry, to buy a great coat, 1 g.; 25th Sept., to pay lodging and diet, 3 gs. ...	4	11	0
,,	20.	Mr. Cooke, for Joyce	5	13	9
		C[arried] forward, ...	£604	5	7

£11 7 6
77 17 10
15 10 6

£104 15 10 — C[arried] f[orward].

ACCOUNT OF SECRET SERVICE MONEY, IRELAND, 1797. 5

	1797.		PAID.	£	s.	d.
£104 15 10 — B. F.			Per amount brought forward,	604	5	7
	Sepr.	21.	Kerr's wife, 1 g.—23rd, Grey, 1 g.; Mitchell, 1 g.; 26th, Mr. Cooke, for Magowan, 1 g.	4	11	0
	,,	26.	Mr. Cooke, for M.	200	0	0
	,,	29.	Major Sirr, for Sandys	5	13	9
	,,	,,	Watkins, for diet of sundry persons, June and July, '97, viz., Newell, Murdock, Lowry, Hayes, Kane, Harpur, Shaw, O'Brien, M'Dermott, Kavanagh, Sandys,			
228 9 11¼			etc., etc., per account and receipt ...	228	9	11½
	,,	30.	Mr. Cooke, for Medlicott	5	13	9
	,,	,,	Sent to Newell, per post	10	0	0
	,,	,,	Mitchell and Grey	2	5	6
	Octor.	5.	Mr. Cooke, for Magowan, 2 gs.; 7th, Mitchell and Grey, 2 gs.	4	11	0
	,,	7.	Do., for Boyle	10	4	9
	,,	10.	Mitchell for M'Cann, 1 g.; 11th, Lowry, 5 gs.; 12th, Major Sirr, for M'Cann, 2 gs.	9	2	0
	,,	13.	Mary Camble, for 12 weeks' lodging, coals,			
6 16 6			etc., for Newell and Mr. Murdock ...	6	16	6
	,,	,,	Mitchell, 1 g.; Grey, 1 g.; 14th, Mitchell, 1 g.	3	8	3
1 12 9	,,	19.	Hassett's bill for washing for Hayes and Lowry	1	12	9
	,,	,,	Mr. Cooke, for Mr. Verner	22	15	0
	,,	,,	Mitchell, 2 gs.; 20th, Mr. Cooke for Grey, 1 g.; 21st, Mitchell and Grey, 2 gs. ...	5	13	9
	,,	23.	John Cochlan of Clonard, per Mr. Tyrrell's letter	20	0	0
	,,	,,	Mr. Dawes, for O'Brien's cloaths ...	4	18	9½
	,,	26.	Mr. Gallaher of Dundalk, bill of expenses	72	17	10½
	,,	28.	Mitchell and Grey, 2 gs.; Lowry, 2 gs.; Newell, 5 gs.	10	4	9
	,,	31.	Mr. Dawes, to send Smith to bring him to town	11	7	6
	Novem.	1.	Keeper of Bridewell for Bell Martin's diet,			
12 16 10½			21 weeks	12	16	10½
	,,	2.	Mitchell, 1 g.; O'Brien, 1 g.	2	5	6
	,,	3.	Bell Martin, to take her out of town, etc. ...	5	13	9

£354 11 11 — C. F.   C. F. £1,265 8 7

ACCOUNT OF SECRET SERVICE MONEY, IRELAND, 1797.

	1797.		PAID	£	s.	d.
£354 11 11 — B. F.			Per amount brought forward,	1,265	8	7
	Novem.	4.	Mr. Dutton, by desire of Lord Carhampton,	11	7	6
	,,	6.	Mitchell, 1 g.; Grey, 2 gs.; 6th, Smith, per Mr. Dawes, 5 gs.	9	2	0
	,,	9.	Lowry, 5 gs.; Newell, per Mr. Dawes, 3 gs.; 10th Nov., Newell, to go out of town, 10 gs.	18	4	0
42 12 6½	,,	8.	Mr. Rea, acct. of expenses of military, parties, prisoners, etc.	42	12	6½
	,,	10.	J. Pollock, esq., per r[eceipt]	100	0	0
	,,	6.	Allowance in lieu of diet to 13 men in the Tower, etc., for one week from this date, per Major Sirr	14	15	9
	,,	11.	J. Hassett, keeper of the Tower, on account (this makes 32 gs.)...	3	8	3
	,,	,,	Mitchell and Grey, 2 gs.; J. Dowling, 1 g.; 18th, Mitchell and Grey, 2 gs. ...	5	13	9
1 2 9	,,	14.	C. Stuart, for lodging, etc., for 2 Mr. Murdocks, Newell and Dutton, 3 days	1	2	9
	,,	13.	Subsistence of 13 men in the Tower, etc., per Hassett	14	15	9
11 7 6	,,	15.	Captain Sterling, on acct. of Hamilton and Kirwan, Barracks, James-street ...	11	7	6
	,,	,,	J. Pollock, esq., per r[eceipt]	50	0	0
	,,	13.	Dowling, 1 g.; Mitchell, 1 g.; Grey, 1 g.	3	8	3
	,,	20.	Subsistence of 13 men in the Tower, etc. ...	14	15	9
8 13 9	,,	,,	Mrs. Morris, account of Smith's lodging, 5 gs.; 21st, Lowry, 2 gs.	7	19	3
	,,	22.	Mr. Cooke, for Nicholls	10	0	0
5 13 9	,,	,,	Mrs. Morris, on further account of Smith's lodging	5	13	9
	,,	23.	Serjeant Dunn of the invalids, going with Grey to Derry	3	8	3
	,,	,,	Mr. Cooke, for Nugent	5	13	9
	,,	,,	J. Pollock, esq.	25	13	9
	,,	24.	Grey, Mitchell and Dowling, 1 g. each ...	3	8	3
	,,	,,	Mr. Cooke, for two men	2	5	6
	,,	27.	Captain A. Macnevin, per r[eceipt] ...	150	0	0
	,,	28.	Mr. Cooke, for McCarry	50	0	0
£421 2 2½ — C. F.			C. F.	£1,830	4	10½

ACCOUNT OF SECRET SERVICE MONEY, IRELAND, 1797.

	1797.		PAID.	£	s.	d.
			Per amount brought forward,	1,830	4	10½
	Novem.	28.	Watkins, for diet of sundry persons in the Castle, etc., in August and September, per account	176	9	5½
	,,	29.	J. Pollock, esq.	20	0	0
	,,	,,	Mr. Cooke, for Mr. Carry's nephew ...	5	13	9
	,,	27.	Subsistence of 13 men in the Tower, viz., 10 at 1 g. and 3 at ½ g.	13	1	7½
	,,	30.	Smith	5	13	9
	Decr.	1.	A. Worthington, esq., balance of an account to 1st Dec.	3	18	9
	,,	,,	Dº an advance of	45	10	0
	,,	2.	Mrs. Morris, on further account of lodging, etc., Smith and wife	11	7	6
	,,	,,	Mitchell and Grey, 2 gs.; Dowling, 1 g.; Mr. Cooke for Lindsay, 2 gs. ...	5	13	9
	,,	4.	Subsistence of men in the Tower, etc., 10 at 1 g., 3 at ½ g.	13	1	7½
	,,	5.	Lowry, 2 gs., and on the 8th going out of town, 5 gs.	7	19	3
	,,	9.	Grey, 1 g.; Mitchell, 1 g.; Mr. Cooke, for Lindsay, etc., 2 gs.	4	11	0
	,,	11.	Subsistence of 11 men at 1 g. and 3 at ½ g.	14	4	4½
	,,	,,	John Pollock, esq., per r[eceipt] ...	300	0	0
	,,	12.	O'Brien, for a great coat, 1 g.; 16th, Grey, 1 g.; Mitchell, 1 g.; Wheatley and Lindsay, 2 gs.	5	13	9
	,,	,,	Mr. Cooke, to send to Newell ...	20	0	0
	,,	13.	Mrs. Morris, in full for diet and lodging Mr. Smith and wife	11	7	6
	,,	,,	Wm. Patrickson, esq., for diet, lodging, etc., in the County of Wicklow, for Smith and wife, 4 weeks	9	2	0
	,,	14.	W. B. Swan, esq., to defray expenses in search of offenders	20	0	0
	,,	15.	Mr. Darcy Mahon, per r[eceipt] ...	50	0	0
	,,	18.	Smith, per his note	10	0	0
	,,	,,	Subsistence of 12 men at 1 g. and 3 at ½ g.	15	7	1½
	,,	,,	Mr. Cooke for F——y	11	7	6
			C. F.	£2,610	7	7

ACCOUNT OF SECRET SERVICE MONEY, IRELAND, 1797.

	1797.		PAID.	£	s.	d.
£023 8 8 — B. F.			Per amount brought forward,	2,610	7	7
	Decem.	19.	R. Marshall, esq., by direction of Mr. Pelham	159	5	0
	,,	21.	Col. Longfield, for soldiers of the Cork Militia	127	8	0
	,,	22.	Mrs. Morris, for 15 days' diet and lodging			
14 9 3			Smith and wife, to 21st Dec. ...	14	9	3
	,,	23.	Mr. Collins, per bill sent to him in London, £100, English, exchange 8 per cent. ...	108	0	0
	,,	,,	Grey, 2 gs.; Mitchell, 2 gs.; Lindsay and Wheatley, 2 gs.	6	16	6
	,,	,,	Subsistence of 11 men at 1 g. and 3 at ½ g.	14	4	4½
	,,	,,	J. Hassett, keeper of the Tower (this makes 37 gs.)	5	13	9
	,,	20.	Joseph Nugent, by direction of Mr. Cooke	5	13	9
	,,	23.	Smith, for cloaths, by d^{o.} d^{o.}	20	0	0
	,,	,,	W. Atkinson, of Belfast, expenses and allowance for going to England in search			
65 0 0			of Magee, per his account and receipt ...	65	0	0
	,,	,,	Earl Carhampton, for Feris (Feris to have £100 per annum from 1st December) ...	200	0	0
	,,	,,	Pat Joyce, by direction of Mr. Cooke ...	10	4	9
	,,	28.	Earl of Altamont, per James Clarke's receipt	22	15	0
	,,	29.	Ben Eves, of Blessington, what he advanced to Johnston, alias Smith	14	4	4½
	,,	,,	Mitchell, M'Cann and O'Brien, 1 g. each extra	3	8	3
	,,	30.	Subsistence of 11 men at 1 g. and 3 at ½ g., per Hassett	14	4	4½
	,,	,,	Mitchell, Grey, Lindsay and Wheatley, 1 g. each	4	11	0
287 12 10	,,	,,	Watkins, for diet of sundry persons in October and November, per his account	287	12	10
	1798.					
	January	1.	Lindsay, of the Fifeshire Fencibles, returning to Glasgow	20	0	0
	,,	2.	John Hanlon, per receipt	5	13	9
	,,	4.	Captain Coulson, per receipt	30	0	0
	,,	,,	Serjeant Chapman, 3 gs.; John Connell, 5 gs.	9	2	0
	,,	5.	Mitchell, by Mr. Cooke's directions ...	4	11	0

£996 10 9 — C. F.   C. F.   £3,763   5   6½

ACCOUNT OF SECRET SERVICE MONEY, IRELAND, 1798.

	1798.		PAID.	£	s.	d.
£996 10 9 — B. F.			Per amount brought forward,	3,763	5	6½
	January	5.	Lord Enniskillen, for Captain Henry St. George Cole, by direction of Mr. Pelham	100	0	0
	,,	6.	Subsistence of 14 men, 11 at 1 g. and 3 at ½ g., per account	14	4	4½
	,,	,,	Grey, Mitchell and Wheatley, 1 g. each	3	8	3
1 12 11	,,	,,	Hassett, for washing sheets, etc., for men in the Tower	1	12	11
13 13 0	,,	,,	Mrs. Morris, for diet and lodging Mr. Smith and wife, 2 weeks	13	13	0
	,,	,.	Mr. Cooke	25	0	0
	,,	8.	Serjeant Denis M'Cawly of the Roscommon Militia, by desire of Lord Carhampton	22	15	0
	,,	,,	Travers, 1 g.; 9th, Grey, 5 g.; 11th, Wheatley, 3 g.	10	4	9
	,,	6.	Mr. Marshall, by desire of Mr. Pelham	113	15	0
	,,	13.	Subsistence of 7 men at 1 g. and 3 at ½ g.	9	13	4½
	,,	,,	Mitchell, 4 g.; Grey, 1 g.; Travers, 1 g.; Joyce's brother, 1 g.; Wheatley, 1 g.	6	16	6
	,,	,,	Mr. Dutton	68	5	0
	,,	,,	Mr. Cooke, for Mr. Higgins	100	0	0
100 0 0	,,	18.	Surgeon-General, for attendance on prisoners	100	0	0
	,,	,,	Mr. Cooke, for Justice Bell	50	0	0
13 13 0	,,	19.	Mrs. Morris, diet and lodging Smith and wife	13	13	0
	,,	,,	Mr. Cooke, for soldiers of the Kildare Militia	5	13	9
	,,	20.	Wheatley, Mitchell, Grey, Chapman, Baynham and Travers, 1 g. each	6	16	6
	,,	,,	Subsistence of 5 men in the Tower at 1 g. and 3 at ½ g.	7	7	10½
	,,	,,	Mr. Smith	10	0	0
	,,	22.	Major Sirr, for Bourke	5	13	9
	,,	23.	Wheatley, to take him home	20	0	0
,125 9 8 — C. F.			C. F.	£4,471	18	7

B

ACCOUNT OF SECRET SERVICE MONEY, IRELAND, 1798.

£1,125 9 8 — D. F.

6 7 10

£1,131 17 6 — C. F.

1798.		PAID.	£	s.	d.
		Per amount brought forward,	4,471	18	7
January	25.	Mr. Cooke, for Corbett	20	0	0
,,	27.	Major Sirr, for M°Cann	5	13	9
,,	,,	Grey, 1 g.; Mitchell, 2 g.; Chapman, 1 g.; Travers, 1 g.	5	13	9
,,	,,	Subsistence of 4 men at 1 g. and 1 at ½ g.	5	2	4½
,,	29.	Mr. Cooke, for Warren	2	5	6
Feb.	2.	Mrs. Morris, balance for diet and lodging Smith and wife	6	7	10
,,	,,	Mr. Cooke, for Mr. Bell	40	13	9
,,	,,	Honorable C. Skeffington, what he paid Newell	22	15	0
,,	,,	Mr. O'Bren from the north	13	13	0
,,	3.	Grey, 2 g.; Chapman, 1 g.; Travers, 1 g.; Mitchell, 1 g.; Newell, 5 g. ...	11	7	6
,,	,,	Subsistence of 4 men at 1 g. and 2 at ½ g.	5	13	9
,,	8.	Major Sirr, to release Mitchell, 2 g.; for M°Cann, 5 g.	7	19	3
,,	,,	Mr. Dawes, for Joyce's cloaths	4	15	2½
,,	9.	T. M°Cue, a trumpeter of the 5 dragoon guards	1	2	9
,,	,,	Mr. Cooke, for B.	10	0	0
,,	10.	Gray, Mitchell, Chapman and Travers, 1 g. each	4	11	0
,,	,,	Subsistence of 4 men at 1 g. and 3 at ½ g.	6	5	1½
,,	16.	Newell, on going to England	56	17	6
,,	17.	Grey, Mitchell, Chapman and Travers, 1 g. each	4	11	0
,,	,,	Subsistence of 4 men at 1 g. and 3 at ½ g.	6	5	1½
,,	22.	Major Sirr, for Brennan, by direction of Mr. Cooke	22	15	0
,,	24.	Mr. Pollock for J. W. H.	56	17	6
,,	,,	Grey, Mitchell, Chapman and Travers, 1 g. each	4	11	0
,,	,,	Subsistence of 4 men at 1 g. and 3 at ½ g.	6	5	1½
,,	,,	Major Sirr, for a printer in the *Telegraph* office	1	2	9
		C. F.	£4,805	3	1½

ACCOUNT OF SECRET SERVICE MONEY, IRELAND, 1798. 11

	1798.		PAID.	£	s.	d.
£1,131 17 6 — B. F.			Per amount brought forward,	4,805	3	1½
	Feb.	27.	Mr. Cooke (Mr. Cope), 300 guineas and 5½	341	5	5½
	,,	28.	Poyle, for Monks	1	2	9
	March	2.	Subsistence of 4 men at 1 g. and 3 at ½ g.	6	5	1½
	,,	,,	Grey, Mitchell, Chapman and Trevors, 1 g. each	4	11	0
	,,	,,	Jer. Hassett, keeper of the Tower (this makes 42 g.)	5	13	9
	,,	,,	Mitchell, extra, 1 g.; Brien Lennon, 1 g.	2	5	6
	,,	6.	Captain Sterling, on account of subsistence for Hamilton, Kirwan and Donnelly, in			
30 0 0			the Barracks, James's-street... ...	30	0	0
	,,	,,	Rev. Mr. Vignoles, by direction of Mr. Pelham	6	16	6
	,,	10.	Subsistence of 4 men at 1 g. and 3 at ½ g.	6	5	1½
	,,	,,	Grey, Mitchell, Chapman and Travers, 1 g. each	4	11	0
	,,	13.	Wm. Logan, police constable, on going to			
22 15 0			the country	22	15	0
	,,	14.	Philip Gahan, by direction of Mr. Cooke...	1	2	9
	,,	15.	Serjeant Chapman, to send his wife to Cork and bring her back...	11	7	6
	,,	16.	Mr. Swan's expenses of coaches, guards,			
23 13 6			etc., at Mr. Bond's...	23	13	6
	,,	,,	Mr. Geo. Murdock, by direction of Mr. Cooke	150	0	0
	,,	17.	Subsistence of 4 men at 1 g. and 3 at ½ g. per each	6	5	0
	,,	,,	Grey, Mitchell, Chapman and Travers, 1 g. each	4	11	0
	,,	,,	Brien Lenehan from Athlone	1	2	9
	,,	20.	Lowry, by direction of Mr. Cooke, on Lord Castlereagh's letter	5	13	9
	,,	,,	Watkins, for diet of sundry persons, De-			
80 10 7½			cember,'97, and January,'98, per account	80	10	7½
	,,	,,	The two Joyces, to take them home ...	11	7	6
	,,	21.	Mr. Lees, 220 guineas, by direction of Mr. Cooke	250	5	0
	,,	,,	Major Sirr, for D'Evelyn	1	2	9
£1,288 16 7½ — C. F.			C. F.	£5,783	16	7

ACCOUNT OF SECRET SERVICE MONEY, IRELAND, 1798.

£1,288 16 7½ – B. F.

1798.		PAID.	£	s.	d.
		Per amount brought forward,	5,783	16	7
March	24.	Advance to J. Richardson, keeper of Kilmainham Gaol, for support of State prisoners	400	0	0
,,	,,	Subsistence of 4 men at 1 g. and 3 at ½ g.	6	5	1½
,,	,,	Grey, Mitchell, Chapman and Travers, 1 g. each	4	11	0
,,	26.	J. Walsh, expense of bringing Kelaher and Wilson from Cork	34	2	6
,,	27.	Mr. Trevor, Royal Infirmary, diet, etc., necessary for the two Joyces, from 29 January to 21 March	11	16	3½
,,	,,	Mr. Godfrey, expense of coach-hire, etc., to Wicklow, etc.	3	19	1
,,	28.	Serjeant Usher, 7 D. G., expenses with prisoners from Athlone	4	11	0
,,	,,	Chapman, to buy cloaths on his going to Cork	3	8	3
,,	,,	Mr. A. Neilson, expense of bringing up Joseph M'Anally, a witness from Monaghan	12	10	3
,,	,,	Major Sirr, for Lennon and his sons, who attended at Roscommon	5	13	9
,,	,,	Mr. Cooke, for Darcy Mahon	100	0	0
,,	29.	Mr. Lindsay, for Mrs. Bell	20	0	0
,,	,,	Mr. Cooke, for Mr. Swan	100	0	0
,,	30.	Tho. Tyler, gaoler of Roscommon, for expenses bringing up John Cummings, prisoner	11	7	6
,,	,,	Travers, to buy cloaths on his going to Trim	4	11	0
,,	,,	Grey, Mitchell, Chapman and Travers, 1 g. each	4	11	0
,,	,,	Subsistence of 4 men at 1 g. and 5 at ½ g.	7	7	10½
,,	31.	Major Sirr, for Brennan	22	15	0
April	2.	Lord Enniskillen, for Captain Henry St. George Cole	160	0	0
,,	,,	J. Welsh, expense of bringing Sweeny from Cork	28	8	9
,,	,,	Monks, 1 g.; Coughlan, 1 g., by desire of Mr. Cooke	2	5	6

£1,795 12 0 — C. F.

C. F. £6,732 0 5½

ACCOUNT OF SECRET SERVICE MONEY, IRELAND, 1798.

	1798.		PAID.	£	s.	d.
£1,795 12 0 — B. F.			Per amount brought forward,	6,732	0	5½
	April	3.	Mr. Cooke, for Mr. Verner	11	7	6
	,,	4.	Stephen Robson, a soldier, by Mr. Cooke's desire	0	11	4½
	,,	6.	Mr. Cooke, per his note	100	0	0
	,,	7.	Major Sirr, for 3 Lennons, Doran, M'Allaster and Magrath, expenses coming from the assizes	10	4	9
	,,	,,	Grey, Mitchell and Travers, 1 g. each	3	8	3
	,,	,,	Subsistence of 4 men at 1 g. and 5 at ½ g.	7	7	10½
115 0 0	,,	,,	Oliver Carleton, esq., on going to Mr. O'Connor's trial in England	115	0	0
11 7 6	,,	,,	Sir George Hill, for a man going to do.	11	7	6
	,,	,,	Cahill, by desire of Mr. Cooke	1	2	9
11 7 6	,,	11.	Campbell, lodging, etc., for prisoners, Lower Castle Yard	11	7	6
34 11 0	,,	,,	Mr. Dutton, going to England to attend Quigley's trial	34	11	0
	,,	,,	Mr. Verner	28	8	9
	,,	13.	Lowry, by desire of Mr. Cooke	1	14	1½
21 9 8	,,	14.	Mr. Swan, balance of an account of expenses in search for and apprehending sundry persons	21	9	8
	,,	,,	Subsistence of 5 men at 1 g. and 5 at ½ g.	8	10	7½
	,,	,,	Mitchell, Grey, Travers and Coughlan, 1 g. each	4	11	0
	,,	16.	Major Sandys	2	5	6
	,,	18.	Mitchell, to pay his lodging	2	5	6
27 6 0	,,	19.	Duignan, dieting State prisoners, 17th January to 14th March, per account	27	6	0
8 16 0½	,,	,,	C. Stuart, diet, lodging and wine for Mr. Taaffe, 10 days	8	16	0½
22 15 0	,,	20.	J. Armit, esq., account of Oliver Carleton, esq., what he paid a man in London sent by Sir G. Hill to attend the trials	22	15	0
25 0 0	,,	,,	Mr. Trevor, on account of expenses, State prisoners, Kilmainham	25	0	0
£2,073 4 9½— C. F.			C. F.	£7,191	11	2

ACCOUNT OF SECRET SERVICE MONEY, IRELAND, 1798.

1798.		PAID.	£	s.	d.
£2,073 4 8½— B. F.		Per amount brought forward,	7,191	11	2
	April 20.	Mr. Archer, expenses of bringing persons from Co. Wicklow ...	3	19	10
	,, 21.	Subsistence of 4 men at 1 g. and 10 at ½ g.	10	4	9
	,, ,,	Mitchell and Grey, 1 g. each	2	5	6
	,, ,,	Major Bruce, for two soldiers of the Cork Militia looking for Trainor ...	1	2	9
74 5 10½	,, 23.	Mich. Vaughan, for medicines for State prisoners at Kilmainham, per his account to 8th February, 1798	74	5	10½
110 8 9	,, ,,	Watkins, diet of sundry persons, etc., in the Castle, etc., in February and March, per account	110	8	9
	,, ,,	Mr. Brownlow, going to Whitehaven about Sampson ...	11	7	6
	,, ,,	Mr. Poyle, for cloaths for John Moncks ...	2	17	5
27 4 4	,, ,,	M'Kenzie, keeper of the Castle Guard House, for bedding, fire and candle for sundry prisoners, from November, '97, per account vouched by Major Nicholls	27	4	4
20 0 0	,, 25.	Captain Sterling, on further account for subsistence of men in the Barracks, James's-street ...	20	0	0
	,, ,,	Travers' wife, per Grey	1	2	9
	,, 26.	J. Hassett, keeper of the Tower (this makes 47 g.)	5	13	9
	,, 27.	Mr. Darcy Mahon, by direction of Mr. Cooke	100	0	0
	,, ,,	J. Pollock, esq., on his going to England	110	0	0
	,, ,,	Subsistence of 4 men at 1 g. and 10 at ½ g.	10	4	9
	,, ,,	Grey, Mitchell and Travers, 1 g. each	3	8	3
	,, ,,	Mr. Brewer, expense of sending F. Provost, a French prisoner, to Liverpool	2	2	2½
	May 1.	Alex. Worthington, esq.	45	10	0
	,, ,,	Lowry, by desire of Lord Castlereagh	2	5	6
	,, 3.	Geo. Hobbs, by desire of Mr. Rochford, Co. Carlow	20	0	0
	,, ,,	Grey, for lodging and cloaths, by desire of Mr. Cooke	4	11	0
£2,309 3 6 — C. F.		C. F.	£7,760	6	1

ACCOUNT OF SECRET SERVICE MONEY, IRELAND, 1798.

1798.		PAID.	£	s.	d.
£2,309 3 6 — B. F.		Per amount brought forward,	7,760	6	1
May	3.	Lord Carhampton's bill to Mr. Luttrell, on account of James Feris, to 1 May (ought to be 1 June), £50	54	3	4
,,	5.	Subsistence of 4 men at 1 g. and 10 at ½ g.	10	4	9
,,	,,	Mitchell, Grey and Travers, 1 g. each ...	3	8	3
,,	,,	Major Sirr, for Bourke's widow, 3. g.; Edward Joyce, 1 g.	4	11	0
,,	,,	Philip Cahill	1	2	9
,,	8.	Hunt and Kiernan, for medicines for prisoners in the Castle	20	2	5
,,	10.	Subsistence of 4 men at 1 g. and 10 at ½ g.	10	4	9
,,	,,	Mitchell, Grey and Travers, 1 g. each ...	3	8	3
,,	,,	Mr. Medlicott, by desire of Mr. Cooke ...	5	13	9
,,	,,	Honorable A. Annesley, per Mr. Swan ...	50	0	0
,,	,,	Mr. Philip Godfrey, on account, for attendances — Kilmainham	25	0	0
,,	,,	Major Sirr, for Brennan	11	7	6
,,	14.	Counsellor Townsend, what he advanced in Cork to two persons going from thence to O'Connor's trial...	34	2	6
,,	15.	J. Lees, esq., for Mr. Sproule	20	0	0
,,	16.	Bremer and Cahill, 1 g. each	2	5	6
,,	17.	Mr. Hyde, expenses of bringing up Mr. Caulfield, 1 g., and Doyle from Kilcullen, £1 10s. 0½d., chaise, guards, etc. ...	2	12	9½
,,	19.	Lowry, to buy cloaths, and in full, by Mr. Cooke's desire	5	13	9
,,	,,	Grey, Mitchell and Travers, 1 g. each ...	3	8	3
,,	,,	Subsistence of 7 men at 1 g. and 5 at ½ g.	10	16	1½
,,	23.	C. Stuart, for diet, lodging and wine for Mr. FitzGerald, 2 weeks, 18 May ...	12	5	11
,,	,,	Chaise, serjeant and soldiers with [blank] from Kilcullen	2	5	6
,,	24.	Bill remitted to Wright (alias Lawler), £30, Eng., ex. 9½	32	17	0
,,	26.	J. Lees, esq., for Mr. Sproule	50	0	0
		C. F.	£8,136	0	2

£2,405 12 7½ — C. F.

1798.		PAID.	£	s.	d.
		Per amount brought forward,	8,136	0	2
May	26.	Mr. M'Naghten's draft, 3 April, for subsistence of John Chambers	6	16	6
,,	,,	Grey, Mitchell, Travers and Cahill, 1 g. each	4	11	0
,,	,,	Subsistence of 6 men at 1 g. and 7 at ½ g.	10	16	1½
,,	31.	C. Brennan	22	15	0
,,	,,	Mr. W. Edgar, by Mr. Cooke's desire ...	100	0	0
June	2.	Subsistence of 7 men at 1 g. and 7 at ½ g. each	11	18	10½
,,	,,	Mitchell, Grey and Travers, 1 g. each; O'Neil, per Mr. Cooke, 2 g.	5	13	9
,,	5.	Joseph Wall, keeper of the Prison, Smithfield, for diet of State prisoners, 31 May, per account	56	12	1
,,	6.	Mr. Jennings, per Mr. Lees	50	0	0
,,	9.	Subsistence of 7 men at 1 g. and 7 at ½ g.	11	18	10½
,,	,,	Mitchell, 2 g.; Grey, 1 g.; Travers, 1 g.; 10th, Cahill, 1 g.	5	13	9
,,	,,	Major Sandys, for men in the barracks ...	3	8	3
,,	,,	Chaise with 3 men sent to Naas, per Merchants' cavalry	1	2	9
,,	12.	Do. with J. Connellan from Dundalk, and expenses on the road	3	9	10½
,,	,,	Mr. Dutton, by desire of Lord Castlereagh	50	0	0
,,	,,	Dean of Killala, per Lord Altamont, expenses of B. Warren, Castlebar ...	8	0	0
,,	13.	Mr. Swan, by Mr. Cooke's desire ...	100	0	0
,,	,,	Mr. Dennis, for Mr. Ryan's widow, per d°.	100	0	0
,,	,,	Charles M'Fallen, going to Derry, per d°.	6	16	6
,,	,,	Lenehan, by the Lord Lieutenant's direction, per Major Bruce	11	7	6
,,	,,	Watkins, diet of prisoners, April and May, per account	389	15	2½
,,	15.	J. Pollock's bill from London, 30 May, £100, English, ex. 9⅜	109	7	6
,,	,,	Alderman James, on account of his office, etc.	200	0	0
,,	20.	F. H., discovery of L. E. F.	1,000	0	0
		C. F.	£10,406	3	8½

ACCOUNT OF SECRET SERVICE MONEY, IRELAND, 1798.

	1798.		PAID.	£	s.	d.
£2,863 9 0½— B. F.			Per amount brought forward, 10,406	3	8½
	June	16.	Subsistence of 7 men at 1 g. and 7 at ½ g.	11	18	10½
	,,	,,	Grey, 2 g.; Mitchell, 1 g.; Travers, 1 g.; O'Neill, 2 g.	6	16	6
0 17 4	,,	17.	Chaise from the 'Man of War,' with Bird, alias Johnston	0	17	4
	,,	18.	Cahill, 1 g.; 30th do., 1 g.; O'Neill, 2 g.	4	11	0
	,,	20.	Mr. Sproule	50	0	0
	,,	21.	Mr. Stewart, Surgeon-General, for attendants on Lord Edward Fitzgerald in gaol, viz.: Mr. Garnett, who sat in the room, £22 15s.; Mr. Kinsley, attending him while in a delirium, £4 11s.; Surgeon Leake, 16 days' attendance, twice a day,			
47 6 0			£20	47	6	0
	,,	23.	Subsistence of 7 men at 1 g., and 7 at ½ g.	11	18	10½
	,,	,,	Grey, Mitchell and Travers, 1 g. each ...	3	8	3
	,,	26.	Mr. Godfrey, on account, for attendance at			
20 0 0			Kilmainham	20	0	0
	,,	27.	Sir Henry Echlin, for Nugent	5	13	9
	,,	,,	Mr. Cooke, Sunday, 20th May, not before entered	11	7	6
	,,	30.	Subsistence of 7 men at 1 g. and 7 men at ½ g.	11	18	10½
	,,	,,	Grey, Mitchell and Travers, 1 g. each	3	8	3
	,,	,,	Frederick Trench, esq., for Bergin ...	50	0	0
	July	4.	J. C. Beresford, esq.	50	0	0
	,,	,,	Major Sirr, for provisions, etc., for prisoners in the old Custom House and Royal			
22 15 0			Exchange, at different times	22	15	0
	,,	,,	Ensign Murray (York Regiment), expenses			
5 13 9			of bringing priest Martin from Rathdrum	5	13	9
	,,	,,	T. M'Donald, for 8 horses with Dr. Esmond			
4 6 8			from Naas, etc., 8th June, &c. ...	4	6	8
	,,	7.	Subsistence of 7 men at 1 g. and 7 at ½ g.	11	18	10½
	,,	,,	Grey, Mitchell and Travers, 1 g. each ...	3	8	3
1 1 8	,,	11.	Chaise, etc., with a prisoner from Naas ...	1	1	8
£2,963 9 5½— C. F.			C. F. £10,744	13	1½

ACCOUNT OF SECRET SERVICE MONEY, IRELAND, 1798.

	1798.		PAID.	£	s.	d.
£2,965 9 5½ — B. F.			Per amount brought forward,	10,744	13	1½
	July	13.	James Hutchinson, by Lord Castlereagh's directions...	2	5	6
49 3 8	,,	,,	C. Stuart, for diet, lodging and wine for Mr. FitzGerald, 8 weeks from 18th May to 13th July, per account ...	49	3	8
	,,	14.	Grey, Mitchell and Travers, 1 g. each ...	3	8	3
	,,	,,	Subsistence of 8 men at 1 g. and 6 at ½ g. ...	12	10	3
	,,	,,	O'Brien, washing for prisoners, 16/5, coach hire he paid, 8s. 1½d. ...	1	4	6½
0 11 4½	,,	18.	Lieutenant Simmons, Leixlip Cavalry, chaise with a prisoner ...	0	11	4½
	,,	,,	J. Pollock's bill from London, dated 3rd July, £150, ex. 9½ per cent. ...	164	5	0
20 0 0	,,	19.	Captain Sterling, account of subsistence of men in James's street ...	20	0	0
100 0 0	,,	,,	Major Sandys, on account of prisoners in the provost ...	100	0	0
	,,	,,	Earl of Enniskillen, for Captain Henry St. George Cole	37	10	0
	,,	21.	Subsistence of 8 men at 1 g. and 4 at ½ g. ...	11	7	6
	,,	,,	Grey, 2 g.; Mitchell, 1 g.; Trevors, 1 g.	4	11	0
124 1 11	,,	23.	J. Wall, keeper of the Prison in Smithfield, for diet of State prisoners from 1st June to 9th July, per account ...	124	1	11
200 0 0	,,	25.	Major Sandys, on further account of prisoners in the Provost ...	200	0	0
	,,	26.	Major Sirr, for pistols for Mr. Reynolds ...	9	2	0
	,,	,,	T. Collins' bill, dated London, 23rd June, £50, Eng., ex. 9¾ ...	54	17	6
	,,	28.	Subsistence of 8 men at 1 g. and 3 at ½ g.	10	16	1½
	,,	,,	Grey, Mitchell and Travers, 1 g. each ...	3	8	3
30 0 0	,,	,,	Mr. Joshua Manders, on account of expenses attending prisoners in the Castle ...	30	0	0
	,,	30.	Mitchell to pay his rent and buy cloaths ...	5	13	9
	,,	31.	Mr. Sproule	20	0	0
£3,489 6 5 — C. F.			C. F. £11,609		9	9

ACCOUNT OF SECRET SERVICE MONEY, IRELAND, 1798.   19

	1798.		PAID.	£	s.	d.
£3,489 6 3 — B. F.			Per amount brought forward,	11,609	9	9
	August	1.	Rd. Herbert, for subsistence of Geraghty, an approver at Clonmel	5	15	0
	,,	2.	Major Sirr, for Leech	2	5	6
	,,	4.	Subsistence of 8 men at 1 g. and 3 at ½ g. each	10	16	1½
	,,	,,	Grey, Mitchell and Travers, 1 g. each ...	3	8	3
	,,	7.	Major Sirr, for Serjeant M'Dowall of the Dumbartons	11	7	6
16 5 0	,,	,,	Mr. Wigelsworth, steward, Royal Infirmary, subsistence of Mr. Hugh Jackson, from 5 April to 4 June	16	5	0
	,,	,,	E. O'Neal, by Mr. Cooke's desire ...	1	2	9
	,,	11.	Subsistence of 8 men at 1 g. and 3 at ½ g.	10	16	1½
	,,	,,	Grey, Mitchell, Travers and Cahill, 1 g. each	4	11	0
	,,	13.	Mr. A. Worthington, balance of an account	5	13	9
	,,	,,	Do., advances	34	2	6
3 8 3	,,	,,	Capt. Smyth, Drogheda Corps, expenses with Jackson, a prisoner	3	8	3
	,,	14.	James Lardner, per Mr. Cooke's note ...	20	0	0
12 5 11	,,	,,	C. Stuart, for diet, lodging and wine for Mr. Fitzgerald, 13 to 27 July ...	12	5	11
0 11 4½	,,	,,	Carriage with a prisoner from Swords, 13 July	0	11	4½
6 5 1½	,,	16.	Col. Handfield, for chaises, etc., from Montgomery Mills, with Aylmer, Fitzgerald, and other prisoners, July	6	5	1½
	,,	,.	J. Magin, per receipt	700	0	0
	,,	17.	Do., per do.	56	17	7
2 3 4	,,	,,	Chaises, horses, etc., with Sir Tho. Esmonde and Capt. Doyle, from Bray in [blank], and returning with the officers who guarded them	2	3	4
	,,	,,	Hanlon, extra 1 g.; 18th, Grey, Mitchell, Travers and O'Neil, 1 g. each ...	5	13	9
	,,	18.	O'Brien, for 8 men at 1 g. and 3 at ½ g. ...	10	16	1½
0 18 8	,,	,,	Major Sirr, expenses of Connolly from Drogheda to Belfast, in July; and Connolly and Martin from Drogheda to Dublin, 18 August	6	18	8
£3,537 4 1 — C. F.			C. F.	£12,540	13	3½

1798.		PAID.	£	s.	d.
£3,537 4 1 — D. F.		Per amount brought forward,	12,540	13	3½
	August 18.	J. Pollock, esq., bill to F. Carleton, esq., dated Newry, 10 August	56	17	6
28 2 3	,, 21.	Mr. James Dowis, Commander of the 'Prince Augustus,' Scotch Revenue cutter, for a pilot on the Wexford coast, and subsistence of prisoners, by order of General Needham, per receipt ...	28	2	3
	,, ,,	Serjeant Lodwick Hamilton, of the Roscommon Militia, by desire of Lord Carhampton, in January '98, when Sergt. M'Cauly was paid the same for attendance at assizes, etc., to prosecute ...	22	15	0
	,, 23.	Serjeant Gleeson, Co. Limerick Militia, who brought a prisoner from Cork, to pay his expenses back	3	8	3
	,, 25.	O'Brien, for 8 men at 1 g. and 3 at ½ g. ...	10	16	1½
	,, ,,	Grey, Mitchell, Travers and O'Neil, 1 g. each; Joyce, 2 g.	6	16	6
	,, 27.	Mr. Taggart, from Newtownardes, by desire of Lord Castlereagh	10	0	0
638 18 5½	,, ,,	Watkins, for diet of State prisoners in the Castle, etc., for June and July, per account	638	18	5½
	,, 28.	Cahill, 1 g.; Ch. M'Fillan, per Mr. Marsden's note, 3 g.	4	11	0
	,, ,,	Mr. Sproule, per Mr. Cooke's note ...	50	0	0
	,, ,,	Mr. Pollock's bill, dated Belfast, 20 June	56	17	6
	,, 31.	John Chambers, per Mr. Cooke's note ...	2	5	6
	Sept.	O'Brien, for 8 men at 1 g. and 3 at ½ g. ...	10	16	1½
		Grey, Mitchell, Travers, O'Neal and Phelan, 1 g. each	5	13	9
	,, 3.	Mr. Cooke	30	0	0
	,, 6.	James Ormsby, esq., per receipt ...	18	4	0
	,, ,,	Charles M'Fillan, by Mr. Cooke's desire...	20	0	0
54 11 0	,, 7.	Mr. Taggart and three others, from Co. Down, attending secret committee, balance of account of expenses and return, with £10 each for loss of time, per account	54	11	0
£1,258 15 9½— C. F.		C. F.	£13,571	6	3

ACCOUNT OF SECRET SERVICE MONEY, IRELAND, 1798.

	1798.		PAID.	£	s.	d.
£4,258 15 9¼ — B. F.			Per amount brought forward,	13,571	6	3
	Septem.	7.	O'Brien, for 8 men at 1 g. and 3 at ½ g. ...	10	16	1½
	,,	,,	Grey, Mitchell, Travers, O'Neill, Cahill and Phelan, 1 g. each	6	16	6
	,,	12.	Major Sandys, balance of an account for subsistence of prisoners at the barracks, to 27 July			
58 16 8½				58	16	8½
5 13 9	,,	,,	Capt. Smyth, expenses with a prisoner from Newry	5	13	9
	,,	14.	J. Pollock, esq., bill, dated Belfast, 8 Sept.	56	17	6
16 14 10	,,	,,	Lieut. Atkinson, of the Louth Militia, expenses of bringing La Roche and Teeling, French officers, to Dublin	16	14	10
100 0 0	,,	,,	Major Sandys, on account of subsistence of prisoners	100	0	0
	,,	15.	O'Brien, for 8 men at 1 g. and 3 at ½ g. ...	10	16	1½
	,,	,,	Grey, Mitchell, Travers and O'Neil, 1 g. each; 17th, Bourke, 1 g. ...	5	13	9
	,,	21.	M. Bourke, 1 g.; 22nd, Grey, Mitchell, Travers and O'Neil, 1 g. each ...	5	13	9
	,,	22.	O'Brien, for 8 men at 1 g. and 3 at ½ g. ...	10	16	1½
	,,	,,	Mr. Sproule	24	14	7
208 2 2	,,	,,	Joseph Wall, keeper of Bridewell, for maintenance of State prisoners to the 10th September, per account	208	2	2
	,,	,,	John Chambers, by Mr. Cooke's desire ...	2	5	6
	,,	26.	Mr. Ellis, from Enniskillen, for his expenses	20	0	0
	,,	24.	Mr. Cooke	10	0	0
	,,	28.	Alderman James, for expenses of his office	200	0	0
	,,	,,	Lindsay and Mr. Burke, 1 g. each, by direction of Mr. Cooke	2	5	6
	,,	29.	O'Brien, for 8 men at 1 g. each, and 3 at ½ g.	10	16	1½
	,,	,,	Grey, Mitchell, Travers and O'Neill, 1 g. each	4	11	0
	,,	,,	Mr. Tho. Reynolds	1,000	0	0
13 5 5	October	2.	J. Haggarty, pilot on board the 'Prince of Wales,' Scotch Revenue cruiser, from 28 July to 15 Sep. '98, 49 days at 5s. 5d.	13	5	5
£4,661 8 9— C. F.			C. F. £15,356		1	8½

	1798.		PAID.	£	s.	d.
£4,661 8 8 — B F.			Per amount brought forward,	15,356	1	8½
	October	6.	O'Brien, for 9 men at 1 g. and 3 at ½ g ...	11	18	10½
	,,	,,	Grey, Mitchell, Travers, O'Neal and Burke, 1 g. each ...	5	13	9
	,,	,,	J. Chambers, £1 2s. 9d., 8th, Mr. Nugent, £5 13s. 9d. ...	6	16	6
	,,	9.	F. Dutton, by direction of Lord Castlereagh	50	0	0
	,,	13.	O'Brien, for 9 men at 1 g. and 3 at ½ g. ...	11	18	10½
	,,	,,	Grey, Mitchell, Travers, O'Neal, Lindsay, Burke, Chambers and Cahill, 1 g. [each]	7	19	3
74 4 9		22.	Bill drawn by Robert Harding, esq., Cork, for subsistence of the Hills, witnesses for the Crown ...	74	4	9
	,,	,,	Tho. Collins, bill, dated London, 19th Sep., £50, English ...	54	3	4
	,,	24.	Mr. Tucker of Ringsend, for Mr. Carry ...	20	0	0
	,,	27.	O'Brien, for 10 men at 1 g. and 3 at ½ g. ...	13	1	7½
	,,	,,	Grey, Mitchell, Travers, O'Neal, Burke, Chambers and Lindsay, 1 g. ...	7	19	3
	,,	30.	Goaler of Limerick, by order of Lord Castlereagh, compensation for trouble attending prisoners by courts martial ...	50	0	0
812 13 5½	,,	,,	Watkins, for diet of State prisoners, August and Sep., per account ...	812	13	5½
	Nov.	3.	O'Brien, for 10 men at 1 g. and 3 at ½ g. ...	13	1	7½
	,,	,,	Grey, Lindsay, Mitchell, Travers, Bourke and O'Neal, Chambers, 1 g. ...	7	19	3
	,,	,,	Cahill, by direction of Mr. Cooke ...	2	16	10½
£5,548 6 10½				16,568	12	9
			Deduct the amount of the several sums per margin in red ink, received at the Treasury, 16th Nov, '98, per letter, being the amount of subsistence of State prisoners from January to Sep., '98, £4,526 14s. 3d. Do. of expenses of carriages, guards, etc., with prisoners, £1,021 12s. 7½d. ...	5,548	6	10½
			C. F.	£11,020	5	10½

ACCOUNT OF SECRET SERVICE MONEY, IRELAND, 1798.

	1798.		PAID.	£	s.	d.
			Per amount brought forward,	11,020	5	10½
	November	10.	Surgeon-General, for his attendance on			
£200 0 0			State prisoners	200	0	0
	,,	,,	Oliver Carleton, esq., expenses of car-			
5 8 4			riages, etc., with prisoners	5	8	4
	,,	,,	O'Brien, for taking care of the Tower and washing for prisoners, from 14 May to 5 Nov., '98, 25 weeks at 11s. 4½d. ...	14	4	4½
	,,	,,	Do. for 10 men at 1 g. and 3 at ½ g. ...	13	1	7½
	,,	,,	Grey, Mitchell, Travers, Lindsay, Burke, O'Neal and Chambers, 1 g.	7	19	3
	,,	12.	Major Thackary, his expenses from Derry			
28 8 9			with T. W. Tone, and return ...	28	8	9
28 8 9	,,	,,	Captain Williams, do. do. do.	28	8	9
	,,	13.	Mr. Holmes, expense of carriages bringing			
9 2 0			Rev. Mr. Dease from Sligo	9	2	0
	,,	16.	Mr. T. Reynolds	2,000	0	0
	,,	17.	O'Brien, for 10 men at 1 g. and 3 at ½ g. ...	13	1	7½
	,,	,,	Grey, Mitchell, Travers, O'Neal, Lindsay, Chambers, Burke and Cahill, 1 g. ...	9	2	0
	,,	,,	Lord Carhampton's bill for Feris, half-year, £50, English	54	3	4
	,,	,,	Mr. Holmes, for his own expenses from			
25 11 10½			Sligo with Mr. Dease, and his return ...	25	11	10½
	,,	19.	Mr. Philip Godfrey, balance of his account for attendance on State prisoners at Kilmainham, for six months, by order of Government, and for coach-hire with			
53 10 0			prisoners	53	10	0
	,,	20.	Captain Williams, expenses in town, de-			
17 1 3			tained on account of Tone	17	1	3
	,,	,,	Mr. Nugent, to take him to England ...	5	13	9
	,,	,,	Bill remitted to Wright, alias Lawler, £30, English, exch. 9 p. c.	32	14	0
	,,	24.	Rt. Honble. Denis Browne, for Flattelly, who prosecuted F. French, esq., at Castlebar, for high treason	100	0	0
	,,	,,	O'Brien, for 9 men at 1 g. and 3 at ½ g. ...	11	18	10½
	,,	,,	Grey, Mitchell, O'Neal, Lindsay, Chambers, Bourke and Cahill, at 1 g.	7	19	3
	,,	29.	Bryan Lennon, by direction of Lord Castlereagh	30	0	0

£367 10 11½— C. F.

C. F. £13,687 14 11

24 ACCOUNT OF SECRET SERVICE MONEY, IRELAND, 1798.

	1798.		PAID.	£	s.	d.
£367 10 11½— B. F			Per amount brought forward,	13,687	14	11
	Decemr.	1.	O'Brien, for 9 men at 1 g. and 3 at ½ g. per week ...	11	18	10½
	,,	,,	Grey, Mitchell, O'Neal, Lindsay, Chambers, Burke and Cahill, 7 at 1 g. ...	7	19	3
	,,	5.	Lieut. Hutton of the Wingfield cavalry, expenses of bringing prisoners from Athlone to Dublin by sea, in June last	22	10	0½
22 10 0½						
	,,	,,	Major Sirr, for O'Kean	5	13	9
	,,	,,	E. Cooke, esq.	500	0	0
	,,	8.	O'Brien, for 10 men at 1 g. and 3 at ½ g. ...	13	1	7½
	,,	,,	Grey, Mitchell, O'Neal, Lindsay, Chambers, Burke and Cahill, 7 at 1 g. ...	7	19	3
	,,	,,	O'Brien, for care of the Tower, washing, etc., 4 weeks, 5th Nov. to 3rd Dec. ...	2	5	6
	,,	15.	Major Sirr, for informer respecting O'Neal	11	7	6
	,,	,,	O'Brien, for 10 men at 1 g. and 3 at ½ g.	13	1	7½
	,,	,,	Grey, Mitchell, O'Neal, Lindsay, Chambers, Burke and Cahill, 7 at 1 g. ...	7	19	3
	,,	,,	Mr. John Mahon, by direction of Mr. Cooke	200	0	0
244 16 8	,,	,,	Joseph Wall for subsistence of prisoners, Smithfield, to 29th Nov.	244	16	8
227 10 0	,,	,,	Wm. Plunkett, esq., for attending courts martial at Castlebar	227	10	0
	,,	22.	O'Brien, for 10 men at 1 g. and 3 at ½ g. ...	13	1	7½
	,,	,,	Grey, Mitchell, O'Neal, Lindsay, Burke, Cahill, T. Lennon and Chambers ...	9	2	0
	,,	29.	Mr. Logan, expenses to Kilkenny, etc., per account	14	19	0½
14 19 0½						
	,,	,,	O'Brien, for 10 men at 1 g. and 3 at ½ g. ...	13	1	7½
	,,	,,	Grey, Mitchell, O'Neal, Lindsay, Burke, Chambers, Lennon and Cahill ...	9	2	0
	,,	,,	Major Sirr, for six men as Christmas boxes	6	16	6
	,,	31.	Mr. Pollock, for two persons, £50 each, per receipt	100	0	0
	1799.					
	Juny.	1.	A. Worthington, esq., balance of an account to 29th December	5	13	9
	,,	,,	Do., advance	34	2	6
	,,	,,	Major Sirr, per receipt	500	0	0
£977 6 8¼— C. F.			C. F.	£15,669	17	3½

ACCOUNT OF SECRET SERVICE MONEY, IRELAND, 1799.

	1799.		PAID.	£	s.	d.
£877 6 8¼— B. F.			Per amount brought forward,	15,669	17	3½
	January	2.	Alex. M'Kenzie, keeper of the guard house, for the use of his rooms from 22 February to 30 October, '98, for			
9 15 0			prisoners, thirty-six weeks at 5s. 5d. ...	9	15	0
	,,	4.	W. B. Swan, for W. Edmond, his clerk, at the office in Exchange Court, etc., per account and receipt	27	5	5½
	,,	5.	Tho Lennon, to take him to England, by direction of Lord Castlereagh ...	12	0	0
	,,	,,	O'Brien, for subsistence of 10 men at 1 g. and 3 at ½ g.	13	1	7½
	,,	,,	Grey, Mitchell, Bourke, O'Neal, Lindsay, Chambers and Cahill	7	19	3
	,,	9.	Alderman James, for expenses of office kept by him for receiving informations,			
200 0 0			issuing passes, etc.	200	0	0
	,,	12.	O'Brien, for taking care of the Tower, etc., 3 December to 7 January, 5 weeks ...	2	16	10½
	,,	,,	Do., for 10 men at 1 g. and 3 at ½ g. ...	13	1	7½
	,,	,,	Grey, Mitchell, Bourke, O'Neal, Lindsay and Chambers	6	16	6
	,,	,,	R. Harding, esq., of Cork, bill for the subsistence of the Hills to 5 January,			
29 11 6			per account	29	11	6
	,,	18.	W. B. Swan, esq., per Mr. Cooke's note	100	0	0
	,,	19.	Mr. T. Reynolds, per receipt ...	1,000	0	0
	,,	,,	O'Brien, for 11 men at 1 g. and 3 at ½ g.	14	4	4½
	,,	,,	Grey, Mitchell, Bourke, O'Neal, Lindsay and Chambers	6	16	6
	,,	23.	J Pollock, esq., per receipt	1,137	10	0
	,,	24.	Cahill, to take him to the country ...	5	13	9
	,,	,,	Grey, per advance, 11 October last, for rent, etc., not before charged ...	6	16	6
	,,	,,	Rev. Geo. Lambart, per Mr. Cooke's note	300	0	0
	,,	26.	Mr. Collins, bill, dated London, 23 December, '98, £50, ex. 10½ per cent.	55	5	0
	,,	,,	O'Brien, for 11 men at 1 g. and 3 at ½ g.	14	4	4½
	,,	,,	Grey, Mitchell, Bourke, O'Neal, Lindsay, and Chambers	6	16	6
£1,116 13 2¼— C. F.			C. F.	£18,639	12	1½

ACCOUNT OF SECRET SERVICE MONEY, IRELAND, 1799.

	1799.		PAID.	£	s.	d.
£1,116 13 2½— B. F.			Per amount brought forward,	18,639	12	1½
	February 2.		Mr. Manders, on further account of			
20 0 0			expenses for prisoners in the Castle ...	20	0	0
	,,	,,	O'Brien, for 10 men at 1 g. and 3 at ½ g. each	13	1	7½
	,,	,,	Grey, Mitchell, Chambers, Lindsay, Burke and O'Neal, 1 g. each ...	6	16	6
30 0 0	,,	6.	Mr. Trevor, account of expenses of prisoners, Kilmainham	30	0	0
	,,	9.	Mr. Cooke, for N.	22	15	0
	,,	,,	O'Brien, for 10 men at 1 g. and 3 at ½ g. each	13	1	7½
	,,	,,	Grey, Mitchell, Chambers, Lindsay, Burke and O'Neal, 1 g. each ...	6	16	6
	,,	,,	O'Brien, expenses of 3 men to Bray, 2 days, and coach-hire	1	19	0
			Do., for care of the Tower, 4 weeks to 4 February	2	5	6
413 5 5½	,,	,,	Watkins, for diet of prisoners, Castle, etc., October and November	413	5	5½
	,,	12.	Sir J. Blaquiere, for Leonard Cornwall	22	15	0
	,,	15.	Serjeant Daly, per Mr. Cooke's note ...	10	0	0
	,,	16.	J. Pollock, esq., for T. W. £150 ; G. M. £50	200	0	0
	,,	,,	O'Brien, for 10 men at 1 g. and 3 at ½ g.	13	1	7½
	,,	,,	Do., for Wm. Edmonds	2	5	6
	,,	,,	Grey, Mitchell, Chambers, Lindsay, Bourke and O'Neal	6	16	6
	,,	18.	Alderman Manders, for subsistence of an evidence	4	17	6
	,,	20.	Earl of Enniskillen, for Capt. R. St. Geo. Cole's receipt to 31 December, '98 ...	75	0	0
	,,	22.	Major Sirr, for O'Kean, to take him away	10	0	0
	,,	23.	Mr. Crofton, for 3 men of Mohill, Co. Leitrim, per receipt	34	2	6
	,,	,,	O'Brien, for 11 men at 1 g. and 3 at ½ g.	14	4	4½
	,,	,,	Grey, Mitchell, Chambers, Lindsay, Burke and O'Neal	6	16	6
	March	4.	Mr. Reynolds, to complete £5,000 (viz., Sept. 29, '98, £1,000 ; Nov. 16, '98, £2,000 ; and Jan. 19, '99, £1,000)	1,000	0	0

£1,579 18 8 — C. F.   C. F.   £20,569 12 10

ACCOUNT OF SECRET SERVICE MONEY, IRELAND, 1799.   27

	1799.		PAID.	£	s.	d.
£1,579 18 8 —B. F.			Per amount brought forward,	20,569	12	10
	Feb.	27.	Campbell, balance of his account for lodging, fire, candles and attendance on sundry persons in his house in the Castle yard, in 1797 and 1798, per account			
15 18 6				15	18	6
	March	2.	O'Brien, for 11 men at 1 g. and 3 at ½ g.	14	4	4½
	,,	,,	Grey, Mitchell, Chambers, Lindsay, Burke and O'Neal	6	16	6
	,,	,,	Lindsay, to pay his lodgings, by direction of Mr. Cooke	2	5	6
	,,	,,	Tho. Jones Atkins, per Mr. Marsden's note	113	15	0
	,,	5.	J. Pollock, for McG., sent by post to Belfast	60	0	0
338 18 1	,,	,,	Watkins, for diet of prisoners, Castle, etc., December, '98, and January, '99	338	18	1
18 4 0	,,	6.	Doctor Harding's bill for subsistence of the Hills at Cork	18	4	0
27 18 11½	,,	8.	Mr. Manders, balance of his account to 31st December, '98, for attendance, washing, etc., for prisoners in the Castle, from 12 March, '98	27	18	11½
	,,	,,	O'Brien, for taking care of the Tower, 4 weeks to March 4, '99	2	5	6
	,,	9.	Do. for 11 men at 1 g. and 3 at ½ g.	14	4	4½
	,,	,,	Grey, Mitchell, Burke, O'Neill, Lindsay and Chambers	6	16	6
	,,	12.	Colonel Jackson, for Mr. Moran, by direction of Lord Castlereagh	100	0	0
	,,	15.	Marquess of Waterford, for Doctor Hearn	70	0	0
	,,	16.	Lord Boyle, by direction of Mr. Cooke	100	0	0
	,,	,,	O'Brien, for 11 men at 1 g. and 3 at ½ g.	14	4	4½
	,,	,,	Grey, Mitchell, Bourke, O'Neal, Lindsay and Chambers	6	16	6
	,.	19.	Oliver Carleton, esq., for Shee, diet and lodging for Flannagan, who was to prosecute pikemakers, 18 May to 18 November, '98	20	0	10
	,,	23.	O'Brien, for 11 men, at 1 g. and 3 at ½ g.	14	4	4½
	,,	,,	Grey, Mitchell, Bourke, Lindsay, O'Neal and Chambers	6	16	6
£1,980 18 2½— C. F.			C. F.	£21,523	2	8½

ACCOUNT OF SECRET SERVICE MONEY, IRELAND, 1799.

	1799.		PAID.	£	s.	d.
£1,080 18 2½ — B. F.			Per amount brought forward,	21,523	2	8½
	March	25.	Mr. Marshall, for Frederick Dutton, per Robinson and Pim's bill on Harris and Co., London, £500, English; exchange 10 per cent.	550	0	0
	,,	,,	Cornet Blackmore, 5th dragoon guards, what he paid at Drogheda for chaises			
2 12 0			with 4 persons from Dublin, per receipt	2	12	0
	,,	28.	J. Kelly, per Mr. Cooke's note ...	5	13	9
	,,	,,	Joseph Wall, for the subsistence of State prisoners in Bridewell, from 30 Nov.,'98,			
277 4 6			to 28 Feb., '99, per account ...	277	4	6
	,,	,,	Chapman, by direction of Mr. Cooke ...	3	8	3
	,,	,,	O'Brien, for 12 men at 1 g. and 3 at ½ g.	15	7	1½
	,,	,,	Grey, Mitchell, Bourke, Lindsay, O'Neal and Chambers, 1 g.	6	16	6
	April	6.	O'Brien, for 11 men at 1 g. and 3 at ½ g.	14	4	4½
	,,	,,	Grey, Mitchell, Bourke, Lindsay, O'Neal, Chambers and Chapman	7	19	3
	,,	,,	O'Brien, for taking care of the Tower, 4 weeks to 1 April	2	5	6
		12.	Ensign Smith, Fermanagh Militia, chaises and expenses of bringing Monks from the Castle to Wicklow, to prosecute			
7 19 3			rebels, and back	7	19	3
	,,	13.	O'Brien, for 12 men at 1 g. and 3 at ½ g.	15	7	1½
	,,	,,	Grey, etc., as before, 7 at 1 g. ...	7	19	3
	,,	18.	Mr. Pollock, per receipt	50	0	0
	,,	20.	John Kelly	5	13	9
	,,	,,	O'Brien, for 12 men at 1 g. and 3 at ½ g.	15	7	1½
	,,	,,	Grey, etc., as before, 7 at 1 g. ...	7	19	3
	,,	,,	R. Honourable Denis Browne, for Michael Geraghty	50	0	0
	,,	25.	Sir John Carden, for Brown and Cahill	100	0	0
	,,	27.	Thos. Collins, bill, dated London, 25 March	55	10	0
£2,268 13 11¾ — C. F.			C. F.	£22,724	9	8½

ACCOUNT OF SECRET SERVICE MONEY, IRELAND, 1799.

	1799.		PAID.	£	s.	d.
£2,268 13 11¼— B. F			Per amount brought forward,	22,724	9	8½
	April	27.	O'Brien, for 12 men at 1 g. and 3 at ½ g.	15	7	1½
	,,	,,	Grey, etc., as before, 7 at 1 g.	7	19	3
	,,	29.	The Attorney-General, for people at Finglass, who took several rebels and robbers...	34	2	6
316 4 7½	,,	,,	Watkins, for diet of prisoners, February and March, per account	316	4	7½
	May	1.	Thomas Kearney, recommended by Sir J. Parnell, from the Queen's county	56	17	6
	,,	3.	J. Pollock, esq., for G. M. I.	50	0	0
12 8 9	,,	4.	Mr. Trevor, for subsistence of persons sent from the Castle to the royal military infirmary, per account	12	8	9
	,,	,,	O'Brien, for 14 men at 1 g. and 3 at ½ g.	17	12	7½
	,,	,,	Grey, etc., as before, 7 at 1 g.	7	19	3
	,,	,,	R. Cornwall, esq., amount advanced by him last year to Kellys and Nowlan for information, etc., per account	73	18	9
	,,	8.	Mr. Cooke, an advance	400	0	0
	,,	,,	Bill remitted to Wright, alias Lawler, at Bath, £50; exchange 9¾	54	17	6
	,,	9.	Henry St. George Cole, esq., per Lord Enniskillen, 1 quarter to 1st April	37	10	0
	,,	,,	John Kelly, by direction of Mr. Cooke	5	13	9
	,,	11.	O'Brien, for 14 men at 1 g. and 3 at ½ g.	17	12	7½
	,,	,,	Grey, etc., as before, 7 at 1 g.	7	19	3
	,,	,,	O'Brien, for care of the Tower, 6 weeks, to 14 May	3	8	3
	,,	,,	Keeper of Bridewell, Smithfield, for subsistence of Mary Keating, from 20 March to 20 April, 4 weeks at 16/3	3	5	0
	,,	13.	Commins, by direction of Mr. Cooke	5	13	9
	,,	16.	Grey, to pay rent, etc.	5	13	9
	,,	,,	O'Brien, for 14 men at 1 g. and 3 at ½ g.	17	12	7½
	,,	,,	Grey, etc., as before, 7 at 1 g.	7	19	3
£2,597 7 4 — C. F.			C. F.	£23,884	5	10

	1799.		PAID.	£	s.	d.
£2,507 7 4 — B. F.			Per amount brought forward,	23,884	5	10
			Deduct the amount of the several sums per margin, in red ink, received at the Treasury to May, per letter, being the amount of subsistence of State prisoners, from Sep., '98, to March, '99, £1,680 13s. 9d. D°· expenses of carriages, guards, provisions, etc., of d°· to April, '99, £916 13s. 9d.	2,597	7	4
				£21,286	18	6
	May	20.	Mr. Marshall, repayment of what he paid in London, by Lord Castlereagh's directions, to F. Dutton, 50 g., and to R. Jennings, £50, English ...	111	0	10
	,,	,,	Mr. Cooke, for K.	50	0	0
	,,	,,	Mr. Richard Jennings, of London, per Mr. Robert Norman, of Trinity-street, per receipt and Mr. Jennings' letter...	200	0	0
	,,	24.	Mr. Darcy Mahon, per Mr. Cooke's desire	100	0	0
	,,	25.	O'Brien, for 14 men, at 1 g. and 3 at ½ g.	17	12	7½
	,,	,,	Grey, etc., as before, 7 at 1 g. ...	7	19	3
	,,	,,	O'Brien, for taking care of the Tower, 4 weeks, to 11th June, at 11/4½ ...	2	5	6
	,,	27.	Mr. Sproule, by direction of Mr. Cooke, 25 g.	28	8	9
	,,	,,	Alex. Worthington, esq.	50	0	0
4 12 6	,,	,,	Alderman Manders, subsistence of Owen Tiernay and James Gavin	4	12	6
	June	1.	John Kelly, by direction of Mr. Cooke	5	13	9
	,,	,,	O'Brien, for 14 men, at 1 g. and 3 at ½ g.	17	12	7½
	,,	,,	Grey and others, as before, 7 at 1 g. ...	7	19	3
12 0 6	,,	3.	Mr. Noble, Under-sheriff, Queen's county, expenses of bringing up M'Manus and Bergan, in April, 1798	12	0	6
27 6 0	,,	4.	Dr. Harding, of Cork, for support of the Hills, to May 25	27	6	0
	,,	,,	Mrs. Carey, in full discharge of Mr. Carey's demands	100	0	0
	,,	5.	Mr. Pollock, account of G. M. I. ...	50	0	0
£13 19 0 — C. F.			C. F.	£22,079	10	1

ACCOUNT OF SECRET SERVICE MONEY, IRELAND, 1799.   31

1799.			PAID.	£	s.	d.
£43 19 0 — B. F.			Per amount brought forward,	22,079	10	1
	June	8.	O'Brien, for 14 men at 1 g. and 3 at ½ g.	17	12	7½
	,,	,,	Grey, etc., as before, 7 at 1 g. ...	7	19	3
	,,	10.	Captain D'Auvergne, expense of boat-hire, and for attendance at Holyhead, from November, '97, to April, '99, on account of the rebellion	166	13	4
33 3 8½	,,	,,	R. Warren, keeper of Bridewell, for subsistence of John Mahon and Michael Edwards, per account ...	33	3	8½
	,,	14.	Mr. Reynolds, in full, to 25 March, 1799	1,000	0	0
	,,	,,	Lord Carhampton, for Feris, half-year to 10th May, £50, English	54	3	4
	,,	15.	O'Brien, for 13 men at 1 g. and 3 at ½ g.	16	9	10½
	,,	,,	Grey, etc., as before, 7 at 1 g. ...	7	19	3
	,,	,,	J. Kelly, by direction of Mr. Cooke ...	5	13	9
	,,	18.	Earl of Altamont, by direction of Lord Castlereagh, for Jennings and Conmee, 2 priests, £50 each; Rafferall, £20; Clerk, £11 7s. 6d.; Sheriff of Co. Mayo, £53 3s. 6d.—in all	184	11	0
	,,	19.	Mr. Darcy Mahon, for B., per Mr. Cooke's directions	100	0	0
353 5 10	,,	,,	Watkins, for diet of prisoners in the Castle, etc., April, May and June ...	353	5	10
16 3 0½	,,	,,	Do., coach-hire, etc., paid by directions of Major Sirr, per account	16	3	0½
	,,	22.	O'Brien, for 13 men at 1 g. and 3 at ½ g.	16	9	10½
37 4 3	,,	,,	Do., subsistence of prisoners in the Tower, etc., from 11 June, when Watkins stopped, to 22 June, per account	37	4	3
2 16 10½	,,	,,	Do., for coaches with Monks, etc., to courts martial, per d°·	2	16	10½
	,,	,,	Grey, &c., as before, 7 at 1 g.	7	19	3
	,,	28.	T. Collins, bill, dated London, 14 May, at six weeks, £50, English	55	10	0
	,,	29.	O'Brien, for 13 men at 1 g. and 3 at ½ g.	16	9	10½
	,,	,,	Grey, etc., as before, 7 at 1 g. ...	7	19	3
£486 12 8½— C. F.			C. F.	£24,187	14	5½

ACCOUNT OF SECRET SERVICE MONEY, IRELAND, 1799.

	1799.		PAID.	£	s.	d.
£186 12 8½ — B. F.			Per amount brought forward,	24,187	14	5½
	July	2.	Bryan Forde, expenses attending the prosecution of the murderers of Mrs. Grattan, etc., at Lord Harberton's			
23 11 4½				23	11	4½
	,,	,,	Mr. Edward Trevor, medical attendant on the State prisoners at Kilmainham, from 1 April, '98, to 30 June, '99, 456 days at 10s.			
228 0 0				228	0	0
	,,	5.	J. Kelly, by direction of Mr. Cooke	5	13	9
	,,	6.	O'Brien, for 12 men at 1 g. and 3 at ½ g.	15	7	1½
	,,	,,	Do., subsistence of State prisoners in the Tower, &c., 22 June to 6 July			
46 16 0				46	16	0
	,,	,,	Grey, etc., as before, 7 at 1 g.	7	19	3
	,,	8.	Mr. Cooke, for Nicholson	20	0	0
	,,	9.	Ross Mahon, esq., for the discoverers of the Hardimens	68	5	0
	,,	12.	O'Brien, for 14 men at 1 g. and 3 at ½ g.	17	12	7½
	,,	,,	Do., for subsistence of prisoners, etc., at the Castle, 6 to 13 July			
12 16 9				12	16	9
	,,	,,	Grey, etc., as before, 7 at 1 g.	7	19	3
	,,	17.	T. Collins, bill, dated London, 14 May, at 2 months, £50, English	55	10	0
	,,	20.	O'Brien, for 14 men at 1 g. and 3 at ½ g.	17	12	7½
	,,	,,	Do., subsistence of prisoners, 13 to 20 July			
13 9 9				13	9	9
	,,	,,	Grey, etc., as before, 7 at 1 g.	7	19	3
	,,	,,	Mr. Marshall, what he paid Lord Altamont for printed notices	4	11	0
	,,	24.	Major Sirr, for Hugh McLoughlin, per receipt	22	15	0
	,,	25.	J. Lindsay, to take him home, and in full of all demands	100	0	0
	,,	,,	H. McLoughlin, per Mr. Marsden's note	20	0	0
	,,	,,	Harpur, to take him to Mr. Price's, Saintfield, Co. Down	11	7	6
	,,	27.	Joseph Wall, subsistence of prisoners in Smithfield, from 25 February to 26 June, per account			
251 0 2				251	0	2
	,,	,,	O'Brien, for subsistence of prisoners, Castle, etc., 20 to 27 July			
12 13 6				12	13	6
	,,	,,	Do., for 14 men at 1 g. and 3 at ½ g	17	12	7½
	,,	,,	Grey, etc., as before, except Lindsay, 6 at 1 g.	6	16	6
£1,075 0 3 — C. F.			C. F.	£25,183	3	6

ACCOUNT OF SECRET SERVICE MONEY, IRELAND, 1799.   33

	1799.		PAID.	£	s.	d.
£1,075 0 3 — B. F.			Per amount brought forward,	25,183	3	6
	August	3.	O'Brien, for subsistence of prisoners in the Castle, 28 July to 3 August ...	15	8	9
15 8 9						
	,,	,,	Do., for 14 men at 1 g. and 3 at ½ g. ...	17	12	7½
	,,	,,	Grey, etc., as before, 6 at 1 g. ...	6	16	6
	,,	,,	Mr. Pollock, for G. M. I.	100	0	0
	,,	9.	John Kelly, by direction of Mr. Cooke	5	13	9
	,,	10.	O'Brien, for subsistence of prisoners in the Tower, etc., 3rd to 10th Aug. ...	17	14	8
17 14 8						
	,,	,,	Do., 15 men at 1 g. and 2 at ½ g. ...	18	4	0
	,,	,,	Grey, etc., as before, 6 at 1 g. ...	6	16	6
	,,	17.	O'Brien, for subsistence of prisoners in the Castle, 10 to 17 Aug.	12	10	3
12 10 3						
	,,	,,	Do., 15 men at 1 g. and 2 at ½ g. ...	18	4	0
	,,	,,	Grey, etc., as before, 6 at 1 g. ...	6	16	6
	,,	23.	Tho. Collins, bill, dated 20 June, 2 months	55	15	0
	,,	24.	O'Brien, for subsistence of prisoners in the Tower, etc., 17 to 24 Aug. ...	11	14	0
11 14 0						
	,,	,,	Do., 15 men at 1 g. and 2 at ½ g. ...	18	4	0
	,,	,,	Grey, etc., as before, 6 at 1 g. ...	6	16	6
	,,	27.	Mr. Trevor, subsistence of Butler and Monk, Royal Infirmary	1	15	7
1 15 7						
	,,	,,	Do., cloaths for the attendant on prisoners, Kilmainham	3	19	11½
3 19 11½						
	,,	29.	Henry St. George Cole, esq., per Lord Enniskillen, quarter to 1 July ...	37	10	0
	,,	30.	Mr. Vaughan, apothecary, Kilmainham, for medicines for State prisoners, for 8 Feb., '98, to 13 April, '98 ...	15	6	0½
15 6 0½						
25 0 0	,,	,,	Do., for his attendance in full ...	25	0	0
	,,	,,	Mr. Trevor, on account of expenses of State prisoners, Kilmainham ...	50	0	0
50 0 0						
	,,	31.	O'Brien, for diet of State prisoners [in the] Tower, etc., 24 to 31 Aug. ...	15	2	3
15 2 3						
	,,	,,	Do., 14 men at 1 g. and 4 at ½ g. ...	18	4	0
	,,	,,	Grey, etc., as before, 6 at 1 g. ...	6	16	6
	,,	,,	Watkins, for diet and lodging for Mr. Dease and Mr. Waldron, from 1 June to 31 July, per account	69	7	9
69 7 9						
£1,312 19 6 — C. F.			C. F.	£25,744	12	7½

E

ACCOUNT OF SECRET SERVICE MONEY, IRELAND, 1799.

	1799.		PAID.	£	s.	d.
£1,312 19 6 — B. F.			Per amount brought forward,	25,744	12	7½
13 0 0	Sepr.	7.	O'Brien, for diet of prisoners, etc., in the Castle, etc., 1 to 7 Sep.	13	0	0
	,,	,,	Do., for 15 men at 1 g. and 4 at ½ g. ...	19	6	9
	,,	,,	Grey, etc., as before, 6 at 1 g. ...	6	16	6
	,,	11.	John Kelly, 5 weeks' allowance ...	5	13	9
	,,	12.	Nichs. Price, esq., expenses of bringing J. Townley and Wm. Wallace to assizes, Co. Down, to prosecute rebels, per account			
28 6 1				28	6	1
	,,	14.	O'Brien, for diet of prisoners, etc., 8 to 14 Sep.			
15 5 6				15	5	6
	,,	,,	Do., for 15 men at 1 g. and 4 at ½ g. ...	19	6	9
	,,	,,	Grey, etc., as before, 6 at 1 g. ...	6	16	6
	,,	21.	O'Brien, for diet of prisoners, etc., 15 to 21 September			
15 12 0				15	12	0
	,,	,,	Do., for 15 men at 1 g. and 4 at ½ g. ...	19	6	9
	,,	,,	Grey, etc., as before, 6 at 1 g. ...	6	16	6
	,,	24.	O'Brien, for taking care of the Tower, washing for prisoners, 11 June to 24 September, 15 weeks at 11s. 4d. ...	8	10	7½
£1,385 3 1				£25,909	10	4
			Deduct the amount of the several sums in margin, in red, received at the Treasury, being amount of subsistence of State prisoners, from March to Sep., [17]99, £979 19s. 2½d. Do., expenses for carriages, guards, medical assistance, etc., to do., £405 3s. 10½d.	1,385	3	1
				£24,524	7	3
17 11 0	,,	28.	O'Brien, for diet of State prisoners, 22nd to 28th September	17	11	0
	,,	,,	Do., for 15 men at 1 g. and 4 at ½ g. ...	19	6	9
	,,	,,	Grey, etc., as before, 6 at 1 g. ...	6	16	6
	,,	30.	Major Naughton, of Belfast, expenses and subsistence of Dresdon, taken up by order of the Government ...			
7 10 7				7	10	7
	,,	,,	McGuckin, of Belfast, per post, by direction of Mr. Cooke	50	0	0
£25 1 7 — C. F.			C. F.	£24,625	12	1

ACCOUNT OF SECRET SERVICE MONEY, IRELAND, 1799. 35

	1799.		PAID.	£	s.	d.
£25 1 7 — B. F.			Per amount brought forward,	24,625	12	1
	October	5.	O'Brien, for diet of State prisoners, etc.,			
13 13 0			29 Sept. to 5 Oct....	13	13	0
	,,	,,	Do., for 15 men at 1 g., 4 at ½ g.	19	6	9
	,,	,,	Grey, etc., as before, 6 at 1 g. ..	6	16	6
	,,	9.	John Kelly, for 5 weeks, 11 Sep. to 16 Oct.	5	13	9
	,,	12.	Captain Perry, expenses of trials and			
24 10 0			executions of prisoners, Baltinglass ...	24	10	0
	,,	,,	O'Brien, for diet of State prisoners, 5 to			
13 16 3			12 Oct. ...	13	16	3
	,,	,,	Do., for 15 men at 1 g., 4 at ½ g.	19	6	9
	,,	,,	Grey, etc., as before, 6 at 1 g.	6	16	6
	,,	14.	Mr. A. Worthington, for Boyle, &c.	50	0	0
	,,	19.	Henry St. George Cole, esq., high sheriff, Co. Waterford, expense in apprehending and convicting rebels, Co. Waterford, per Col. Uniacke...	100	0	0
	,,	,,	O'Brien, for subsistence of prisoners,			
15 5 6			12 to 19 Oct. ...	15	5	6
	,,	,,	Do., for 15 men at 1 g., 4 at ½ g.	19	6	9
	,,	,,	Grey, etc., as before, 6 at 1 g.	6	16	6
	,,	22.	Sir G. F. Hill, for McFillan, Murphy, Houston and Burck, per receipt	460	0	0
	,,	24.	Sir Cha. Asgill, for Anglen, a priest, per Mr. Marsden	50	0	0
	,,	26.	O'Brien, for subsistence of prisoners, 19			
13 13 0			to 26 Oct.	13	13	0
	,,	,,	Do., for 15 men at 1 g., 4 at ½ g.	19	6	9
	,,	,,	Grey, etc., as before, 6 at 1 g.	6	16	6
	,,	30.	John Kelly, 2 weeks to this day	2	5	6
	,,	,,	Watkins, for diet and lodging for Mr. Dease and Mr. Waldron, from 1			
69 13 2			August to 30 September, per account	69	13	2
	Novem.	2.	O'Brien, for subsistence of prisoners, 26			
15 12 0			Oct. to 2nd Nov. ...	15	12	0
	,,	,,	Do., for 15 men at 1 g. and 4 at ½ g.	19	6	9
	,,	,,	Grey, etc., as before, 6 at 1 g.	6	16	6
£191 4 6 — C. F.			C. F.	£25,590	10	6

ACCOUNT OF SECRET SERVICE MONEY, IRELAND, 1799.

1799.			PAID.	£	s.	d.
			Per amount brought forward,	25,590	10	6
4:01 4 6 – L. F.	Novem.	5.	Tho. Collins, bill, dated Gosport, 2nd Sept., at 2 months	56	2	6
	,,	6.	Gustavus Rochfort, esq., for Gerraghty...	100	0	0
8 2 3	,,	9.	Mr. Manders, washing for prisoners, 31 Dec. '98, to March, '99	8	2	3
13 16 3	,,	,,	O'Brien, for subsistence of prisoners, 3 to 9 Nov.	13	16	3
	,,	,,	Do., for 15 men at 1 g. and 4 at ½ g. ...	19	6	9
	,,	,,	Grey, etc., as before, 6 at 1 g. ...	6	16	6
	,,	,,	Major Sirr, for the discoverer of an attempt to break the New Gaol ...	22	15	0
	,,	,,	Mr. Marsden, to remit to [blank] an English bank note for £50, exchange 12 per cent.	56	0	0
11 7 6	,,	,,	R. Warren, keeper of Bridewell, diet, washing, etc., for Wm. Mangan, an informer, for 14 weeks, per account ...	11	7	6
		14.	J. Kelly, 5 weeks from 3 October to 4 December	5	13	9
12 10 3	,,	16.	O'Brien, for diet of prisoners, 10 to 16 Nov.	12	10	3
	,,	,,	Do., for 15 men at 1 g. and 4 at ½ g. each	19	6	9
	,,	,,	Grey, etc., as before, 6 at 1 g. ...	6	16	6
12 10 3	,,	23.	O'Brien, for diet of prisoners, 16 to 20 Nov.	12	10	3
	,,	,,	Do., for 15 men at 1 g. and 4 at ½ g. each	19	6	9
	,,	,,	Grey, etc., as before, 6 at 1 g. ...	6	16	6
	,,	26.	Mr. Cooke	20	0	0
3 0 2	,,	29.	Justice Drury, hire of chaise, etc., in search of Tallant	3	0	2
12 10 3	,,	30.	O'Brien, for diet of prisoners, 23 to 30 Nov.	12	10	3
	,,	,,	Do., for 15 men at 1 g. and 4 at ½ g. ...	19	6	9
	,,	,,	Grey, etc., as before, 6 at 1 g. ...	6	16	6
£285 1 5 – C. F.			C. F.	£26,029	11	8

ACCOUNT OF SECRET SERVICE MONEY, IRELAND, 1799.

1799.		PAID.	£	s.	d.
		Per amount brought forward,	26,029	11	8
Dec.	3.	Grey, for rent of his lodging, by direction of Mr. Cooke	6	16	6
,,	,,	Coleman, by d°	1	2	9
,,	4.	J. Kelly, 5 weeks, from 4 December to 15 January, 1800	5	13	9
,,	5.	Henry St. George Cole, esq., 1 qr. to 1 October	37	10	0
,,	,,	Watkins, diet and lodging for Ross, an English messenger, and six assistants from London, with Napper Tandy and other prisoners, per account	24	16	0½
,,	7.	O'Brien, for diet of prisoners, 1 to 7 December	11	1	0
,,	,,	Do., for 15 men at 1 g. and 4 at ½ g. each	19	6	9
,,	,,	Grey, etc., as before, 6 at 1 g.	6	16	6
,,	13.	Mr. Cooke	50	0	0
,,	14.	O'Brien, diet of prisoners, [from] 7 to 14 December	9	2	0
,,	,,	Hanlon, for 16 men at 1 g. and 4 at ½ g. each	20	9	6
,,	,,	Grey, etc., as before, 6, and Conlan, 1 g.	7	19	3
,,	18.	Surgeon-General, for attendance on State prisoners this year	200	0	0
,,	19.	James Flannagan, by order of the Lord Lieutenant	20	0	0
,,	21.	Major Sirr, for the person who discovered Bermingham	17	1	3
,,	,,	O'Brien, for diet of prisoners, 15 to 21 December	10	1	6
,,	,,	Do., for 16 men at 1 g. and 4 at ½ g. each	20	9	6
,,	,,	Grey, etc., as before, and Coleman, 7 at 1 g.	7	19	3
,,	27.	Serjeant John Lee, by direction of Mr. Cooke	100	0	0
,,	28.	O'Brien, for diet of prisoners, 22 to 28 Dec.	10	14	6
,,	,,	Hanlon, for 16 men at 1 g. and 4 at ½ g.	20	9	6
,,	,,	Grey, etc., as before, 6 at 1 g.	6	16	6
,,	,,	Royal Military Infirmary, for subsistence of men sent there	3	3	9
,,	,,	Watkins, for diet and lodging for Mr. Dease and Mr. Waldron, Oct. and Nov.	69	7	9
,,	,,	O'Brien, for care of the Tower, 24 Sept. to 4 Dec., 10 weeks at ½ g.	5	13	9
		C. F.	£26,722	2	11½

ACCOUNT OF SECRET SERVICE MONEY, IRELAND, 1800.

	1800.		PAID.	£	s.	d.
£60 1 8½ — D. F.			Per amount brought forward,	26,722	2	11½
	January	3.	Mr. Trevor, medical attendant on State prisoners in Kilmainham, etc., from 1 July, '99, to 30 June, 1800, 10s. per day			
182 10 0				182	10	0
	,,	,,	Mr. Cooke, for N. ...	5	13	9
	,,	,,	O'Brien, amount paid by him for coach-hire with prisoners, etc., per account vouched by Major Sirr			
19 4 0				19	4	0
11 7 6	,,	4.	Do., for diet of prisoners, 29 Dec. to 4 Jan.	11	7	6
	,,	,,	Hanlon, for 16 men at 1 g. and 4 at ½ g. each	20	9	6
	,,	,,	Grey, etc., as before, 6, and Coleman 1 g.	7	19	3
	,,	6.	J. Kelly, 5 weeks from 8 January to 12 Feb.	5	13	9
	,,	7.	Mr. Cooke, for K. ...	50	0	0
	,,	11.	Honourable W. W. Pole, for bullocks and sheep for the army, in June, 1798			
18 8 6				18	8	6
	,,	,,	O'Brien, for diet of prisoners, 5 to 11 January			
14 15 6				14	15	6
	,,	,,	Hanlon, for 15 men at 1 g. and 4 at ½ g.	19	6	9
	,,	,,	Grey, &c., as before, 6, and Coleman, 1 g.	7	19	3
	,,	17.	Lennan, per Mr. Marshall's note	5	13	9
	,,	19.	Col. Uniacke, for H. St. George Cole, esq., by directions of Mr. Cooke	200	0	0
	,,	,,	Justice Drury, by do. ...	100	0	0
	,,	,,	O'Brien, for diet of prisoners, 12 to 18 January			
17 11 3				17	11	3
	,,	,,	Hanlon, for 15 men at 1 g. and 4 at ½ g.	19	6	9
	,,	,,	Grey, etc., and Coleman, as before, 7 at 1 g.	7	19	3
	,,	21.	Mr. Pollock, for McGuckin ...	100	0	0
	,,	22.	J. Boyce, for printing "Fall of Underwald," Dec. '98, per account	5	13	9
	,,	25.	O'Brien, for diet of prisoners, 19 to 25 January			
15 12 0				15	12	0
	,,	,,	Hanlon, for 15 men at 1 g. and 4 at ½ g.	19	6	9
	,,	,,	Grey, etc., as before, 6	6	16	6
	,,	,,	Coleman, to take him out of town	11	7	6

£888 10 5¼ — C. F.   C. F. £27,594 18 2½

ACCOUNT OF SECRET SERVICE MONEY, IRELAND, 1800.

		1800.	PAID.	£	s.	d.
£888	10	5¼—B. F.	Per amount brought forward,	27,594	18	2½
		January 29.	Col. Unincke, for prosecutors in the Co. of Waterford	200	0	0
		,, 30.	Shaw Cartland, esq., for discoverers of mail robbers, etc., King's Co. ...	56	17	6
		,, 31.	Henry St. George Cole, esq., quarter to 31st Dec., '99	37	10	0
		February 1.	O'Brien, for diet of prisoners, 26 Jan. to 1 Feb.			
15	18	6		15	18	6
		,, ,,	Hanlon, for 15 men at 1 g. and 4 at ½ g.	19	6	9
		,, ,,	Do., for care of the Tower, 4 Dec. to 29 Jan., 8 weeks at ½ g.			
4	11	0		4	11	0
		,, ,,	Grey, etc., as before (except Chapman), 5 at 1 g.	5	13	9
		,, 7.	Lord Carhampton's bill for Feris' allowance, ½ year to 1 Nov., '99, £50, English	54	3	4
12	16	9	,, 8.	O'Brien, for diet of prisoners, 2 to 8 Feb.	12	16	9
		,, ,,	Hanlon, for 15 men at 1 g. and 4 at ½ g.	19	6	9
		,, ,,	Grey, Bourke, Mitchell, Chambers and O'Neil, 5 at 1 g.	5	13	9
		,, 9.	Mr. Cooke, for Fitzgerald	250	0	0
		,, 10.	J. Kelly, 5 weeks, 12 Feb. to 19 March	5	13	9
		,, 15.	O'Brien, coach-hire with prisoners, per account vouched by Major Sirr ...			
2	3	0		2	3	0
13	16	3	,, ,,	Do., diet of prisoners, 9 to 15 Feb. ...	13	16	3
		,, ,,	Hanlon, for 15 men at 1 g. and 4 at ½ g.	19	6	9
		,, ,,	Grey, etc., as before, 5 at 1 g. ...	5	13	9
		,, 19.	Gaoler of the County of Limerick, for subsistence and transmitting prisoners convicted before courts martial, by order of General Lake, April to June, '99, per receipt			
39	17	2		39	17	2
		,, 22.	O'Brien, for diet of prisoners, 16 to 22 Feb.			
12	13	6		12	13	6
		,, ,,	Hanlon, for 15 men at 1 g. and 4 at ½ g.	19	6	9
		,, ,,	Grey, etc., as before, 5 at 1 g. ...	5	13	9
		,, 24.	Col. FitzGerald, of North Cork militia, for the mother of Serjeant Moore, who was killed in taking a rebel	25	0	0
		,, 27.	Mr. Cooke, for M. N.	100	0	0
		March 1.	Mr. Bell, late Sheriff of Drogheda, expenses of court-martial prisoners, '98 ..			
21	11	2		21	11	2
		,, ,,	O'Brien, for diet of prisoners, 23 Feb. to 1 March			
11	7	6		11	7	6
		,, ,,	Hanlon, for 14 men at 1 g. and 4 at ½ g.	18	4	0
£1,023	5	3¼—C. F.	C. F.	£28,577	3	7½

				PAID.	£	s.	d.
£1,023	5	3½ — B. F.	1800.	Per amount brought forward,	28,577	3	7½
			March 1.	Hanlon, for taking care of the Tower, 1 Feb. to 1 March, 4 weeks ...			
2	5	6			2	5	6
			,, ,,	Grey, etc., as before, 5 at 1 g. ...	5	13	9
			,, 6.	S. Baker, per Col. Uniacke's note	100	0	0
			,, 8.	O'Brien, for diet of prisoners, 2 to 8 March ...			
12	0	6			12	0	6
			,, ,.	Hanlon, for 14 men at 1 g. and 4 at ½ g.	18	4	0
			,. ,,	Grey, etc., as before, 5 at 1 g. ...	5	13	9
			,. 14.	Captain W. Faris, of the Killashandra cavalry, expense of bringing up Mathias Tone, September, '98, per receipt ...			
20	6	3			20	6	3
			,, ,,	Watkins, for Mr. Deuse and Mr. Waldron's diet and lodging, Dec., January, and to 24 Feb., when discharged ; apothecary etc., per account			
105	18	5			105	18	5
			,, 15.	Arthur Campbell, for his apartments in the Castle yard, for State prisoners, etc., and attendance upon them, from August, '98, on account			
22	15	0			22	15	0
			,, ,.	O'Brien, for diet of prisoners, 9 to 14 March ...			
14	19	0			14	19	0
			,, ,,	Hanlon, for 15 men at 1 g. and 4 at ½ g.	19	6	9
			,, ,.	Grey, etc., as before, 5 at 1 g. ...	5	13	9
			,, 18.	J. Kelly, -5 weeks, from 19 March to 23 April ...	5	13	9
			,, ,,	Mr. Archer, High Sheriff, County Wicklow ...	100	0	0
			,, 21.	W. Wright, alias Lawler, per bill remitted to him in London, £50, English, 11½ per cent.	55	15	0
			,, ,,	J. Pollock, esq., for T. W. ...	200	0	0
			,, 22.	Mr. Dwyer, for Corporal Bell ...	20	0	0
			,, ,,	O'Brien, for diet of prisoners, 16 to 22 March ...			
16	17	0			16	17	0
			,, ,,	Hanlon, for 15 men at 1 g. and 4 at ½ g. ...	19	6	9
			,, ,.	Grey, &c., as before, 5 at 1 g. ...	5	13	9
			,, 29.	O'Brien, for diet of prisoners, 23 to 29 March ...			
18	10	6			18	10	6
			,, ,,	Hanlon, for 15 men at 1 g. and 4 at ½ g.	19	6	9
			,, ,,	Grey, etc., as before, 5 at 1 g. ...	5	13	9
£1,236	17	5½			£29,376	17	6½
				Deduct amount of the several sums in the margin in red, received at the Treasury, April, 1800, being amount paid for subsistence of prisoners, from 21 Sep., '99, to 29 March, 1800, £615 1s. 10d. ; for carriage, guards, medical assistance, etc., etc., do., £621 15s. 7½d.,	1,236	17	5½
				C. F.	£28,140	0	1

ACCOUNT OF SECRET SERVICE MONEY, IRELAND, 1800.   41

	1800.		PAID.	£	s.	d.
			Per amount brought forward,	28,140	0	1
	April	1.	Mr. Marsden, to remit to McGuckin ...	50	0	0
	,,	3.	Coleman, by direction of Mr. Cooke, per letter from E. D. Wilson, esq. ...	11	7	6
£11 0 6	,,	5.	O'Brien, for diet of prisoners, 29 March to 5 April	11	0	6
	,,	,,	Hanlon, for 15 men at 1 g. and 4 at ½ g.	19	6	9
	,,	,,	Grey, etc., as before, 5 at 1 g.	5	13	9
3 9 1	,,	,,	Cloaths for Burns and Coleman in the Tower, per Major Sirr	3	9	1
	,,	8.	Mr. Thomas Collins' bill, dated Dominica, 20 Dec., '99, £50, English; exchange 11¾ per cent. ...	55	17	6
	,,	10.	Alex. Worthington, esq., balance of an account to 29 March	14	6	4½
	,,	,,	Do., in advance	34	2	6
20 3 0	,,	12.	O'Brien, for diet of prisoners, 5 to 12 April	20	3	0
	,,	,,	Hanlon, for 15 men at 1 g. and 4 at ½ g.	19	6	9
2 5 6	,,	,,	Do., for taking care of the Tower, 1 to 29 March, 4 weeks at ½ g.	2	5	6
	,,	,,	Grey, etc., as before	5	13	9
	,,	16.	J. Kelly, 5 weeks, 23 April to 28 May	5	13	9
	,,	,,	Sir Richard Musgrave, for Michael Burke, to take him to England	5	13	9
	,,	,,	Do., for do., 13 weeks' allowance in advance, from 12th April	14	15	9
	,,	19.	Chapman, 12 weeks' allowance from 25 Jan. to 19 April, per Mr. Turner ...	13	13	0
	,,	,,	Hon. W. Wesley Pole, for informers, Queen's County	100	0	0
16 11 6	,,	,,	O'Brien, for diet of prisoners, 13 to 19 April	16	11	6
	,,	,,	Hanlon, for 15 men at 1 g. and 4 at ½ g.	19	6	9
	,,	,,	Grey, Mitchell, O'Neill and Chambers, 4 at 1 g.	4	11	0
	,,	21.	Mr. Ram, for Serjeant Tuttle, who prosecuted rebels, Wexford	22	15	0
4 3 0	,,	26.	O'Brien, for hire of carriages with prisoners, etc., per account	4	3	0
14 6 0	,,	,,	Do., for diet of prisoners, 20 to 26 April	14	6	0
	,,	,,	Hanlon, for 15 men at 1 g. and 4 at ½ g.	19	6	9
	,,	,,	Grey, etc., as before, 4	4	11	0
£71 18 7 — C. F.			C. F.	£28,638	0	3½
				F		

ACCOUNT OF SECRET SERVICE MONEY, IRELAND, 1800.

	1800.		PAID.	£	s.	d.
£71 18 7 — B. F.			Per amount brought forward,	28,638	0	3½
	May	2.	Lord Rossmore, for the widow Partland, whose house at Newtown Mountkennedy was destroyed by order of the officer commanding, when the rebels attacked the town	10	0	0
	,,	,,	Henry St. George Cole, quarter to 1 April	37	10	0
	,,	3.	O'Brien, for diet of prisoners, 29 April to 3 May	14	19	0
14 19 0						
	,,	,,	Hanlon, for 5 men at 1 g. and 4 at ½ g.	19	6	9
	,,	,,	Grey, Mitchell, O'Neill and Chambers...	4	11	0
	,,	5.	Col. Uniacke, for Henry St. Geo. Cole, esq.	200	0	0
13 6 6	,,	10.	O'Brien, for diet of prisoners, 4 to 10 May	13	6	6
	,,	,,	Hanlon, for 16 men at 1 g. and 3 at ½ g.	19	18	1½
	,,	,,	Grey, Mitchell, O'Neill and Chambers...	4	11	0
	,,	,,	Hanlon, for diet of prisoners, etc., 11 to 17 May...	17	4	6
17 4 6						
	,,	,,	Do., for 16 men at 1 g. and 3 at ½ g. ...	19	18	1½
	,,	,,	Grey, Mitchell, O'Neill and Chambers ...	4	11	0
	,,	20.	Wm. Greenshields, expense of apprehending Wexford rebels	9	2	0
9 2 0						
	,,	22.	Mr. Cooke	40	0	0
	,,	,,	Andrew Macnevin, esq., per post to Carrickfergus	300	0	0
	,,	23.	Mr. Cooke, for N.	10	0	0
	,,	24.	Hanlon, for diet of prisoners, 18 to 24 May	17	17	6
17 17 6						
	,,	,,	Do., for 16 men at 1 g. and 3 at ½ g. ...	19	18	1½
	,,	,,	Grey, etc., as before, 4	4	11	0
	,,	27.	Hamilton M'Dowall, by direction of Lord Castlereagh	1	2	9
	,,	,,	J. Kelly, 5 weeks, from 28 May to 2 July	5	13	9
	,,	,,	Col. MacDonnell, for subsistence of prisoners at Hacketstown	19	9	0
19 9 0						
14 6 0	,,	31.	Hanlon, for diet of prisoners, 25 May to 31	14	6	0
	,,	,,	Do., 17 men at 1 g. and 3 at ½ g. ...	21	0	10½
	,,	,,	Grey, Mitchell, Chambers, O'Neill and M'Dowall, 5	5	13	9
£178 3 1 — C. F.			C. F.	£29,472	11	0½

ACCOUNT OF SECRET SERVICE MONEY, IRELAND, 1800.

	1800.		PAID.	£	s.	d.
£178 3 1 — B. F.			Per amount brought forward,	29,472	11	0½
	May	31.	Hanlon, for taking care of the Tower,			
5 2 4½			29 March to 31 May, 9 weeks, 11/4½	5	2	4½
11 14 0	June	7.	Do. for diet of prisoners, 1 to 7 June ...	11	14	0
	,,	,,	Do., 17 men at 1 g., 3 at ½ g. ...	21	0	10½
	,,	,,	Grey, Mitchell, O'Neil, Chambers and M'Dowall, 5	5	13	9
		10.	Mr. Erskine, steward of the Royal Infirmary, on account for the diet of Mr.			
56 17 6			Mumford	56	17	6
	,,	11.	The Hills, from Cork, for subsistence ...	11	7	6
	,,	,,	Mr. Marsden, for M°Guckin	50	0	0
	,,	,,	Coleman	11	7	6
16 18 0	,,	14.	Hanlon, for diet of prisoners, 8 to 14 June	16	18	0
	,,	,,	Do., 17 men at 1 g. and 3 at ½ g. ...	21	0	10½
	,,	,,	Grey, etc., as before, 5	5	13	9
	,,	17.	Col. Jones, of Leitrim Militia, expenses of executing Dunn and Cotton, two rebels, at Naas and Ballymore Eustace,			
10 0 0			Dec., '99	10	0	0
	,,	19.	Joseph Nugent, per M. Lee's application	5	13	9
	,,	20.	Hugh Whitley (who prosecuted Orr), subsistence	11	7	6
16 5 0	,,	,,	Hanlon, for diet of prisoners, 15 to 21 June	16	5	0
	,,	,,	Do., 17 men at 1 g. and 3 at ½ g. ...	21	0	10½
	,,	,,	Grey, etc., as before, 5 at 1 g. ...	5	13	9
	,,	,,	Hanlon, for coach hire, per account vouched			
5 7 2½			by Major Sirr	5	7	2½
	,,	23.	Philip Cahill, from the Co. Tipperary ...	1	2	9
	,,	26.	Earl Carhampton, for Feris, to 1 May, half-year, £50, English	54	3	4
	,,	,,	Sir R. Musgrave, for Burke, 5 weeks, from 12 July to 16 Aug.	5	13	9
	,,	,,	R. Kilpatrick, from Col. Anstruther, Ballymore	2	5	6
16 11 6	,,	28.	Hanlon, for diet of prisoners, 22 to 28 June	16	11	6
	,,	,,	Do., 17 men at 1 g. and 3 at ½ g. ...	21	0	10½
	,,	,,	Grey, etc., as before, 5 at 1 g. ...	5	13	9
£316 18 8 — C. F.			C. F.	£29,871	6	8½

	1800.		PAID.	£	s.	d.
£316 12 8 — B. F.			Per amount brought forward,	29,871	6	8½
	June	28.	J. Kelly, for 5 weeks, 2 July to 6 August	5	13	9
	July	1.	Bryan Lennan, in full and positive discharge of all demands	11	7	6
	,,	3.	The 3 Hills, from Cork, for subsistence	11	7	6
	,,	5.	Hanlon, for diet of prisoners, June 29 to July 5			
19 18 8				19	18	8
	,,	,,	Do., 17 men at 1 g. and 3 at ½ g. ...	21	0	10½
	,,	,,	Grey, Mitchell, O'Neill, Chambers and McDowall, 5	5	13	9
21 17 8	,,	12.	Hanlon, for diet of prisoners, 6 to 12 July	21	17	8
	,,	,,	Do., 17 at 1 g. and 3 at ½ g.	21	0	10½
	,,	,,	Grey, etc., as before, 5	5	13	9
	,,	15.	Kilpatrick, from Ballymore	3	8	3
	,,	16.	Alex. M'Donnell, per Mr. Marsden, per receipt	150	0	0
	,,	17.	Major Sirr, for Edward Boyle, Michael Fagan, Michael Higgins, Dan. Gore, Ja. Murphy and John Kearney, 30 guineas each, in full discharge of their claims for services, 180 g.	204	15	0
	,,	18.	Hugh Wheatley, for subsistence ...	5	13	9
21 11 2	,,	19.	Hanlon, for diet of prisoners, 13th to 19th	21	11	2
	,,	,,	Do., 11 men at 1 g. and 3 at ½ g. ...	14	4	4½
	,,	,,	Grey, etc., as before, 5	5	13	9
	,,	21.	Mr. Pollock, for M^{c}G.	100	0	0
	,,	23.	Dr. Harding, from Cork, by desire of Lord Castlereagh	500	0	0
	,,	24.	Mr. Pollock, for T. W.	100	0	0
	,,	26.	Isaac Heron, a young man taken up and confined in the Tower instead of another person, who dropped a paper in England, signed Colclough ...	11	7	6
22 4 2	,,	,,	Hanlon, for diet of prisoners, 20th to 26th	22	4	2
	,,	,,	Do., for 11 at 1 g. and 3 at ½ g. ...	14	4	4½
	,,	,,	Grey, etc., as before, 5	5	13	9
£402 10 4 — C. F.			C. F.	£31,153	17	1½

ACCOUNT OF SECRET SERVICE MONEY, IRELAND, 1800. 45

	1800.		PAID.	£	s.	d.
£402 10 4 — B. F.			Per amount brought forward,	31,153	17	1½
	July	26.	Mr. Marsden, for 4 men who came from England relative to Mr. Colclough and Heron	17	1	3
	Aug.	2.	The Hills, from Cork	11	7	6
	,,	,,	Major Sirr, to take men to Hacketstown, etc.	22	15	0
17 17 6	,,	,,	Hanlon, for diet of prisoners, 26 July to 2 August	17	17	6
	,,	,,	Do., for 11 men at 1 g. and 3 at ½ g. ...	14	4	4½
	,,	,,	Grey, etc., as before, 5	5	13	9
	,,	4.	R. Harpur, to take him to the assizes, Co. Down and back	17	1	3
	,,	,,	J. Kelly, 5 weeks, from 6 August to 10 Sep.	5	13	9
	,,	7.	H. St. Geo. Cole, esq., 1 qr. to 1 July...	37	10	0
	,,	9.	Hugh Wheatly, for subsistence ...	11	7	6
56 17 6	,,	,,	Mr. Erskine, steward of the Royal Infirmary, account of Mumford... ...	56	17	6
13 13 0	,,	,,	Hanlon, for diet of prisoners, 3 to 9 Aug.	13	13	0
	,,	,,	Do., for 11 men at 1 g. and 3 at ½ g. ...	14	4	4½
	,,	,,	Grey, etc., as before, 5	5	13	9
14 12 6	,,	16.	Hanlon, for diet of prisoners, 10 to 16 August...	14	12	6
	,,	,,	Do., for 11 men at 1 g. and 3 at ½ g. ...	14	4	4½
	,,	,,	Grey, etc., as before, 5	5	13	9
	,,	12.	Joseph Nugent, to take him to the country	5	13	9
	,,	18.	Mr. Edward Trevor, medical attendant on prisoners at Kilmainham, for 1 year from 1 July, 1800, to 3 June, 1801, at 10s. per day			
182 10 0				182	10	0
	,,	,,	James Edward Hill from Cork ...	5	13	9
	,,	21.	Sir R. Musgrave, for Bourke, 5 weeks, 16 Aug. to 20 Sep.	5	13	9
15 5 6	,,	23.	Hanlon, for diet of prisoners, 17 to 23 Aug.	15	5	6
	,,	,,	Do., 11 at 1 g., and 3 at ½ g.	14	4	4½
£708 6 4 — C. F.			C. F. £31,668	9	4½	

ACCOUNT OF SECRET SERVICE MONEY, IRELAND, 1800.

1800.		PAID.	£	s.	d.
£703 6 4 — B. F.		Per amount brought forward,	31,668	9	4½
Aug.	23.	Grey, Mitchell, Cahill, Chambers and McDowall, 5	5	13	9
,,	,,	O'Neil, 4 weeks in advance, to 20 Sep. ...	4	11	0
,,	25.	The Hills, from Cork, viz., Philip, John and widow of William	5	13	9
,,	26.	Mr. Worthington, balance of an account	7	7	10½
,,	,,	Do., in advance	22	15	0
,,	27.	Major Sirr, per Mr. Trevor for [blank]	56	17	6
,,	30.	Hanlon, for diet of prisoners, 24 to 30 August...	18	17	0
18 17 0					
,,	,,	Do., for 11 at 1 g. and 3 at ½ g. ...	14	4	4½
,,	,,	Grey, Mitchell, Chambers and McDowall, 4	4	11	0
Sept.	6.	The 3 Hills, from Cork, Philip, John, and widow of William	5	13	9
,,	,,	J. Kelly, for 5 weeks, 10 Sep. to 15 Oct.	5	13	9
,,	3.	Mitchell, to send his child to the country	1	2	9
,,	6.	Hanlon, for diet of prisoners, 1 Aug.— 6 Sep.	15	12	0
15 12 0					
,,	,,	Do., 11 men at 1 g. and 3 at ½ g. ...	14	4	4½
,,	,,	Grey, Mitchell, Chambers and McDowall, 4	4	11	0
,,	,,	Hanlon, for hire of carriages, 23 June to 23 August, and expense of O'Brien's funeral, per account	11	3	9
11 3 9					
,,	8.	James Edward Hill from Cork ...	5	13	9
,,	11.	Magan, per Mr. Higgins	300	0	0
,,	13.	Wheatley...	11	7	6
,,	,,	Hanlon, for diet of prisoners, 7 to 13 Sep.	11	1	0
11 1 0					
,,	,,	Do., 11 at 1 g., and 3 at ½ g.	14	4	4½
,,	,,	Grey, Mitchell, Chambers and McDowall, 4	4	11	0
,,	15.	The Hills, from Cork (this makes 45 g. to them 4 June to 10 Sep., at 1 g. per week each)	5	13	9
,,	,,	Do., in advance from 10 Sep. ...	5	13	9
,,	16.	Mr. Erskine, Royal Infirmary, subsistence of men there	7	7	2
7 7 2					
£767 7 3 — C. F.		C. F. £32,232	14	3½	

ACCOUNT OF SECRET SERVICE MONEY, IRELAND, 1800.

	1800.		PAID.	£	s.	d.
£767 7 3 — B. F.			Per amount brought forward,	32,232	14	3½
	Sept.	18.	Mr. Marsden, for a man sent from England by Mr. King	11	7	6
9 15 0	,,	20.	Hanlon, for diet of prisoners, 13 to 20 September	9	15	0
	,,	,,	Do., for 11 at 1 g. and 3 at ½ g. ...	14	4	4½
	,,	,,	Grey, Mitchell, Chambers and McDowall, 4	4	11	0
	,,	26.	Sir Richard Musgrave, for Burke, 5 weeks, 20 Sept. to 25 Oct.	5	13	9
	,,	27.	The 3 Hills, from Cork, for subsistence to 10 October	4	11	0
	,,	,,	Do., in advance to the 15 'do.	6	16	6
16 18 0	,,	,,	Hanlon, for diet of prisoners, 21 to 27 September	16	18	0
	,,	,,	Do., 11 at 1 g. and 3 at ½ g.	14	4	4½
	,,	,,	Grey, Mitchell, Chambers and McDowall	4	11	0
5 8 2	,,	29.	Richardson, for coals sent to the Tower in February	5	8	2
	,,	30.	Wheatley, per his wife	11	7	6
	,,	,,	O'Neill, per post to Shane's castle, from 20 Sep. to 20 Oct.	5	13	9
	,,	,,	James Edward Hill, from Cork ...	11	7	6
£789 8 5				£32,359	3	8½

Deduct the amount of the several articles marked in the margin in red received at the Treasury, being amount paid for subsistence of prisoners, from 29 March to 30 September £560 17s. 4d.
Do., for medical attendance and carriages, guards, etc., do. £235 11s. 1d.

				799	8	5
				£31,559	15	3½
	Oct.	1.	Mr. Marsden, for Murphy, who was sent from London	20	0	0
9 18 3	,,	4.	Hanlon, for taking care of the Tower, 1 June to 30 Sep., 17 weeks 3 days at 11s. 4½d. ...	9	18	3
18 10 6	,,	,,	Do., for diet of prisoners, 27 Sep. to 4 Oct.	18	10	6
	,,	,,	Do., for 12 at 1 g. and 2 at ½ g. ...	14	15	9
	,,	,,	Grey, Mitchell, Chambers and McDowall	4	11	0
0 11 4½	,,	6.	Officers at Blessington, expenses in search of Reilly, 12 July	0	11	4½
	,,	10.	Mr. Marsden, for Sheriff, Co. Waterford, per Mr. Turner	100	0	0
£29 0 1½ — C. F.			C. F.	£31,728	2	2

ACCOUNT OF SECRET SERVICE MONEY, IRELAND, 1800.

	1800.		PAID.	£	s.	d.
£29 0 1¼— B. F.			Per amount brought forward,	31,728	2	2
22 2 0	October	11.	Hanlon, for diet of prisoners, 4 to 11 Oct.	22	2	0
	,,	,,	Do., for 12 at 1 g. and 2 at ½ g. ...	14	15	9
	,,	,,	Grey, Mitchell, Chambers and McDowall, 4	4	11	0
	,,	13.	Mr. Cooke	200	0	0
	,,	,,	J. Kelly, 5 weeks in advance, from 15 Oct. to 19 Nov.	5	13	9
	,,	14.	The three Hills, from Cork, from 15 Oct. to 29 Oct.	6	16	6
	,,	,,	Captain Fitzgerald, per Mr. Cooke ...	100	0	0
14 17 11	,,	17.	Mr. Dwyer, for Major Uniacke, Limerick, expenses previous to Sir James Duff's command there	14	17	11
	,,	,,	Kilpatrick, from Carrickfergus, by Mr. Cook's directions	5	13	9
	,,	18.	Murphy, from London, by desire of Mr. Marsden	11	7	6
20 9 6	,,	,,	Hanlon, for diet of prisoners, 12 to 18 Oct.	20	9	6
	,,	,,	Do., for 12 at 1 g. and 2 at ½ g. ...	14	15	9
	,,	,,	Grey, Mitchell, Chambers and McDowall	4	11	0
	,,	23.	Murphy, to return to London, per Mr. Marsden	22	15	0
	,,	,,	Coleman, from Carrickfergus	11	7	6
	,,	24.	Major Sirr, to send Halpen's wife to the country	3	8	3
	,,	,,	Mr. Cooke, for N.	20	0	0
	,,	,,	Henry Laverty, from Portaferry, by Lord Castlereagh's desire	5	13	9
	,,	25.	Hugh Wheatley	5	13	9
16 18 0	,,	,,	Hanlon, for diet of prisoners, 19 to 25 October	16	18	0
	,,	,,	Do., 12 at 1 g. and 2 at ½ g. ..	14	15	9
	,,	,,	Grey, Mitchell, Chambers and McDowall	4	11	0
	,,	,,	Three Hills, from Cork, 5 weeks each, to 3rd December	17	1	3
	,,	,,	James Edward Hill, do., to 21 January	5	13	9

£103 7 6½— C. F.   C. F. £32,281 14 7

	1800.		Paid.	£	s.	d.
£103 7 6½ – B. F.			Per amount brought forward,	32,281	14	7
	October	28.	Coleman, in advance for subsistence, to 6 January	11	7	6
	"	"	Stamps, from Aug., '99, to Oct., 1800, 6 at 6d.	0	3	0
	"	"	Do., do., do., for repayment, 2 d°. ...	0	1	0
	Novem.	1.	O'Neill, 5 weeks, 25 Oct. to 29 Nov. ...	5	13	9
	"	"	Sir R. Musgrave, for Burke, 7 weeks, 25 Oct. to 19 Dec.	7	19	3
12 1 0	"	"	Hanlon, for diet of prisoners, 25 Oct. to 1 Nov.	12	1	0
	"	"	Do., 12 men at 1 g., 2 at ½ g. ...	14	15	9
	"	"	Do., for 2 men in the county of Wicklow, per Major Sirr	4	11	0
	"	"	Mitchell, Chambers and Grey ...	3	8	3
	"	2.	N., per Mr. Cooke's note	30	0	0
47 11 3½	"	7.	Captain Nesbitt, Londonderry regiment, per Mr. Shepherd, for subsistence and necessaries for Patrick Donohue ...	47	11	3½
	"	"	H. St. George Cole, esq., 1 quarter, to 1 October	37	10	0
16 5 0	"	8.	Hanlon, for diet of prisoners, 1 to 8 Nov.	16	5	0
	"	"	Do., for 12 at 1 g. and 2 at ½ g. ...	14	15	9
	"	"	Do., for 2 men in the country, per Major Sirr	2	5	6
	"	"	Grey, Mitchell and Chambers ..	3	8	3
	"	13.	Wheatley...	11	7	6
	"	14.	Lord Carhampton, for Feris, half-year to 1 Nov., £50, English	54	3	4
	"	15.	J. Kelly, 5 weeks, 19 Nov. to 24 Dec.	5	13	9
18 17 0	"	"	Hanlon, for diet of prisoners, 9 to 15 Nov.	18	17	0
	"	"	Do., for 14 at 1 g. and 2 at ½ g. ...	17	1	3
	"	"	Grey, Mitchell and Chambers ...	3	8	3
	"	18.	Mr. Cooke	200	0	0
	"	"	Mr. Neville, for Anne Lewis, £300; W. Pollen, £200, per receipt	500	0	0
	"	22.	Hamilton M'Dowall, 4 weeks, 25 Oct. to 22 Nov.	4	11	0
£198 1 10 — C. F.			C. F.	£33,308	12	11½

ACCOUNT OF SECRET SERVICE MONEY, IRELAND, 1800.

	1800.		PAID.	£	s.	d.
£168 1 10 — B. F.			Per amount brought forward,	33,308	12	11½
	Novem.	22.	Hanlon, for diet of prisoners, 16 to 22 Nov.	14	19	0
	,,	,,	Do., for 14 at 1 g. and 2 at ½ g. ...	17	1	3
	,,	,,	Grey, Mitchell and Chambers ...	3	8	3
	,,	24.	Kilpatrick, from Carrickfergus, by direction of Mr. Cooke	5	13	9
	,,	27.	Harpur, on account of his sickness ...	2	5	6
	,,	,,	Hunt and Kernan, apothecaries, for medicines furnished to State prisoners, etc., by order of Government, from			
55 19 10			1798 to 1800	58	19	10
14 12 0	,,	29.	Hanlon, for diet of prisoners, 23 to 29 Nov.	14	12	6
	,,	,,	Do., for 14 at 1 g. and 2 at ½ g. ...	17	1	3
	,,	,,	Grey, Mitchell and Chambers ...	3	8	3
	Decem	1.	Mr. Marsden, repayment of what he advanced J. —	100	0	0
	,,	2.	Wheatley...	11	7	6
	,,	3.	Three Hills, from Cork, from 3 Dec. to 7 January	17	1	3
3 8 3	,,	6.	Major Hardy, expense of subsisting rebel prisoners at Hacketstown, May, '98 ...	3	8	3
17 17 6	,,	,,	Hanlon, for diet of prisoners, 30 Nov. to 6 Dec.	17	17	6
	,,	,,	Do., for 14 at 1 g. and 2 at ½ g. ...	17	1	3
	,,	,,	Grey, Mitchell, Chambers and O'Neill...	4	11	0
	,,	3.	Geo. Clibborn, esq., per receipt ...	500	0	0
	,,	,,	Grey, per advances to him, not charged before, viz., 31 Aug., '99, 1 g. ; April 19, 1800, 1 g. ; 10 June, 6 g. ; and 15 July, 1 g., in all, 9 guineas ...	10	4	9
18 10 6	,,	13.	Hanlon, for diet of prisoners, 7 to 13 Dec.	18	10	6
	,,	,,	Do., for 14 at 1 g. and 2 at ½ g. ...	17	1	3
	,,	,,	Grey, Mitchell, Chambers and O'Neill...	4	11	0
	,,	16.	Harpur, on account of his sickness ...	2	5	6
£320 9 5 — C. F.			C. F.	£34,170	2	3½

ACCOUNT OF SECRET SERVICE MONEY, IRELAND, 1800—1801.

	1800.		PAID.	£	s.	d.
4326 9 5 — B. F			Per amount brought forward,	34,170	2	3½
	Decem.	19.	Sir Richard Musgrave, for Bourke, 7 weeks, 13 Dec. to 31 Jan.	7	19	3
	,,	,,	Wheatley...	11	7	6
17 4 6	,,	20.	Hanlon, for diet of prisoners, 13 to 20 Dec.	17	4	6
	,,	,,	Do., for 14 at 1 g. and 2 at ½ g. ...	17	1	3
	,,	,,	Grey, Mitchell, Chambers and O'Neil ...	4	11	0
	,,	22.	J. Kelly, 5 weeks, 24 December to 28 January	5	13	9
	,,	24.	W. Wright, remitted to him per his letter, £50, English, exchange 9¼ per cent. ...	54	15	0
	,,	27.	Grey, Mitchell, Chambers and O'Neil, and Coleman, to 13 Jan., 5	5	13	9
22 2 0	,,	,,	Hanlon, for diet of prisoners, 20 to 27 Dec.	22	2	0
	,,	,,	Do., for 14 at 1 g. and 2 at ½ g. ...	17	1	3
	,,	,,	Grey, to pay rent of his lodgings ...	6	16	6
	,,	30.	Judith Ward, alias Carr, from Co. Kildare, per Mr. Tyrrell	1	14	1½
	1801.					
	Jan.	1.	McGuckin, per post to Belfast ...	100	0	0
	,,	,,	A. Macnevin, esq., of Carrickfergus, per his letter, 26 Nov.	140	10	0
	,,	,,	Justice Drury	100	0	0
	,,	3.	Hanlon, for taking care of the Tower, 1 Oct.			
7 9 6			to 31 Dec., 18 weeks 1 day, at 11s. 4½d.	7	9	6
18 17 0	,,	,,	Do., for diet of prisoners, 28 Dec. to 3 Jan.	18	17	0
	,,	,,	Do., for 14 at 1 g. and 2 at ½ g. ...	17	1	3
	,,	,,	Grey, Mitchell, Chambers and O'Neill ...	4	11	0
	,,	5.	Major Swan, per receipt	113	15	0
	,,	6.	Surgeon-general, for one year's attendance			
200 0 0			on State prisoners	200	0	0
	,,	,,	Messrs. Leahy and Blaquiere, for Dobson, per Mr. Gorges' letter, etc.	22	15	0
	,,	,,	Philip Godfrey, in full, for his attendance			
40 0 0			on State prisoners	40	0	0
	,,	7.	Mr. Alex. Worthington, balance of an account...	30	14	3
	,,	,,	Do., in advance	34	2	6
£632 2 5 — C. F.			C. F.	£35,171	17	8

ACCOUNT OF SECRET SERVICE MONEY, IRELAND, 1801.

	1801.		PAID.	£	s.	d.
£632 2 5 — B. F.			Per amount brought forward,	35,171	17	8
	Jan.	9.	Three Hills, from 7 to 21 January ...	6	16	6
14 19 0	,,	10.	Hanlon, for diet of prisoners, 3 to 10 Jan.	14	19	0
	,,	,,	Do., for 14 at 1 g. and 2 at ½ g. ...	17	1	3
	,,	,,	Grey, Mitchell, Chambers, O'Neill and Coleman, 5	5	13	9
	,,	14.	Wheatley	11	7	6
15 17 0	,,	17.	Hanlon, for diet of prisoners, 11 to 17 Jan.	18	17	0
	,,	,,	Do., for 14 at 1 g. and 2 at ½ g. ...	17	1	3
	,,	,,	Grey, Mitchell, Chambers, O'Neill and Coleman	5	13	9
	,,	20.	Mr. Erskine, of the Royal Infirmary, balance of his account for Lewis			
27 4 7			Mumford, to the 5 January, 1801 ...	27	4	7
56 17 6	,,	,,	Do., in advance on same account ... -	56	17	6
	,,	22.	The four Hills, from Cork, 21 Jan. to 1 Feb.	9	2	0
	,,	23.	J. Kelly, 5 weeks, from 28 Jan. to 4 March	5	13	9
14 19 0	,,	24.	Hanlon, for diet of prisoners, 18 to 24 Jan.	14	19	0
	,,	,,	Do., for 14 at 1 g. and 2 at ½ g. ...	17	1	3
	,,	,,	Grey, Mitchell, Chambers, O'Neill and Coleman	5	13	9
	,,	,,	Mr. Erskine, Royal Infirmary, subsistence			
3 18 6			of men sent there	3	18	6
17 17 6	,,	31.	Hanlon, for diet of prisoners, 25 to 31 Jan.	17	17	6
	,,	,,	Do., for 14 men at 1 g. and 2 at ½ g. ...	17	1	3
	,,	,,	Grey, Mitchell, Chambers, O'Neil and Coleman	5	13	9
	Feb.	1.	Mr. Dudley Hill, of Carlow, amount of expenses incurred under the orders of Major-General Sir Charles Asgill, in			
55 17 2			1798	55	17	2
	,,	3.	Four Hills, from Cork, 4 to 18 Feb. ...	9	2	0
	,,	4.	Henry St. George Cole, esq., 1 quarter, to 1 January	37	10	0
	,,	5.	Wheatley, 1 g., and [on] the 6th, in full of all demands, £150	151	2	9
£812 12 8 — C. F.			C. F.	£35,704	2	5

ACCOUNT OF SECRET SERVICE MONEY, IRELAND, 1801.   53

	1801.		PAID.	£	s.	d.
£812 12 8 — B. F.			Per amount brought forward,	35,704	2	5
	Feb.	6.	Mitchell, the 24 Dec., '99, 1 g.; and this day, 1 g., both on account of the sickness of his family	2	5	6
19 10 0	,,	7.	Hanlon, for diet of prisoners, 1 to 7 Feb.	19	10	0
	,,	,,	Do., for 14 at 1 g. and 2 at ½ g. ...	17	1	3
	,,	,,	Grey, Mitchell, O'Neill, Chambers, 4 ...	4	11	0
	,,	10.	Captain Rawson, of Athy, expenses of John Cranny, approver	6	8	0
	,,	12.	Mr. Manders, on account for washing, etc., for Hughes and Conlon ...	11	7	6
11 7 6						
	,,	13.	Mr. Cooke, for N.	20	0	0
	,,	,,	Joseph Nugent, by direction of Mr. Cooke	10	0	0
	,,	14.	Sir Rich. Musgrave, for Burke, 10 weeks, 31 Jan. to 11 April	11	17	6
16 5 0	,,	,,	Hanlon, for diet of prisoners, 8 to 14 Feb.	16	5	0
	,,	,,	Do., for 14 at 1 g., 2 at ½ g.	17	1	3
	,,	,,	Grey, Mitchell, O'Neill and Chambers, 4	4	11	0
	,,	18.	The Hills, 18 Feb. to 4 March, 4 at 2 g.	9	2	0
	,,	,,	Col. Dive, of the Duke of York's Highlanders, expenses attending the execution of Ginoud, at Baltinglass, the 27 December	5	9	5½
	,,	21.	Hanlon, for Coleman, 3 weeks, from 31 January	3	8	3
19 10 0	,,	,,	Do., for diet of prisoners, 14 to 21 Feb.	19	10	0
	,,	,,	Do., for 14 at 1 g., 2 at ½ g. ...	17	1	3
	,,	,,	Grey, Mitchell, O'Neill and Chambers, 4	4	11	0
	,,	28.	J. Kelly, 5 weeks, 4 March to 8 April...	5	13	9
22 2 0	,,	,,	Hanlon, for diet of prisoners, 22 to 28 Feb.	22	2	0
	,,	,,	Do., for 14 at 1 g. and 2 at ½ g. ...	17	1	3
	,,	,,	Grey, Mitchell, O'Neill, Chambers and Coleman	5	13	9
	,,	,,	Coleman, 4 weeks in advance, to 28 March	4	11	0
	,,	,,	To bury Chambers	5	13	9
£931 7 2 — C. F.			C. F. £35,964	7	10½	

ACCOUNT OF SECRET SERVICE MONEY, IRELAND, 1801.

	1801.		PAID.	£	s.	d.
£931 7 2 — B. F.			Per amount brought forward,	35,964	7	10½
	March	3.	The 4 Hills, from Cork, 2 weeks to 18 March	9	2	0
7 9 6	,,	4.	Expenses of bringing prisoners from Ardee to Dublin...	7	9	6
	,,	6.	Bryan Forde, from Lord Harberton's, Co. Kildare	3	8	3
20 16 0	,,	7.	Hanlon, for diet of prisoners, 1 to 7 March	20	16	0
	,,	,,	Do., for 14 at 1 g., 2 at ½ g. ...	17	1	3
	,,	,,	Grey, Mitchell and O'Neill ...	3	8	3
	,,	,,	O'Neill, 5 weeks in advance, to 11 April	5	13	9
	,,	10.	General Eustace, for Bridget Dolan ...	22	15	0
	,,	12.	Mr. Whitty, by direction of Mr. Cooke, 36 g.	40	19	0
	,,	14.	J. Coughlen, to release his cloaths to go to Trim assizes ...	5	13	9
	,,	,,	Grey and Mitchell ...	2	5	6
21 19 10	,,	,,	Hanlon, for diet of prisoners, 8 to 14 March	21	19	10
	,,	,,	Do., for 14 at 1 g., 2 at ½ g. ...	17	1	3
	,,	16.	The Hills, from 18 March to 1 April ...	9	2	0
3 12 0	,,	,,	Coach, bringing up Tho. Markey from Dundalk to Kilmainham ...	3	12	0
	,,	,,	Hayden, a woman who gave information against the murderers of Col. St. George, per Col. Uniacke ...	20	0	0
11 7 6	,,	20.	Major Sirr, expenses of carriages for witnesses, etc., to Leixlip courts-martial	11	7	6
26 0 0	,,	21.	Hanlon, for diet of prisoners, 15 to 21 March ...	26	0	0
	,,	,,	Do., for 14 at 1 g., 2 at ½ g. ...	17	1	3
	,,	,,	Grey and Mitchell ...	2	5	6
21 2 6	,,	,,	Major Sirr, maintenance, etc., of James O'Brien in gaol ...	21	2	6
£1,043 14 6						
				£36,252	11	11½

Deduct the amount of the several articles in the margin in red, received at the Treasury, 23 April, 1801, being:
Amount paid for subsistence of prisoners from 30 Sep., '99, to 25 March, 1801 ... £550 1 11
Medical assistance, carriages and other expenses, do., do. ... 493 12 7
} 1,043 14 6

C. F. £35,208 17 5½

ACCOUNT OF SECRET SERVICE MONEY, IRELAND, 1801.

	1801.		PAID.	£	s.	d.
			Per amount brought forward,	35,208	17	5½
	March	26.	Mr. Cooke, for F.	200	0	0
	,,	27.	Bryan Forde, from Lord Harberton's, Co. Kildare	5	13	9
£18 17 0	,,	28.	Hanlon, for diet of prisoners, 23 to 28 March	18	17	0
	,,	,,	Do., for 14 at 1 g., 2 at ½ g.	17	1	3
	,,	,,	Grey and Mitchell	2	5	6
	,,	30.	The 4 Hills, from Cork, 1 to 15 April ...	9	2	0
	April	4.	J. Coughlan, from Clonard, in lieu of a warrant of concordatum, which could not be given this year	20	0	0
	,,	,,	J. Kelly, 5 weeks, 8 April to 13 May ...	5	13	9
19 3 6	,,	,,	Hanlon, for diet of prisoners, 29 March to 4 April	19	3	6
	,,	,,	Do., for 14 at 1 g., 2 at ½ g.	17	1	3
	,,	,,	Grey and Mitchell	2	5	6
	,,	10.	Major Sirr, for Nowlan, who prosecuted at Dundalk	17	1	3
16 18 0	,,	11.	Hanlon, for diet of prisoners, 4 to 11 April	16	18	0
	,,	,,	Do., 14 at 1 g., and 2 at ½ g.	17	1	3
	,,	,,	Grey and Mitchell	2	5	6
	,,	15.	The 4 Hills, from Cork, 15 to 29 April ...	9	2	0
19 10 0	,,	18.	Hanlon, for diet of prisoners, 11 to 18 April	19	10	0
	,,	,,	Do., for 15 at 1 g. and 2 at ½ g. ...	18	4	0
	,,	,,	Grey and Mitchell	2	5	6
	,,	,,	Sir R. Musgrave, for Mary Eldon, the 15 Aug., '99, omitted to be charged before	5	13	9
18 4 0	,,	25.	Hanlon, for diet of prisoners, 19 to 25 April	18	4	0
	,,	,,	Do., for 15 at 1 g., and 2 at ½ g. ...	18	4	0
	,,	,,	Grey and Mitchell	2	5	6
			C. F.	£35,672	15	8½

£92 12 6 — C. F

	1801.		PAID.	£	s.	d.
£92 12 6 — D. F.			Per amount brought forward,	35,672	15	8½
	April	27.	Mr. Archer, late Sheriff, Co. Wicklow...	70	0	0
	,,	30.	The 4 Hills, from Cork, 29 April to 13 May	9	2	0
	,,	,,	Henry St. George Cole, esq., 1 quarter to 1 April	37	10	0
	May	2.	Hanlon, for taking care of the Tower, 1			
9 13 4½			Jan. to 30 April, 17 weeks... ...	9	13	4½
	,,	,,	Hanlon, for diet of prisoners, 26 April to			
16 5 0			2 May	16	5	0
	,,	,,	Do., for 15 at 1 g., 2 at ½ g.	18	4	0
	,,	,,	Grey and Mitchell	2	5	6
	,,	4.	Bryan Forde, from the Co. Kildare ..	5	13	9
	,,	5.	Col. Uniacke, for Henry St. Geo. Cole, esq.	200	0	0
	,,	,,	O'Neill, per post, 5 weeks, 11 April to 16 May	5	13	9
	,,	6.	Sir R. Musgrave, for Burke, 10 weeks, 10 April to 20 June	11	7	6
19 4 0	,,	9.	Hanlon, for diet of prisoners, 3 to 9 Aug.	18	4	0
	,,	,,	Do., for 15 at 1 g., and 2 at ½ g. ...	18	4	0
	,,	,,	Grey and Mitchell	2	5	5
	,,	11.	J. Kelly, 5 weeks, 13 May to 27 June ...	5	13	9
	,,	13.	The four Hills, from Cork, 2 weeks, from 13 to 27 May	9	2	0
	,,	16.	Coleman, 15 weeks, from 28 March to 11 July	17	1	3
	,,	,,	Thomas Pope, gaoler of Limerick, on account of expenses of bringing prisoners			
10 0 0			from thence to the court of king's bench	10	0	0
19 4 0	,,	,,	Hanlon, for diet of prisoners, 9 to 16 May	18	4	0
	,,	,,	Do., sundry persons, as before ...	18	4	0
	,,	,,	Grey and Mitchell	2	5	6
	,,	,,	Lord Carhampton's draft for Feris, half-year to 1 May, £50, English ...	54	3	4
£164 18 10½ — C. P.			C. F.	£36,231	17	11

ACCOUNT OF SECRET SERVICE MONEY, IRELAND, 1801.

	1801.		PAID.	£	s.	d.
£164 18 10½— D. F.			Per amount brought forward,	36,231	17	11
	May	21.	Mr. Trevor, for Mr. Redfern's family ...	5	13	9
	,,	23.	T. Pope, gaoler of Limerick, on further account of expenses of bringing up 8 prisoners to the court of king's			
34 2 6			bench, and returning	34	2	6
18 4 0	,,	,,	Hanlon, for diet of prisoners, 16 to 23 May	18	4	0
	,,	,,	Do., for sundry persons, as before ...	18	4	0
	,,	,,	Grey and Mitchell	2	5	6
	,,	27.	The four Hills, from 27 May to 11 June, 2 weeks	9	2	0
	,,	28.	Earl of Shannon, for Rev. Mr. Barry, R. C. priest at Mallow	100	0	0
17 11 0	,,	30.	Hanlon, for diet of prisoners, 23 to 30 May	17	11	0
	,,	,,	Do., for sundries, as before	18	4	0
	,,	,,	Grey and Mitchell	2	5	6
	June	1.	Lord Tyrawley, for Rev. C. Doran, R. C. priest at Monasterevan, instead of a warrant of concordatum for the last year	20	0	0
	,,	4.	Mr. Pollock, per receipt	50	0	0
	,,	6.	Hanlon, for diet of prisoners, 31 May to			
17 4 6			6 June	17	4	6
	,,	,,	Do., sundries, as before	18	4	0
	,,	,,	Grey and Mitchell	2	5	6
	,,	9.	Mr. Marsden, for Cody	200	0	0
	,,	10.	Do.	22	15	0
	,,	,,	The four Hills, 2 weeks, 11 to 25 June	9	2	0
	,,	13.	Bryan Forde, by desire of Mr. Marsden	5	13	9
18 17 0	,,	,,	Hanlon, for diet of prisoners, 7 to 13 June	18	17	0
	,,	,,	Do., sundries, as before	18	4	0
	,,	,,	Grey and Mitchell	2	5	6
	,,	,,	J. Kelly, per Gray, 5 weeks, 17 June to 22 July	5	13	9
£270 17 10½— C. F.			C. F.	£36,847	15	2

ACCOUNT OF SECRET SERVICE MONEY, IRELAND, 1801.

	1801.		PAID.	£	s.	d.
£270 17 10½— B. F.			Per amount brought forward,	36,847	15	2
	June	16.	O'Neill, 5 weeks, 16 May to 20 June, per post	5	13	9
	,,	,,	Mr. Pollock, for T. W. (repaid from pension)	—		
	,,	17.	Nich. Price, esq., for Ja⁵· Gardener and Ch. Young, £10 each; and for Tho. Townley, £15, persons in the Co. Down	35	0	0
	,,	19.	Messrs. Armit and Borough, for Brig.-Gen. Mayrick, subsistence of prisoners moved from Ennis to Galway during			
6 1 4			the assizes in 1800 and 1801 ...	6	1	4
18 4 0	,,	20.	Hanlon, for diet of prisoners, 14 to 20 June	18	4	0
	,,	,,	Do., sundries, as before	18	4	0
	,,	,,	Grey and Mitchell	2	5	6
	,,	23.	Mr. Erskine, of the Royal Hospital, on further account for the subsistence of			
22 15 0			Lewis Munford	22	15	0
	,,	,,	Grey, for Mitchell, while Mitchell and wife were ill	1	14	1½
	,,	,,	Mr. Grenshiels, per Mr. Uniacke's note	22	15	0
	,,	,,	Sir Rich. Musgrave, for Michael Burke, 10 weeks, to 29 August	11	7	6
	,,	25.	The four Hills, 2 weeks, to 9 July ...	9	2	0
17 6 8	,,	27.	Hanlon, for diet of prisoners, 20 to 27 June	17	6	8
	,,	,,	Do., for sundries, as before	18	4	0
	,,	,,	Grey and Mitchell	18	4	0
	,,	,,	Philip Hill, per Sir Richard Musgrave, 5 weeks to 13 Aug.	5	13	9
	July	4.	Messrs. Armit and Borough, for the paymaster of the Tay Fencibles, for subsistence of prisoners at Carrickfergus, Nov., '98, to July, '99, per			
17 8 1			receipt	17	8	1
	,,	,,	Do., for paymaster of the Aberdeenshire Fencibles, for subsistence of prisoners at Leixlip,			
6 18 6			Nov., 1800, to May, 1801, per receipt	6	18	6
	,,	,,	Hanlon, for diet of prisoners, 28 June to			
18 12 8			4 July	18	12	8
	,,	,,	Do., for sundries, as before	18	4	0
	,,	,,	Grey and Mitchell	2	5	6
£378 4 1½— C. F.			C. F.	£37,107	16	0½

ACCOUNT OF SECRET SERVICE MONEY, IRELAND, 1801.

	1801.		PAID.	£	s.	d.
4378 4 1½— B. F.			Per amount brought forward,	37,107	16	0½
	July	8.	James Curran, from Portaferry, per Lord Castlereagh's recommendation ...	20	0	0
	,,	9.	The three Hills, 2 weeks, to 23rd July ...	6	16	6
	,,	,,	Mr. Turner, repayment of what he advanced to Chapman, in Cork, from 19 April, 1800, to 5 July, 1801, 1 year and 11 weeks, at 1 g. per week ...	71	13	3
18 19 2	,,	11.	Hanlon, for diet of prisoners, 4 to 11 July	18	19	2
	,,	,,	Do., for sundries, as before	18	4	0
	,,	,,	Grey and Mitchell	2	5	6
	,,	18.	Do. and do.	2	5	6
17 4 6	,,	,,	Hanlon, for diet of prisoners, 11 to 18 July	17	4	6
	,,	,,	Do., for sundries, as before	18	4	0
	,,	23.	The three Hills, 2 weeks, to 6 August ...	6	16	6
	,,	,,	J. Kelly, per Grey, 5 weeks, to 26 August	5	13	9
	,,	25.	Mr. Cooke, for K.	100	0	0
17 4 6	,,	,,	Hanlon, for diet of prisoners, 19 to 25 July	17	4	6
	,,	,,	Do., for sundries, as before	18	4	0
	,,	,,	Grey and Mitchell	2	5	6
	,,	27.	J. Bell, by direction of Mr. Cooke ...	200	0	0
	,,	,,	Mr. Pollock, do.	10	0	0
4 19 1½	,,	,,	Hanlon, for taking care of the Tower, 1 May to 30 June, 8 weeks 5 days, 11s. 4½d.	4	19	1½
16 18 0	August	1.	Do., for diet of prisoners, 26 July to 1 August	16	18	0
	,,	,,	Do., for sundries, as before	18	4	0
	,,	,,	Grey and Mitchell	2	5	6
	,,	5.	Edmond O'Neill, 10 weeks, from 20 June to 29 August	11	7	6
30 0 0	,,	7.	Mr. Erskine, Military Infirmary, per Mr. Trevor, account of Mumford's subsistence	30	0	0
£483 9 5 — C. F.			C. F. £37,727		6	10

ACCOUNT OF SECRET SERVICE MONEY, IRELAND, 1801.

1801.		PAID.	£	s.	d.
£483 9 5 — B.F.		Per amount brought forward,	37,727	6	10
August	8.	For Belfast Newsletter, furnished to Mr. Pollock, by direction of Government, from March, '95, to January, 1801	9	16	9
,,	,,	The three Hills, from 6 to 20 August	6	16	6
11 14 0	,,	,, Hanlon, for subsistence of prisoners, 1 to 8 August	11	14	0
,,	,,	Do., for sundries, per list	20	9	6
,,	,,	Grey and Mitchell	2	5	9
,,	,,	Mr. Pollock, for Stockdale	5	13	9
,,	10.	Mr. Marshall, what he paid for the "Beauties of the Press"	1	2	9
,,	14.	Philip Hill, per Sir Richard Musgrave, 5 weeks, to 17 September	5	13	9
12 0 6	,,	15. Hanlon, for subsistence of prisoners, 9 to 15 August	12	0	6
,,	,,	Do., for sundries	20	9	6
,,	,,	Grey and Mitchell	2	5	6
,,	11.	Coleman, by direction of Mr. Cooke	1	2	9
,,	18.	Alex. Worthington, esq., balance of an account	29	11	6
,,	,,	Do., in advance	34	2	6
,,	20.	W. Corbett, by direction of Mr. Cooke	358	10	0
,,	,,	Mr. Cooke	50	0	0
,,	21.	The three Hills, two weeks, to 3 Sep.	6	16	6
12 13 6	22.	Hanlon, for diet of prisoners, 15 to 22 August	12	13	6
,,	,,	Do., for sundries, per list	20	9	6
,,	,,	Grey and Mitchell	2	5	6
,,	21.	Edward Lennan, to take him out of town, per Mr. Trevor	3	8	3
,,	27.	Henry St. George Cole, esq., 1 quarter, to 1 July	37	10	0
,,	28.	J. Kelly, per Grey, 5 weeks, to 30 Sep.	5	13	9
,,	,,	M. Burke, per Sir R. Musgrave, 5 weeks, to 3 October	5	13	9
4 11 0	,,	,. Serjeant of Clare Militia, who came with Hide, with a prisoner from Limerick	4	11	0
£524 8 5 — C.F.		C. F.	£38,398	3	4

ACCOUNT OF SECRET SERVICE MONEY, IRELAND, 1801.

	1801.		PAID.	£	s.	d.
£524 8 5 — D. F.			Per amount brought forward,	38,398	3	4
	August	29.	Hanlon, for diet of prisoners, 22 to 29 August			
15 9 10				15	9	10
	,,	,,	Do., for sundries, per list	19	6	9
	,,	,,	Mitchell	1	2	9
	Septem.	5.	Do.	1	2	9
	,,	,,	Hanlon, for diet of prisoners, 30 Aug. to 5 September			
15 7 8				15	7	8
	,,	,,	Do., for sundries, as before	19	6	9
	,,	,,	The three Hills, from Cork, 2 weeks, 3 to 17 Sept.	6	16	6
	,,	9.	Sir Richd Musgrave, for Michael Burke, 5 weeks, from 3 Oct. to 8 Nov. ...	5	13	9
13 10 10	,,	12.	Hanlon, for diet of prisoners, 6 to 12 Sep.	13	10	10
	,,	,,	Do., for sundries	19	6	9
	,,	,,	Mitchell	1	2	9
	,,	16.	Dr. Macartney, of Antrim, for candles and firing for a guard in 1796 ...			
1 13 0				1	13	0
	,,	17.	The four Hills, from Cork, 2 weeks, 17 Sep. to 1 Oct.	9	2	0
11 7 6	,,	19.	Hanlon, for diet of prisoners, 13 to 19 Sep.	11	7	6
	,,	,,	Do., for sundries	19	6	9
	,,	,,	Mitchell	1	2	9
	,,	,,	Gaoler of Enniskillen, expenses bringing up John Jenkinson, alias Ward ...			
1 15 2				1	15	2
	,,	21.	Lord Longueville, for the Rev. Mich^l Barry, priest at Middleton ...	100	0	0
	,,	,,	P. Prendergast, a police officer, who went with Hide to Chester, with Fitzgerald, a prisoner			
2 5 6				2	5	6
	,,	,,	Tho. King, esq., of Rathdrum, by order of the Marquis Cornwallis... ...	300	0	0
15 5 6	,,	26.	Hanlon, for diet of prisoners, 20 to 26 Sep.	15	5	6
	,,	,,	Do., for sundries	19	6	9
	,,	,,	Mitchell	1	2	9
	,,	29.	Hanlon, for care of the Tower, 1 July to 29 Sep., 13 weeks at 11s. 4½d. ...			
7 7 10¼				7	7	10½
£608 11 3¼ — C. F.			C. F.	£39,006	5	11½

	1801.		PAID.	£	s.	d.
£608 11 3½ — B. F.			Per amount brought forward,	39,006	5	11½
	September.		Mr. Cooke, what he gave Whelan, in London, £20, English	21	13	4
£608 11 3½				£39,027	19	3½
			Deduct the amount of the several articles in the margin in red, received at the Treasury, 23 Oct., 1801, being: Amount paid for subsistence of prisoners from 25 March to 29 Sep.... £532 3 9 Other expenses, do., do. ... 76 7 6½	608	11	3½
			Total amount applied according to the act of parliament, from 20 August, 1797, to the 30 September, 1801, per affidavit of Edward Cooke, esq., lodged in the Treasury	38,419	8	0
			Balance carried to new account ...	1,580	12	0
				£40,000	0	0
	October	3.	Hanlon, for diet of prisoners, 26 Sep. to 3 Oct.			
16 11 6				16	11	6
	,,	,,	Do., for sundries	20	9	6
	,,	,,	Mitchell and Coleman, 1 g. each ...	2	5	6
	,,	8.	The Hills, 1 week to this date ...	4	11	0
	,,	10.	J. Kelly, five weeks, from 30 Sep. to 4 Nov.	5	13	9
	,,	,,	Mitchell, Coleman and Cranny, from Athy, 1 g. each ...	3	8	3
	,,	,,	Bryan O'Reilly, of Lord Mathew's yeomanry, who apprehended Wm. Moroney, per Sir Ch. Asgill's letter, etc. ...	56	17	6
22 15 0	,,	,,	Hanlon, for diet of prisoners... ...	22	15	0
	,,	,,	Do., for sundries	20	9	6
	,,	16.	The Hills, from Cork, 1 week, to 15 Oct.	4	11	0
20 16 0	,,	17.	Hanlon, for diet of prisoners, 11 to 17 Oct.	20	16	0
	,,	,,	Do., for sundries	20	9	6
	,,	,,	Mitchell and Coleman, 1 g. each ...	2	5	6
	,,	19.	Hanlon, to bury Edward Lennon ...	1	2	9
	,,	23.	The Hills, 1 week, to 22 Oct. ...	4	11	0
	,,	,,	Cranny, from Athy, by desire of Mr. Cooke	1	2	9
22 2 0	,,	24.	Hanlon, for diet of prisoners, 18 to 24 Oct.	22	2	0
	,,	,,	Do., for sundries	20	9	6
	,,	,,	Mitchell, 1 g. ; Cranny, the 29th, 1 g.	2	5	6
£82 4 6 — C. F.			C. F.	£252	17	0

	1801.		PAID.	£	s.	d.
£82 4 5 — B. F.			Per amount brought forward,	252	17	0
	Oct.	30.	J. Keogh, per receipt	100	0	0
	,,	,,	The Hills, four, 1 week, to 29 October ...	4	11	0
	,,	31.	Edward O'Neill, per post to Antrim, 10 weeks, 29 Aug. to 7 Nov. ...	11	7	6
18 10 6	,,	,,	Hanlon, for diet of prisoners, 24 to 31 Oct.	18	10	6
	,,	,,	Do., for sundries	20	9	6
	,,	,,	Mitchell, 1 g.; Bryan Forde, 2 g.; 6 Nov., Cranny, 1 g.	4	11	0
	,,	,,	The Hills, 1 week, to 5 November ...	4	11	0
	Novem.	6.	R. Power, esq., Sheriff, Co. Waterford, for the Cushmore corps, for apprehending rebels and robbers, per receipt, 80 g. ...	91	0	0
	,,	7.	Right Hon. Denis Browne, for informers against Rd. Jordan, 90 g.	102	7	6
15 18 6	,,	,,	Hanlon, for diet of prisoners, 1 to 7 Nov.	15	18	6
	,,	,,	Do., for sundries, as before	20	9	6
	,,	,,	Mitchell, 1 g.; 12 Nov., J. Kelly, 5 weeks, to 9 December, £5 13s. 9d. ...	6	16	6
	,,	13.	Sir R. Musgrave, for Michael Burke, 5 weeks, 8 November to 18 December	5	13	9
	,,	,,	The Hills, 1 week, to 12 Nov., £4 11s.; Cranny, £1 2s. 9d.; 14th, Mitchell, £1 2s. 9d. ...	6	16	6
17 11 0	,,	14.	Hanlon, for diet of prisoners, 7 to 14 Nov.	17	11	0
	,,	,,	Do., for sundries	20	9	6
	,,	18.	Henry St. Geo. Cole, esq., 1 quarter's allowance to 1st October	37	10	0
	,,	20.	The Hills, 1 week to 19 Nov., £4 11s.; Cranny, £1 2s. 9d.; 21st, Mitchell, £1 2s. 9d.	6	16	6
17 17 6	,,	21.	Hanlon, for diet of prisoners, 15 to 21 Nov.	17	17	6
	,,	,,	Do., for sundries	20	9	6
	,,	24.	Mr. Erskine, of the Royal Infirmary, balance of account for subsistence, etc., of Mumford, to 5 Nov., in full ...	6	15	4½
6 15 4½	,,	,,	Lord Carhampton's bill for James Feris, half-year to 1 Nov., £50, British ...	54	3	4
	,,	27.	The Hills, 1 week, £4 11s.; Cranny, £1 2s. 9d.; 28th, Mitchell, £1 2s. 9d.	6	16	6
£158 17 4½— C. F			C. F.	£854	8	11½

ACCOUNT OF SECRET SERVICE MONEY, IRELAND, 1801.

	1801.		PAID.	£	s.	d.
£158 17 4½— B. F.			Per amount brought forward,	854	8	11½
	Nov.	28.	Hanlon, for diet of prisoners, 21 to 28 Nov.	17	4	6
	,,	,,	Do., for sundries, as before	20	9	6
	Dec.	4.	The Hills, £4 11s.; Cranny, £1 2s. 9d.; 5th, Mitchell, £1 2s. 9d.	6	16	6
16 11 6	,,	5.	Hanlon, for diet of prisoners, 28 Nov. to 5 Dec.	16	11	6
	,,	,,	Do., for sundries, as before ...	20	9	6
	,,	,,	Wm. Wright, alias Lawler, per bill remitted to him in London, per his letter, B. Clarke and son on Wallis and Co., £50; exchange, 10½ per cent. ...	55	5	0
	,,	7.	Remitted to John King, esq., in repayment of what he advanced to John Lindsay, per Mr. King's letter, etc., £2, British	2	3	4
22 15 0	,,	9.	Campbell, of the Treasury, on further account, for the use of his rooms in the Castle, for Conlan, Hughes, etc., since June, 1798 ...	22	15	0
	,,	12.	J. Kelly, 3 weeks, from 9 to 30 December	3	8	3
	,,	,,	Mitchell, 1 g.; Cranny, 1 g.; the Hills, 4 g.	6	16	6
16 18 0	,,	,,	Hanlon, for diet of prisoners, 5 to 12 Dec.	16	18	0
	,,	,,	Do., for sundries, as before	20	9	6
	,,	,,	Rich. Campsie, in full of all his claims, by direction of Mr. Abbott	56	17	6
	,,	16.	Sir Rich. Musgrave, for Mich. Burke, 5 weeks, to 17 January, 1802	5	13	9
	,,	18.	The Hills, £4 11s.; Cranny, £1 2s. 9d.; Mitchell, £1 2s. 9d.	6	16	6
14 6 0	,,	,,	Hanlon, for diet of prisoners, 12 to 19 Dec.	14	6	0
	,,	,,	Do., for sundries, as before	20	9	6
	,,	26.	The Hills, £4 11s.; Cranny and Mitchell, £2 5s. 6d.	6	16	6
12 0 6	,,	,,	Hanlon, for diet of prisoners, 19 to 26 Dec.	12	0	6
	,,	,,	Do., for sundries, as before	20	9	6
	,,	30.	Coleman, by desire of Mr. Marsden, per letter from General Drummond, etc. ...	5	13	9
	,,	31.	Major Sirr, to discharge two men on his list who were employed in the country, at 1 g. per week each	56	17	6
	,,	,,	The Hills, £4 11s.; Cranny, £1 2s. 9d.; Jan. 2nd., Mitchell, £1 2s. 9d.	6	16	6

£258 12 10½— C. F.   C. F. £1,276 13 6½

ACCOUNT OF SECRET SERVICE MONEY, IRELAND, 1802.

	1802.		PAID.—	£	s.	d.
£258 12 10½— B. F.			Per amount brought forward,	1,276	13	6½
	January	2.	J. Kelly, 5 weeks, from 30 Dec. to 3 Feb.	5	13	9
11 1 0	,,	,,	Hanlon, for diet of prisoners, 26 Dec. to 2 Jan.	11	1	0
	,,	,,	Do., for sundries, as before, deducting 2 men paid off, 31 Dec.	18	4	0
	,,	9.	The Hills, 4; Cranny and Mitchell, 1 g. each	6	16	6
10 1 6	,,	,,	Hanlon, for diet of prisoners, 3 to 9 Jan.	10	1	6
	,,	,,	Do., for sundries, as before	18	4	0
	,,	14.	Sir. Rich. Musgrave, for Michael Boyle (Burke), 5 weeks, 17 Jan. to 21 Feb.	5	13	9
	,,	15.	Surgeon-General, for attendance on prisoners, etc., for 1 year	200	0	0
200 0 0						
	,,	,,	Mr. E. Trevor, for do., from 1 July to 31 Dec., 1801, 184 days, at 10s. per day	92	0	0
92 0 0						
	,,	,,	The Hills, 4 g.; Cranny and Mitchell, 1 g. each	6	16	6
	,,	,,	Alderman Alexander, for Mr. Atkinson, of the Police, for going to Limerick, last summer, to bring up Fitzgerald with a messenger	22	15	0
	,,	16.	Coleman, from Carrickfergus... ...	5	13	9
	,,	,,	E. O'Neill, 10 weeks, from 7 Nov., 1801, to 16 Jan. 1802	11	7	6
12 0 6	,,	,,	Hanlon, for diet of prisoners, 9 to 16 Jan.	12	0	6
	,,	,,	Do., for sundries, as before	18	4	0
	,,	21.	Hunt and Kiernan, for medicines, from September, 1800, to 3 Dec., 1801 ...	46	11	10
46 11 10						
	,,	23.	The Hills, 4; Cranny and Mitchell, 1 g. each	6	16	6
11 7 6	,,	,,	Hanlon, for diet of prisoners, 16 to 23 Jan.	11	7	6
	,,	,,	Do., for sundries, as before	18	4	0
	,,	28.	Mr. Justice Drury	100	0	0
	,,	29.	The Hills, 4 g.; Cranny and Mitchell, 1 g. each	6	16	6
12 0 6	,,	30.	Hanlon, for diet of prisoners, 24 to 30 Jan.	12	0	6
	,,	,,	Do., for sundries, as before	18	4	0
	Feb.	6.	J. Kelly, two weeks, 3 to 17 Feb. ...	2	5	0
	,,	,,	The Hills, 4 g.; Cranny and Mitchell, 1 g. each	6	16	6
£653 15 8½— C. F.			C. F.	£1,950	8	1½

ACCOUNT OF SECRET SERVICE MONEY, IRELAND, 1802.

	1802.		PAID.	£	s.	d.
£653 15 8½ — B. F.			Per amount brought forward,	1,950	8	1½
13 13 0	Feb.	6.	Hanlon, for diet of prisoners, 30 Jan. to 6 Feb.	13	13	0
	,,	,,	Do., for sundries, as before	18	4	0
	,,	,,	Bryan Ford, who came from Lord Harberton's, in full of all claims ...	68	5	0
	,,	,,	Mr. John Hughes, of [blank], do. do. ...	200	0	0
	,,	8.	John Cranny, from Athy, recommended by Captain Rawson, do. do. ...	34	2	6
	,,	10.	Henry St. Geo. Cole, esq., 1 quarter's allowance, to 1 January	37	10	0
	,,	11.	Mitchell, 17 Nov., 1801, and 6 June last, on account of the illness of his family	2	5	6
	,,	,,	Do., to pay off his lodging	5	13	9
	,,	,,	Do., in full of his claims upon Government	100	0	0
	,,	,,	Captain Graham, what he advanced to Henry O'Hara, of Antrim, in full for his services, per Doctor Macartney's letters	56	17	6
	,,	,,	H. B. Cody, per receipt	100	0	0
	,,	13.	Mr. Cassidy, for the Rev. Mr. Doran, of Monasterevan, recommended per Lord Tyrawley	50	0	0
	,,	,,	Coleman, from Carrickfergus ...	5	13	9
	,,	,,	Major Sirr, for John Beckett, Mr. Lennan, Mr. Dunn, Chas. McGowan, John Kearney, Edward Hayes and Denis Carr, in full of their claims on Government, for services in the rebellion ...	328	8	9
10 1 6	,,	,,	Hanlon, for diet of prisoners, 6 to 13 Feb.	10	1	6
	,,	,,	Do., for 10 persons remaining on his list	11	7	6
	,,	19.	The Hills, 4 g.; J. Kelly, 2 weeks, 17 Feb. to 1 March, 2 g.	6	16	6
	,,	20.	J. McGuckin, to replace £100, advanced to him, 16 May, 1801, but afterwards stopped out of his pension... ...	100	0	0
	,,	,,	Mr. Wm. Corbett, per agreement by Mr. Pollock, relative to Stockdale ...	100	0	0
8 2 6	,,	,,	Hanlon, for diet of prisoners, 14 to 20 Feb.	8	2	6
	,,	,,	Do., for sundries, as before	11	7	6
7 7 10½	,,	,,	Do., for his care of the Tower, etc., from 29 Sep. to 25 Dec., 1801, 13 weeks...	7	7	10½
£693 0 7 — C. F.			C. F.	£3,226	5	3

	1802.		PAID.	£	s.	d.
£693 0 7 — B. F.			Per amount brought forward,	3,226	5	3
	Feb.	26.	Mr. Ball, of Finglas, for the yeomanry there, who took several robbers, etc., per Lord Norbury's letter	22	15	0
	,,	,,	The Hills, from Cork	4	11	0
8 2 6	,,	27.	Hanlon, for diet of prisoners, 21 to 27 Feb.	8	2	6
	,,	,,	Do., for five men, per list	5	13	9
	March	2.	J. Kelly, 2 weeks, 3 to 17 March ...	2	5	6
	,,	5.	The Hills, from Cork, 1 week ...	4	11	0
	,,	6.	Hanlon, for diet of prisoners, 28 Feb. to			
8 2 6			6 March	8	2	6
	,,	,,	Do., for five men, per list	5	13	9
	,,	12.	The Hills, 4 g.; J. Kelly, 2 weeks, 17 to 31 March, 2 g.	6	16	6
7 9 6	,,	13.	Hanlon, for diet of prisoners, 7 to 13 Mar.	7	9	6
	,,	,,	Do., for 5 men, per list	5	13	9
	,,	19.	The Hills, 4	4	11	0
8 2 6	,,	20.	Hanlon, for diet of prisoners, 14 to 20 Mar.	8	2	6
	,,	,,	Do., for 5 men, per list	5	13	9
	,,	,,	James Coleman, from Carrickfergus ...	11	17	6
	,,	,,	Mr. Worthington, the 11 February, account of Boyle	50	0	0
	,,	,,	Campbell, on further account for lodging,			
22 15 0			etc., for Conlan and Hughes ...	22	15	0
10 0 0	,,	,,	Mr. Manders, for washing, etc., do., do.	10	0	0
	,,	,,	Major Sirr, for Mrs. O'Brien, John Neil, Frederick Develin, John Coughlan, and Thomas Jackson, per receipt in full of their claims	300	0	0
	,,	25.	Sir Richard Musgrave, for Michael Burke, 5 weeks, 21 Feb. to 28 March	5	13	9
	,,	,,	Do., for do., in full of his claims ...	113	15	0
	,,	,,	The Hills	4	11	0
	,,	,,	The Marquess of Waterford, for the Sub-Sheriff, Co. Waterford, 1801, and expenses of the Sheriff	162	0	0
£737 12 7 — C. F.			C. F.	£4,006	9	6

ACCOUNT OF SECRET SERVICE MONEY, IRELAND, 1802.

1802.		PAID.	£	s.	d.
£757 12 7 — B. F.		Per amount brought forward,	4,006	9	6
March	27.	The Earl of Shannon, for the Rev. Mr. Barry, Parish Priest at Mallow	100	0	0
,,	,,	Edm$^{d.}$ O'Neill, 10 weeks' subsistence, 16 Jan. to 27 March	11	7	6
8 2 6	,,	,,	Hanlon, for diet of prisoners, 20 to 27 Mar.	8	2	6
	,,	,,	Do., for 5 men, per list	5	13	9
4 11 0	,,	30.	Hanlon, to be a witness to Trim Assizes	4	11	0
	,,	,,	J. Kelly, 3 weeks, to 7 April	3	8	3
	,,	,,	Captain Rawson, of Athy, what he advanced to J. Cranny	4	11	0
£770 6 1			£4,144	3	6

Deduct the amount of the several articles in the margin in red, received at the Treasury, being:

Amount paid for subsistence of prisoners from 30 Sep., 1801, to 31 March, 1802 ... £364 5 4½
Surgeon-General, and other expenses attending do. ... 406 0 8½

			770	6	1
			£3,373	17	5
	April	2.	The Hills, from Cork, four	4	11	0
	,,	3.	Hanlon, for subsistence of prisoners, 27 March to 3 April	7	3	0
7 3 0	,,	,,	Do., for five men, per list	5	13	9
	,,	9.	The Hills	4	11	0
	,,	10.	Hanlon, for subsistence of prisoners, 4 to 10 April	7	9	6
7 0 6	,,	,,	Do., for five men, per list	5	13	9
	,,	16.	The Hills, £4 11s.; 17, Hanlon, for five men, £5 13s. 9d.	10	4	9
	,,	17.	Hanlon, for subsistence of prisoners, 11 to 17 April	5	17	0
5 17 0	,,	21.	Edm$^{d.}$ O'Neill, 5 weeks, 27 March to 1 May	5	13	9
	,,	,,	J. Kelly, 3 weeks, 7 to 28 April	3	8	3
	,,	23.	The Hills, £4 11s.; Hanlon, for five men, £5 13s. 9d.	10	4	9
3 11 6	,,	24.	Hanlon, for diet of prisoners, 18 to 24 April	3	11	6
£24 1 0 — C. F.		C. F.	£3,447	19	5

ACCOUNT OF SECRET SERVICE MONEY, IRELAND, 1802. 69

1802.		PAID.	£	s.	d.
£24 1 0 — B. F.		Per amount brought forward,	3,447	19	5
April	29.	J. Kelly, 3 weeks, from 28 April to 19 May	3	8	3
,,	30.	The Hills, £4 11s.; 1 May, Hanlon, for 5, £5 13s. 9d.	10	4	9
2 5 6 May	1.	Hanlon, for diet of prisoners	2	5	6
,,	3.	The Lord Mayor (Alderman Manders), for R. Lowther, per receipt ...	22	15	0
,,	6.	The Hills, £4 11s.; 7th, Hanlon, for 5, £5 13s. 9d.; for Conlan, £2 5s. 6d.	12	10	3
,,	7.	E. O'Neill, 5 weeks, 1 May to 5 June ...	5	13	9
45 0 0 ,,	8.	Dr. Trevor, for attendances at Kilmainham, 1 quarter, to 31st March, 1802 ...	45	0	0
,,	,,	J. C. Beresford, esq., amount of an account of money expended for Government, between 1798 and 1802	470	11	8½
,,	14.	The Hills, £4 11s.; Hanlon, 5 g., and for Conlan, 2 g.	12	10	3
7 6 3 ,,	,,	Hanlon, for taking care of the Tower, from 25 December, 1801, to 25 March, 1802 ...	7	6	3
,,	19.	J. Kelly, 5 weeks, from 19 May to 23 June	5	13	9
,,	21.	The Hills, £4 11s.; Hanlon, for 5, £5 13s. 9d.; for Conlan, £2 5s. 6d.	12	10	3
,,	25.	Major Cutting, expenses of prisoners at Athlone, per receipt	8	11	0
8 11 0					
,,	27.	Rich^d. Grandy, per receipt, etc. ...	100	0	0
,,	28.	The Hills, £4 11s.; Hanlon, for 5, £5 13s. 9d.; for Conlan, £2 5s. 6d.	12	10	3
June	2.	Coleman, from Carrickfergus, for subsistence from 20 March	11	7	6
,,	,,	Do., in full of his claims for services (appointed Sub-Tidewaiter) ...	34	2	6
,,	4.	The Hills, £4 11s.; Hanlon, for 5, £5 13s. 9d.; for Conlan, £2 5s. 6d. ...	12	10	3
,,	,,	Henry St. Geo. Cole, esq., 1 quarter allowance, to 1 April, and in full	37	10	0
,,	11.	The Hills, £4 11s.; Hanlon, for 5, £5 13s. 9d.; Conlan, £2 5s. 6d.	12	10	3
,,	15.	E. O'Neill, to 19 June	2	5	6
,,	14.	Captain Wainright, Co. Wicklow, for Bridget Dolan, per Mr. [illegible] ...	22	15	0
£87 3 9 — C. F.		C. F.	£4,312	11	4½

1802.		PAID.	£	s.	d.
£87 3 9 — B. F.		Per amount brought forward,	4,312	11	4½
June	19.	The Hills, £4 11s.; Hanlon, for 5, £5 13s. 9d.; for Conlan, £2 5s. 6d.	12	10	3
,,	24.	Tho. Little, of Court Duff, Co. Kildare, on recommendation of the Grand Jury, for his exertions to bring offenders to justice	100	0	0
,,	25.	J. Kelly, 3 weeks, 23 June to 14 July	3	8	3
,,	,,	The Hills, £4 11s.; Hanlon, for 5, £5 13s. 9d.; for Conlan, £2 5s. 6d.	12	10	3
July	3.	Do., do. do.	12	10	3
7 7 10½ ,,	,,	Hanlon, for care of the Tower, 25 March to 24 June, 13 weeks	7	7	10½
,,	7.	Captain Prendergast, Tipperary Militia, account of his expenses on actions against him for proceedings against rebels, in 1798, per letter, etc.	34	2	6
,,	10.	The Hills, £4 11s.; Hanlon, for 5, £5 13s. 9d.; for Conlan, £2 5s. 6d.	12	10	3
,,	14.	J. Kelly, from Carlow, in full of his claims for services (made a gauger)	113	15	0
,,	,,	James Corran, of Portaferry, an annual allowance to 1 July, 1802, engaged to him by Lord Castlereagh	20	0	0
,,	17.	The Hills, £4 11s.; Hanlon, for 5, £5 13s. 9d.; for Conlan, £2 5s. 6d.	12	10	3
,,	19.	Earl Carhampton's draft for Feris, half-year to [blank] £50 British	54	3	4
45 10 0 ,,	,,	Dr. Trevor, 1 quarter to 30 June	45	10	0
,,	23.	The Hills, £4 11s.; Hanlon, for 5, £5 13s. 9d.; for Conlan, £2 5s. 6d.	12	10	3
,,	,,	W. B. Coady, per receipt by Mr. Marsden's direction	100	0	0
,,	,,	The Auditor-General, his fees for seven warrants for the maintenance of State prisoners, to March, 1802, at 7s. 0½d. each	2	9	3½
,,	30.	The Hills, £4 11s.; Hanlon, for 5, £5 13s. 9d.; for Conlan, £2 5s. 6d.	12	10	3
,,	,,	James Edward Hill, Philip Hill, John Hill and Mary Hill, widow of William Hill, in full, for their claims for services at Cork during the rebellion, etc., £100 each	400	0	0
£140 1 7¼— C. F.		C. F.	£5,280	19	4½

ACCOUNT OF SECRET SERVICE MONEY, IRELAND, 1802.

1802.		PAID.	£	s.	d.
£140 1 7½—B. F.		Per amount brought forward,	5,280	19	4½
August	7.	Conlan, £2 5s. 6d.; Hanlon, for five, £5 13s. 9d.	7	19	3
,,	14.	Do., do.	7	19	3
,,	21.	Do., do.	7	19	3
,,	28.	Do., do.	7	19	3
Sept.	4.	Do., do.	7	19	3
,,	11.	Do., do.	7	19	3
,,	16.	James Mallon, per note from Mr. Sack[ville] Hamilton	5	13	9
,,	18.	Conlan, £2 5s. 6d.; Hanlon, for five, £5 13s. 9d.	7	19	3
,,	25.	Do., do.	7	19	3
7 7 10½	,,	,,	Hanlon, for care of the Tower, from 25 June, 13 weeks	7	7	10½
Oct.	2.	Conlan, £2 5s. 6d.; Hanlon and four others, £5 13s. 9d.	7	19	3
,,	5.	Luke Brien, per Mr. Wickham's directions, for one month	5	13	9
,,	9.	Conlan, Hanlon, etc.	7	19	3
,,	16.	Do., do.	7	19	3
,,	20.	E. O'Neill, his allowance from 19 June last to 23 October	20	9	6
,,	,,	Do., in full of all claims, per his receipt — (made a gauger)	113	15	0
,,	23.	Conlan, Hanlon, etc.	7	19	3
,,	28.	Alex. Worthington, esq., account of Boyle	34	2	6
,,	30.	Conlan, Hanlon, etc.	7	10	3
Novem.	2.	Luke Brien (to pay his fees at the Custom House, per letter)	7	7	10½
,,	6.	Conlan, Hanlon, etc.	7	19	3
,,	10.	Luke Brien, his allowance for November	5	13	9
,,	13.	Conlan, Hanlon, etc.	7	19	3
,,	20.	Do., do.	7	19	3
,,	26.	Lord Carhampton, for Feris, half-a-year, to 1 Nov., £50, British	54	3	4
5 13 9	,,	27.	Gaoler of Drogheda, for bringing up a Frenchman, per Mr. Swan... ...	5	13	9
,,	,,	Conlan, Hanlon, etc.	7	19	3

£153 3 3—C. F.

C. F. £5,676 7 8½

	1802.		PAID.	£	s.	d.
£153 3 3 — B. F.			Per amount brought forward,	5,676	7	8½
1 19 0	Decem.	4.	Conlan, Hanlon, etc., per account	9	18	3
	,,	,,	Mr. Gilbert, for McNevin's pamphlets	34	2	6
	,,	2.	Luke Brien, his allowance for December	5	13	9
	,,	11.	Conlan, Hanlon, etc., per account	8	5	9
	,,	13.	Mr. Oliver, member for Co. Limerick, per Mr. Marsden	34	2	6
	,,	14.	Mr. Flint, by direction of Mr. Marsden, £20, British	21	14	1½
	,,	15.	Fras. Magan, by direction of Mr. Wickham	500	0	0
	,,	16.	Mr. Worthington, for allowance to Boyle, in full, to 18 December	7	8	10½
	,,	,,	Do., for him, in full of all claims	200	0	0
100 0 0	,,	,,	The Surgeon-General, in full, for attendance on prisoners	100	0	0
	,,	18.	Wm. Wright, alias Lawler, per bill remitted to him in London (per his letter), Tho. Henry on Messrs. Johnston and Co., 17 Dec., £50; exchange, 10¾	55	7	6
	,,	,,	Conlan, Hanlon, etc., per account	7	19	3
1 14 1½	,,	,,	Hanlon, for coach-hire with prisoners	1	14	1½
	,,	20.	Major Sirr, by direction of Mr. Marsden	5	13	9
	,,	,,	W. B. Cody, do. do.	100	0	0
	,,	23.	John Conlan, in full of all claims, per receipt	315	0	0
	,,	25.	Hanlon, etc., five	5	13	9
7 7 10½	,,	,,	Do., for care of the Tower, 13 weeks, to 25 December	7	7	10½
	,,	,,	Campbell, for the use of his apartments for Conlan, etc., since Aug., 1798 (this makes 70 guineas)	11	7	6
92 0 0	,,	,,	Mr. Trevor, half-year to 31 Dec., 184 days at 10s.	92	0	0
£356 4 3				£7,199	17	2½

Deduct the amount of the several articles in the margin, in red, received at the Treasury, being:
Amount paid for subsistence of prisoners from 31 March to 30 Sep., 1802 £28 5 6
Surgeon-General, Mr. Trevor, and other expenses, attending do. to do. 327 18 9
} 356 4 3

C. F. £6,843 12 11½

1803.		PAID.	£	s.	d.
		Per amount brought forward,	6,843	12	11½
January	1.	Hanlon and four others, per list	5	13	9
,,	8.	Do. do.	5	13	9
,,	10.	Luke Brien, his allowance for January	5	13	9
,,	15.	Hanlon and four others, per list	5	13	9
,,	19.	Major Sirr, by direction of Mr. Marsden, Carroll	5	13	9
,,	22.	Hanlon and four others, per list	5	13	9
,,	29.	Do. do.	5	13	9
February	1.	Sir Charles Ross [*illegible*], to make with £6 12s. 6d., balance of his account (per letter, 11 Jan.), £50 in repayment of what he paid Mr. Flannery, priest of Cappoquin	43	4	6
,,	,,	Alderman Alexander, for maintenance of John Dejune, a Frenchman, and his passage to Bourdeaux, per receipt	15	14	2
,,	2.	Mr. John Stockdale, of London, for printing Sheares' Trial, in London, 1798, by direction of Lord Castlereagh, per G. Goulding, £42 19s. 6d., British	46	11	1½
,,	5.	Hanlon and four others, per receipt	5	13	9
,,	7.	Richd. Grandy, per Loftus Tottenham, esq., per receipt	50	0	0
,,	10.	Justice Drury, per receipt	100	0	0
,,	12.	Mr. Pollock, for McGuckin, an extra allowance	50	0	0
,,	,,	Luke Brien, his allowance for February	5	13	9
,,	,,	Hanlon and four others	5	13	9
,,	19.	Do. do.	5	13	9
,,	26.	Do. do.	5	13	9
March	4.	Rt. Hon. Col. King, for Francis Long, of Ballina, a yeoman who lost his arm in fighting the rebels, Sept., 1798 (to be continued annually), this for 1802	20	0	0
,,	5.	Hanlon and four others	5	13	9
,,	12.	Do. do.	5	13	9
,,	,,	Major Sirr, Carroll	5	13	9
		C. F.	£7,254	9	0

1803.		PAID.	£	s.	d.
		Per amount brought forward,	7,254	9	0
March	14.	Luke Brien, his allowance for March ...	5	13	9
,,	15.	Major Sirr, } for P. [*illegible*]	2	5	6
,,	16.	Do.	3	8	3
,,	12.	Wm. Corbett (Telegraphe), by Mr. Marsden's directions ...	34	2	6
,,	16.	H. B. Cody (.. P.) do. ...	100	0	0
,,	,,	Mr. Marsden, for T. W. ...	100	0	0
,,	19.	Major Sirr, Carroll ...	5	13	9
,,	,,	Hanlon, etc. ...	5	13	9
,,	25.	Major Sirr, Carroll ...	5	13	9
,,	26.	Hanlon, etc. ...	5	13	9
,,	,,	Hanlon, for care of the Tower, 13 weeks, to 25 March ...	7	7	10½
,,	28.	Captain Bruce, to remit to the Earl of Londonderry, for two years' allowance to Thomas Townley, £30; do. to Jas. Gardner, £20; and do., Charles Young, £20 (see entry, 17 June, 1801) ...	70	0	0
,,	29.	Lord Erris, for the Rev. Mr. Neligan ...	200	0	0
April	2.	Hanlon, etc. ...	5	13	9
,,	,,	F. Magan, per post to Philipston ...	100	0	0
,,	4.	Major Sirr, Carroll ...	5	13	9
,,	5.	Do., Wicklow Mountains ...	7	19	3
,,	4.	Do., for Mrs. Cox ...	11	7	6
,,	9.	Hanlon, etc. ...	5	13	9
,,	14.	Major Sirr, for Carroll ...	5	13	9
,,	,,	Luke Brien, his allowance for April ...	5	13	9
,,	16.	Hanlon, etc. ...	5	13	9
,,	23.	Do. ...	5	13	9
,,	,,	Major Sirr, Wicklow mountains ...	7	19	3
		C. F.	£7,967	4	1½

ACCOUNT OF SECRET SERVICE MONEY, IRELAND, 1803.

1803.		PAID.	£	s.	d.
		Per amount brought forward,	7,967	4	1½
April	30.	Reginald Cocks, by Mr. Marsden's directions, per receipt (42 g.) charged to Civil S. S.	—		
,,	,,	Hanlon, etc.	5	13	9
May	2.	Mr. Marsden, for Quigley	40	0	0
,,	,,	James Mallow, half-a-year's allowance	10	0	0
,,	3.	Major Sirr, for Carroll	5	13	9
,,	7.	Hanlon, etc.	5	13	9
,,	14.	Do.	5	13	9
,,	,,	Mr. Wm. Corbett, for Kennedy	11	7	6
,,	,,	Luke Brien, his allowance for May	5	13	9
,,	,,	Mr. Turner (of the Treasury), in repayment of what he advanced to Chapman in Cork, from 5 July, 1801 (see entry in this book, 9 July, 1801), to 28 February, 1803, 86 weeks at 1 g.	97	16	6
,,	21.	Richd. Chapman, allowance from 28 February to 24 May, 12 weeks	13	13	0
,,	,,	Do., in full of his claims, for his services to Government, per receipt	113	15	0
,,	,,	Hanlon, etc.	5	13	9
,,	27.	W. Corbet, by desire of Mr. Marsden, per receipt	50	0	0
,,	,,	Major Sirr, for Boylan, Carroll, and Smith	22	15	0
,,	28.	Hanlon, etc.	5	13	9
,,	30.	Mr. Giffard, for Mr. Owen, of Co. Wexford	11	7	6
June	1.	Rev. R. Woodward, per Mr. Knox, for the Rev. Tho. Barry, P.P., Mallow	100	0	0
,,	3.	W. Logan (Chief Constable Police), for informers, per receipt	22	15	0
,,	4.	Hanlon, etc.	5	13	9
,,	,,	Do., for subsistence of Hugh Loughlin	2	18	6
,,	6.	Mr. Pollock, for D. and M., per receipt	30	0	0
,,	10.	Henry Ellis, of Rockbrook, Kilkenny, for two years' allowance to 1st May	60	0	0
		C. F.	£8,599	2	1½

ACCOUNT OF SECRET SERVICE MONEY, IRELAND, 1803.

1803.		PAID.	£	s.	d.
		Per amount brought forward,	8,599	2	1½
June	11.	Hanlon and four others	5	13	9
,,	,,	Do., for subsistence of prisoners in the Tower, per receipt	3	5	0
,,	13.	Major Sirr, for Hayden	22	15	0
,,	14.	Lord Carhampton's bill for Feris, half-year, to 1 May, £50, British	54	3	4
,,	,,	L. Brien, allowance for June	5	13	9
,,	18.	Marquis of Sligo, for the persons who apprehended Tho. Gibbons...	56	17	6
,,	,,	Hanlon, etc.	5	13	9
,,	20.	W. B. Cody, per receipt	100	0	0
,,	21.	Colonel Wolfe, by direction of Mr. Marsden, for Catherine Foley	20	0	0
,,	22.	Major Sirr, for [blank]	5	13	9
,,	25.	Hanlon, etc.	5	13	9
,,	,,	J. Pollock, esq., for J. M. G., per receipt	100	0	0
,,	,,	Hanlon, for taking care of the Tower, to 26 June, 1 quarter	7	7	10½
,,	30.	Sir James Cotter, per Mr. Marsden	17	1	3
July	2.	Hanlon and four others	5	13	9
,,	6.	Col. Phaire, for the widow of Jordan, a serjeant of yeomanry, killed at Newtownbarry,—to be continued annually	20	0	0
,,	9.	Hanlon and four others	5	13	9
,,	,,	Do., for subsistence of James Brennan	0	19	6
,,	,,	Major Sirr, for Carroll and Boylan	11	7	6
,,	13.	Luke Brien, his allowance for July	5	13	9
,,	14.	Wm. Wainright, esq., Co. Wicklow, for Bridget Dolan, one year to 24 June	22	15	0
,,	16.	W. Wright, alias Lawler, per bill remitted to him,—Robert Mullin, on Badger, Hudson and Smith, London, for £50, ex. 15 per cent. ...	57	10	0
		C. F.	£9,138	14	1

1803.		PAID.	£	s.	d.
		Per amount brought forward,	9,138	14	1
July	16.	Hanlon and four others	5	13	9
,,	,,	Do., for subsistence of James Brennan	2	5	6
,,	23.	Hanlon and four others	5	13	9
,,	,,	Do., for subsistence of J. Brennan and Edward Talbot	3	11	6
,,	26.	Thos. Smart (per Alderman James)	3	8	3
,,	28.	Major Sirr, for informers, 15 g.	17	1	3
,,	30.	Hanlon and four others	5	13	9
,,	,,	Do., for subsistence of sundry persons in the Tower, per account	14	7	7½
,,	,,	Do., do. of do. in Guard-house	12	15	0
August	5.	Bishop of Killaloe (Dr. Knox), by direction of Mr. Marsden	50	0	0
,,	,,	Mr. Wm. Corbett, per do.	50	0	0
,,	,,	Mr. Hume, repayment of what he advanced on Sunday, the 24th, to Mr. Marsden, for [blank]	100	0	0
,,	6.	Hanlon and four others	5	13	9
,,	,,	Do., subsistence of prisoners in the Tower, £15 10s. 4½d.; Guard-house, £9 2s.	24	12	4½
,,	8.	Major Swan, to pay carriage-hire of prisoners, etc., etc.	22	15	0
,,	11.	N. Sneyd, esq., by direction of Mr. Marsden, expenses of bringing up Ferrall Kiernan, a prisoner	20	0	0
,,	10.	Major Sirr, for expenses	11	7	6
,,	12.	Luke Brien, his allowance for August	5	13	9
,,	10.	Mr. Giffard, for informers	22	15	0
,,	13.	Hanlon and four others	5	13	9
,,	,,	Do., subsistence of prisoners in the Tower, £11 14s.; Guard-house, £7 4s. 6d.	18	18	6
,,	16.	Major Sirr, for expenses	34	2	6
,,	19.	Do., for Guy Smith, who had been detained	3	8	3
		C. F.	£9,584	4	10

ACCOUNT OF SECRET SERVICE MONEY, IRELAND, 1803.

1803.		PAID.	£	s.	d.
		Per amount brought forward,	9,584	4	10
August 20.		Hanlon and four others	5	13	9
,,	,,	Do., subsistence of prisoners in the Tower, £12 17s. 6d.; Guard-house, £7 12s. 6d.	20	10	0
,,	,,	Adjutant Sutherland, of 38th regiment ...	22	15	0
,,	23.	Major Sirr, for W. A. H.	68	5	0
,,	,,	Mr. Paine, what he advanced to Sir James Cotter, by Mr. Marsden's direction	20	0	0
,,	25.	Mr. Pollock, for L. M., £100; [*illegible*] £10, per receipt	110	0	0
,,	26.	Thomas Smart, per his son's receipt ...	3	8	3
,,	,,	Major Sirr, for Boylan, Carroll and Farrell	28	8	9
,,	27.	John Reilly, esq., of the Co. Down ...	50	0	0
,,	,,	Hanlon and four others	5	13	9
,,	,,	Do., for subsistence of prisoners in the Tower, £15 14s. 6d.; Guard-house, £15	30	14	6
,,	28.	Mr. Burnett, of 79th regiment, per note	5	13	9
,,	31.	Mr. Dawes, for Nicholson, by Mr. Wickham's directions	50	0	0
,,	,,	Mr. Giffard, per receipt	22	15	0
,,	,,	Smyth and Ruddle, passengers taken from on board a vessel, 5 g. each ...	11	7	6
Sept.	1.	Mr. Flint, to send to E.	20	0	0
,,	2.	Nugent, per Major Sirr's note ...	11	7	6
,,	,,	Major Sirr, for Fleming	15	0	0
,,	3.	Hanlon, etc.	5	13	9
,,	,,	Do., for diet of prisoners, Tower, £15 11s. 6d.; Guard-house, £21 10s. ...	37	1	6
,,	5.	Earl Annesley, for Mr. Forde ...	50	0	0
,,	8.	Serjeant of a party, for chaise, etc., with a prisoner from Naas	3	8	3
,,	,,	John Byrne, what he gave Smyth, by direction of Mr. Wickham	0	5	5
,,	12.	Hanlon, etc.	5	13	9
,,	,,	Do., diet of prisoners, Tower, £13 19s. 6d.; Guard-house, £19 10s.	33	9	6
		C. F.	£10,221	9	9

ACCOUNT OF SECRET SERVICE MONEY, IRELAND, 1803.

1803.		Paid.	£	s.	d.
		Per amount brought forward,	10,221	9	9
Sept.	13.	W. B. Cody, per Mr. Marsden's note ...	100	0	0
,,	14.	Luke Brien, for September ...	5	13	9
,,	,,	Mr. Marsden, for L. M.	100	0	0
,,	15.	Major Sirr, for Fleming and others ...	40	0	0
,,	,,	Hanlon, for hire of carriages to different places with prisoners	26	10	4
,,	,,	Do., for washing for prisoners in the Tower	3	19	7½
,,	,,	W. Corbett, per Mr. Marsden's note ...	50	0	0
,,	17.	Mr. Paine, what he paid for a chaise with prisoners from the Man-of-war...	1	0	0
,,	,,	Chaise, from Naas, this day, with two prisoners	1	8	8½
,,	,,	Hanlon and four others, per Major Sirr	5	13	9
,,	,,	Anne Hanlon, for diet of prisoners in the Tower, £14 19s.; Guard-house, £20	34	19	0
,,	19.	Mr. Marsden, to send to M^cG. ...	100	0	0
,,	21.	Mr. Samuel Page, his expenses to Dundalk and back	17	1	10½
,,	22.	Major Sirr, for the gaoler of Longford, bringing up [*illegible*]	8	3	3
,,	,,	Mr. Armit, for Brigadier Gen. Colin Campbell, for expenses attending prisoners at Belfast, per account ...	37	11	9½
,,	24.	Anne Hanlon and five others, per list ...	6	16	6
,,	,,	Do., diet of prisoners, Tower, £15 5s. 6d.; Guard-house, £15 10s.	30	15	6
,,	,,	Do., for washing	1	2	9
,,	26.	The coachman taken at Emmet's Depot, compensation for his loss of time, etc., per General Dunne's note... ...	30	0	0
,,	,,	Expense of transmitting F. Kohan (67 reg.) from Dundalk	8	11	8½
,,	,,	Anne Hanlon, for care of the Tower, from 24 June to 29 Sep.	7	7	10½
,,	28.	Major Sirr, for Carroll and others ...	20	0	0
,,	30.	Mr. Dawes, for subsistence and lodging for Doyle, from Ballinascorney ...	28	9	4½
		C. F.	£10,886	15	6½

ACCOUNT OF SECRET SERVICE MONEY, IRELAND, 1803.

1803.		PAID.	£	s.	d.
		Per amount brought forward,	10,886	15	6½
Sept.	30.	A. Hanlon and five others, per list, 1 Oct.	6	16	6
,,	,,	Anne Hanlon, for diet of prisoners, 1 Oct., Tower, £18 4s.; Guard-house, £14 15s.	32	19	0
			£10,926	**11**	**0½**

Deduct the amount of the several articles in the margin, in red, received at the Treasury, being:

Amount paid for the subsistence of prisoners from Jan. 1 to Sep. 30, 1803... £348 6 1¼ }
Hire of carriages and other expenses, for do., same time ... 219 6 11 }   567 12 11½

			£10,358	**18**	**1**
	October	4.	Three post-chaises with prisoners from Naas	4	6	1½
£4 0 1½	,,	7.	Lieut. Sutherland, per post to Baltinglass	34	2	6
	,,	8.	Surgeon Byrne, for attendance on Horsley and Redmond	3	8	3
3 8 3	,,	,,	Mr. Flint, for Major Tatom	8	3	4
	,,	,,	Alexander Worthington, esq., for B. ..	30	0	0
	,,	,,	Anne Hanlon and five others ...	6	16	6
	,,	,,	Do., for diet of prisoners, Tower, £20 16s.; Guard-house, £12 15s.	33	1	0
33 1 0	,,	,,	Do., for washing	1	2	9
1 2 9	,,	12.	Luke Brien, his allowance for October	5	13	9
	,,	,,	Surgeon Byrne, for [blank]	11	7	6
11 7 6	,,	,,	Mrs. McCabe, per Mr. Wickham's note	11	7	6
	,,	13.	Mr. Justice Drury, going to the county	11	7	6
	,,	14.	Lord Dunlo, expenses bringing up Quigly, Stafford and Perrott ...	10	0	0
10 0 0	,,	13.	Dr. Trevor, for Ryan and Mahaffy ...	100	0	0
	,,	15.	Major Sirr, for informer, for Howley and Condon	56	17	6
	,,	,,	Do., for Pat Farrel's family ...	11	7	6
25 0 0	,,	,,	Do., for coach-hire for prisoners, etc. ...	25	0	0
	,,	17.	Captain Hepenstall, for the persons who discovered pikes at [illegible] ...	5	13	9
			C. F. **£10,728**	**13**	**6½**

ACCOUNT OF SECRET SERVICE MONEY, IRELAND, 1803.

	1803.		PAID.	£	s.	d.
			Per amount brought forward,	10,728	13	6½
	October	17.	Mr. Foote, for Toole, of Carlow, by direction of Mr. Marsden, per Mr. Paine ...	3	8	3
£36 6 0	,,	15.	Anne Hanlon, for diet of prisoners, etc., Tower, £20 16s.; Guard-house, £15 10s.	36	6	0
	,,	,,	Do., and five others, weekly allowance...	6	16	6
33 4 6	,,	22.	Do., subsistence of prisoners, etc., Tower, £20 9s. 9d.; Guard-houses, £12 15s.	33	4	6
	,,	,,	Do., and five others, weekly allowance...	6	16	6
1 2 9	,,	,,	Do., for washing, etc., for prisoners ...	1	2	9
	,,	,,	Major Ferrar, for an address to counteract treason, etc., circulated by him (received per the Treasury.)	—		
5 2 4½	,,	23.	Expenses bringing up John Parrot from Loughrea	5	2	4½
6 6 2½	,,	27.	Do. do. Jacob, from Drogheda ...	6	6	2½
	,,	,,	Nugent, by desire of Mr. Marsden ...	5	13	9
15 10 9	Nov.	1.	Col. Alexander, expenses of bringing Finney from Liverpool	15	10	9
2 17 11	,,	,,	Chaises, etc., with six prisoners from Naas, McDermott and others ...	2	17	11
	,,	,,	Mr. Pollock, for P [*illegible*] per receipt	10	0	0
	,,	2.	James Mallow, half-a-year's allowance...	10	0	0
	,,	,,	Major Sirr, for assistant in his office, six weeks, to 31st Oct.	13	13	0
	,,	,,	Do., funeral expenses of Hanlon ...	11	7	6
	,,	,,	Do., for Carrol and Boylan	22	15	0
29 6 6	Oct.	29.	Anne Hanlon, for diet of prisoners, Tower, £19 16s. 6d.; Guard-house, £9 10s.	29	6	6
	,,	,,	Do., and five others	6	16	6
0 3 9½	,,	30.	Coach, with Connor Keevan to the prevost	0	3	9½
	Nov.	4.	W. Corbett, by desire of Mr. Marsden, per receipt	50	0	0
29 18 6	,,	5.	A. Hanlon, for subsistence of prisoners, £22 8s. 6d.; Guard-houses, £7 10s.	29	18	6
	,,	,,	Do., and five others, weekly allowance	6	16	6
	,,	,,	Finlay and Co., account of Richd. Jones, esq. (to be replaced to this account hereafter) ...	1,000	0	0
1 11 5	,,	7.	Chaise from Naas, with Dillon and others	1	11	5
1 6 0	,,	8.	Do., with Ch. Teeling, from the Naul, etc.	1	6	0
	,,	7.	George Wood, who came from Hamburgh, and was confined	11	7	6
			C. F. £12,057		1	3

ACCOUNT OF SECRET SERVICE MONEY, IRELAND, 1803.

	1803.		PAID.	£	s.	d.
			Per amount brought forward,	12,057	1	3
	Novem.	10.	Luke Brien, his allowance for November	5	13	9
	,,	12.	A. Hanlon, for subsistence of prisoners,			
£25 0 6			Tower, £18 4s.; Guard-house, £6 16s. 6d.	25	0	6
1 14 1½	,,	,,	Do., for washing, etc., for do. ...	1	14	1½
	,,	,,	Do., and five others, weekly allowance	6	16	6
	,,	14.	W. D. Harvey, of Maynooth, gauger, per letter and receipt	5	13	9
	,,	15.	Bishop of Derry (Dr. Knox), by direction of Mr. Marsden, per receipt ...	50	0	0
	,,	17.	Serjeant McKay, who came from Workington, with Mr. Dawes and a prisoner	5	13	9
	,,	,,	Mr. Flint, for K. (£100 returned same day)	—		
	,,	,,	Captain Sutherland, Co. Wicklow ...	34	2	6
	,,	18.	Col. Alexander, for subsistence and other expenses of French prisoners, from the West Indies, sent to Liverpool, per			
32 16 5½			receipt	32	16	5½
	,,	19.	Rt. Hon. Col. King, for Long, of Ballina, 1 year's allowance, 1803 (see 4 March, 1803) ...	20	0	0
	,,	,,	A. Hanlon, subsistence of prisoners in the Tower, £19 16s. 6d.; Guard-house,			
25 10 3			£5 13s. 9d.	25	10	3
	,,	,,	Do., and five others, weekly allowance	6	16	6
	,,	23.	Doyle, of Ballymore, for loss of time on trial, etc., per Mr. Flint	35	0	0
	,,	25.	Mr. Flint, for L.	25	0	0
	,,	26.	Murphy, Castle-street, for diet and lodging of Mr. Farrell, Mr. Ross, etc.,			
74 3 2			from 24 Sep. to 5 Nov., per account	74	3	2
	,,	,,	Do., for five days' diet for two men, from			
3 0 1			Fort George, to identify Russell ...	3	0	1
	,,	,,	T. W., by direction of Mr. Marsden ...	100	0	0
	,,	,,	A. Hanlon, for diet of prisoners, Tower,			
25 10 9			£22 8s. 6d.; Guard-house, £3 8s. 3d. ...	25	16	9
1 2 9	,,	,,	Do., for washing	1	2	9
	,,	,,	Do., and five others, weekly allowance	6	16	6
	,,	,,	Mr. Flint, for Fleming and Finerty ...	11	7	6
	,,	,,	Callaghan, who gave information to General Dunne, . . 23rd of July	22	15	0
			C. F.	£12,572	1	1

ACCOUNT OF SECRET SERVICE MONEY, IRELAND, 1803.

	1803.		PAID.	£	s.	d.
			Per amount brought forward,	12,572	1	1
£5 13 9	Novem. 29.		Ralph Smyth, esq., of Drogheda, expenses of sending up Ridgeway and Wood and Mr. Landy, per receipt	5	13	9
	Decem.	1.	Mr. Flint, for Murphy	25	0	0
1 11 5	,,	,,	Chaise with McDermott, from Naas, etc.	1	11	5
	,,	2.	Lord Carhampton's bill for Feris, half-year to 1 Nov.	54	3	4
	,,	3.	Terence Coligan's wife, by desire of Mr. Flint	5	13	9
5 0 0	,,	,,	Chaises and expenses with Hughes, Grey, etc., from Athy	5	0	0
23 4 9	,,	,,	A. Hanlon, for diet of prisoners in the Tower, £19 16s. 6d.; Guard-house, £3 8s. 3d.	23	4	9
	,,	,,	Do., and five others, weekly allowance	6	16	6
	,,	,,	Major Sirr, for Halpin, going to Wicklow	2	5	6
	,,	,,	Do., for a clerk for four weeks in November, per receipt	9	2	0
	,,	5.	J. McGuckin, per Mr. Marsden's note, 30 November, etc.	100	0	0
	,,	6.	Luke Brien, expenses going to England, 5 g.; do., allowance for December, 5 g.	11	7	6
	,,	7.	Sergeant of Downshire militia, with letters from Naas	0	5	5
	,,	8.	Nugent, £2 5s. 6d.; 17th, £1 2s. 9d.; 21st, £2 5s. 6d.	5	13	9
19 6 9	,,	10.	A. Hanlon, for diet of prisoners in the Tower, £18 4s.; washing, £1 2s. 9d.	19	6	9
	,,	,,	Do., and five others, weekly allowance	6	16	6
	,,	13.	Major Sirr, expenses of retaking J. Murray or Morgan, per receipt	23	13	0
	,,	,,	J. Jones, sent over by the Admiralty to identify Morgan, in case he had been one of the crew of the 'Hermione'	11	7	6
	,,	15.	Mr. Flint, for Mr. [illegible]	25	0	0
	,,	16.	Captain Bruce, to remit to the Earl of Londonderry, for one year's allowance, to 1 Nov., for Tho. Townley, £15; J. Gardner, £10; and Ch. Young, £10	35	0	0
	,,	,,	Mr. Flint, per Mr. Wickham's note. Cox	68	5	6
	,,	17.	A. Hanlon, and eight others, per account	10	4	9
4 11 0	,,	,,	Do., subsistence of Mr. Holmes and Cloney, in the Tower	4	11	0
1 14 1½	,,	,,	McCabe, Farrell and Fleming, for subsistence, until placed on the list of [illegible]	1	14	1½
			C. F.	£13,033	17	10½

ACCOUNT OF SECRET SERVICE MONEY, IRELAND, 1803.

	1803.		PAID.	£	s.	d.
			Per amount brought forward,	13,033	17	10½
	Decem.	19.	Mr. Flint, for Farrell's expenses from London, per Mr. Wickham's note ...	50	0	0
	,,	20.	Major Sirr, for a person going to Limerick	11	7	6
	,,	,,	Mr. Flint, for Doyle	22	15	0
£0 16 3	,,	,,	Chaise, some time past, with Dorr from Leixlip ..	0	16	3
	,,	,,	Advance to the late John Hanlon, 16 July, 1802, which was to have been charged to him at a final settlement (not entered before) ...	5	13	9
7 3 0	,,	24.	Anne Hanlon, for diet of prisoners in the Tower, per account	7	3	0
1 2 9	,,	,,	Do., for washing for d⁰·	1	2	9
7 7 10½	,,	,,	Do., for care of the Tower, 1 quarter, to 25 December	7	7	10½
	,,	,,	Anne Hanlon, and eight others, per list	10	4	9
1 6 0	,,	,,	Cologan's subsistence, before sent to Kilmainham, 4 days at 2s. 8d., 10s. 10d.; do., family allowance, per Mr. Wickham's order, 1 week, at 2s. 8d. per day, 15s. 2d.	1	6	0
	,,	25.	Mr. Flint, for Murphy, going to Belfast	25	0	0
	,,	31.	Colgan's wife, one week's allowance, at 2s. 2d. per day	0	15	2
0 10 10	,,	27.	Coaches with Charles Kane and Rourke to Kilmainham, 5s. 5d. each ...	0	10	10
6 16 6	,,	31.	Anne Hanlon, subsistence of prisoners in the Tower	6	16	6
	,,	,,	Do., and eight others, per list, weekly allowance	10	4	9
	,,	,,	Mr. James Cahill, of Hospital, Co. Limerick, per Mr. Wickham's directions, on Baron McClolland's recommendation	50	0	0
	,,	,,	Mr. Flint, for M., going to the Isle of Man	25	0	0
	,,	,,	Do., for Lacy, one month's allowance ...	5	13	9
	1804.					
	January	7.	Colgan's wife, one week's allowance, 2s. 2d. per day	0	15	2
	,,	,,	Luke Brien, his allowance for January	5	13	9
7 9 6	,,	,,	Anne Hanlon, subsistence of prisoners in the Tower	7	9	6
1 2 9	,,	,,	Do., for washing, etc.	1	2	9
	,,	,,	Do., and eight others, per list, weekly allowance	10	4	9
	,,	9.	Lieut. Dunn, by direction of Mr. Wickham, per Mr. Flint's note	11	7	6
			C. F.	£13,312	9	2

ACCOUNT OF SECRET SERVICE MONEY, IRELAND, 1804.

	1804.		PAID.	£	s.	d.
			Per amount brought forward,	13,312	9	2
	January 11.		Captain Cole, of the Fermanagh militia, expenses of bringing up the rebel General Clarke, from Cashel to Dublin, per—[*illegible*]			
£17 10 0				17	10	0
	,,	13.	H. B. Cody, per Mr. Marsden's note ...	100	0	0
	,,	,,	Do., for Campbell, per do.	22	15	0
	,,	,,	J. Pollock, esq., for Col. Wolfe, for men taken up in Co. Kildare	113	15	0
	,,	,,	Major Sirr, for an assistant in his office, from 1 to 31 Dec.	11	7	6
	,,	,,	Do., for Carroll and Boylan, from 1 November to 31 Dec., 9½ g. each ...	21	12	3
	,,	14.	Anne Hanlon, for subsistence of prisoners in the Tower	4	11	0
4 11 0						
	,,	,,	Do., and eight others, per list, weekly allowance	10	4	9
	,,	,,	Colgan's wife, one week's allowance ...	0	15	2
	,,	16.	Surgeon-General, for attendance on prisoners, etc., from July to Dec., 1803 ...	100	0	0
100 0 0						
	,,	,,	Dr. E. Trevor, by directions of Mr. Wickham	200	0	0
	,,	,,	Mr. Edward Wilson, police chief constable, by do.	200	0	0
	,,	20.	Murphy, for diet and lodging of Mr. James Farrell, from 5 November, etc., per account ... ... £80 14 3 Nursetender, 6 weeks, £3 8s. 3d.; Merrett, for attendance in charge, £6 16s. 6d. ... 10 4 9 Apothecary 0 9 3	91	8	3
91 8 3						
	,,	21.	Anne Hanlon, for subsistence of prisoners in the Tower	4	11	0
4 11 0						
1 2 9	,,	,,	Do., for washing	1	2	9
	,,	,,	Do., and eight others, weekly allowance	10	4	9
	,,	,,	Colgan's wife, one week's allowance ...	0	15	2
	,,	24.	Allen and Greene, Town Clerks, for their fees on 55 prisoners discharged—for the sec[ret] service, at £1 13s. 6d. each	91	13	4
	,,	26.	Chaises from Naas, with Fleming, Cox, Keogh, Finnerty and Condon, per account ...	3	1	9
3 1 9						
	,,	25.	W. Corbett, by Mr. Marsden's directions	100	0	0
	,,	27.	Rt. Hon. Col. King, for the Rev. Mr. Nelligan, of Ballina, in full	50	0	0
	,,	28.	Anne Hanlon, for subsistence of prisoners in the Tower	5	4	0
5 4 0						
	,,	,,	Do., and eight others, weekly allowance	10	4	9
	,,	,,	Colgan's wife, one week's do. ...	0	15	2
			C. F.	£14,484	0	9

ACCOUNT OF SECRET SERVICE MONEY, IRELAND, 1804.

	1804.		PAID.	£	s.	d.
			-Per amount brought forward,	14,484	0	9
	February 4.		Colgan's wife, one week's allowance ...	0	15	2
£3 5 0	,,	,,	Anne Hanlon, for subsistence of prisoners in the Tower	3	5	0
1 2 9	,,	,,	Do., for washing, etc., for do. ...	1	2	9
	,,	,,	Do., and eight others, weekly allowance	10	4	9
	,,	,,	W. H. Hume, esq., for Wm. Murray, who assisted in bringing in Dwyer, etc.	34	2	6
	,,	,,	Mr. Kernan, per Mr. Marsden's note ...	11	7	6
	,,	7.	Mr. Pollock, for McG., per receipt ...	500	0	0
	,,	8.	Major Sirr, for Dillon, to Cork ...	11	7	6
	,,	9.	Mr. Flint, for Murphy, per Mr. Marsden's note £20			
	,,	,,	Do., for do., per credit in account for Irish Office ... 180	200	0	0
	,,	10.	Troy, by direction of Mr. Marsden ...	50	0	0
	,,	,,	Luke Brian, his allowance for February	5	13	9
4 11 0	,,	11.	Anne Hanlon, for subsistence of prisoners in the Tower, per account ...	4	11	0
	,,	,,	Do., and eight others, weekly allowance	10	4	9
	,,	,,	Colgan's wife, week's allowance ...	0	15	2
	,,	13.	Richd. Grandy, per Mr. Loftus Tottenham	50	0	0
	,,	14.	Mr. Justice Drury, per [*illegible*] ...	100	0	0
	,,	,,	Mr. Pollock, for E. Hardy	100	0	0
	,,	15.	Mr. Deering, expenses taking Hamilton from Monaghan to Enniskillen, etc. ...	28	8	9
28 8 9	,,	,,	Mr. Flint, for Lacy...	34	2	6
	,,	16.	Mr. Griffith, for Sergeant Cox's wife ...	11	7	6
	,,	18.	Anne Hanlon, for subsistence of prisoners in the Tower	7	3	0
7 3 0						
1 2 9	,,	,,	Do., for washing, etc., ...	1	2	9
	,,	,,	Do., and eight others, weekly allowance	10	4	9
	,,	,,	Colgan's wife, do.	0	15	2
	,,	20.	John W. Hart, by direction of Mr. Marsden, per receipt	30	0	0
	,,	18.	P. Cullen, to take him out of town ...	5	13	9
			C. F.	£15,706	8	9

ACCOUNT OF SECRET SERVICE MONEY, IRELAND, 1804.

	1804.		PAID.	£	s.	d.
			Per amount brought forward,	15,706	8	9
	February		Mr. Crow, repayment of what he gave Mr. Marsden, 31 Dec. last, for men going to the country	10	0	0
	,,	21.	Wm. St. John, per Mr. Marsden's note	22	15	0
	,,	,,	Col. Phaire, for the widow of Serjeant Jordan (see 6 July, 1803), half-year, to Dec., 1803 ...	10	0	0
	,,	24.	Dunn, gaoler of Kilmainham, for Joseph Flannagan	5	13	9
£25 18 0	,,	,,	Justice Godfrey, for carriage-hire and expenses of prisoners, sundry times ...	25	18	0
1 19 5	,,	,,	Col. Aylmer, expenses paid by the ninth regiment, for conveying a prisoner to Dublin ...	1	19	5
1 10 10½	,,	,,	Chaise with Mernagh, etc., from Naas	1	10	10½
	,,	25.	Anne Hanlon, for subsistence of prisoners in the Tower	5	17	0
5 17 0	,,	,,	Do., and eight others, weekly allowance	10	4	9
	,,	,,	Colgan's wife, d°.	0	15	2
	,,	27.	Mr. Pollock, for Pat Karlan	10	0	0
	March	2.	Anne Hanlon, for subsistence of prisoners in the Tower, £7 16s.; Guard-house, £12 10s. ...	20	6	0
20 6 0	,,	,,	Do., and eight others, weekly allowance	10	4	9
	,,	,,	Colgan's wife, d°.	0	15	2
	,,	,,	John Dillon, £2; 10th, £11 7s. 6d.; 15th, £20; 21st, £66 12s. 6d., to make up	100	0	0
	,,	10.	Mr. Marsden, (returned 12 April) ...	—		
	,,	,,	A. Hanlon, for subsistence of prisoners in the Tower, £9 2s.; washing, etc., £1 14s. 1½d. ..	10	16	1½
10 16 1½	,,	,,	Do., and eight others, weekly allowance	10	4	9
	,,	,,	Colgan's wife, d°.	0	15	2
	,,	13.	L. Brien, allowance for March ...	5	13	9
	,,	17.	A. Hanlon, for subsistence of prisoners in the Tower, £8 2s. 6d.; Guard-house, £1 2s. 9d.	9	5	3
9 5 3	,,	,,	Do., and eight others, weekly allowance	10	4	9
	,,	,,	Colgan's wife, d°.	0	15	2
	,,	23.	Mr. Lander, from King's county with Mr. Flattery, his expenses back ...	3	8	3
3 8 3	,,	24.	A. Hanlon, for subsistence of prisoners, etc., £11 1s.; Guard-houses, £1 14s. 1½d.	12	15	1½
12 15 1½	,,	,,	Do., and eight others, weekly allowance	10	4	9
	,,	,,	Colgan's wife	0	15	2
			C. F.	£16,017	6	10½

ACCOUNT OF SECRET SERVICE MONEY, IRELAND, 1804.

	1804.		PAID.	£	s.	d.
			Per amount brought forward,	16,017	6	10½
	March	28.	Per acquittance, remitted to Wm. Rowan, esq., Tralee, to reimburse money advanced by him in sending up Thomas Courtney, £16 7s. 11d.; the two sergeants, who came from Limerick,			
£20 7 6½			with do., £3 19s. 7½d.	20	7	6½
11 7 6	,,	31.	Anne Hanlon, for subsistence of prisoners in the Tower	11	7	6
1 14 1½	,,	,,	Do., washing and making linen for do. ...	1	14	1½
	,,	,,	Do., care of the Tower, quarter to 25			
7 7 10½			March	7	7	10½
	,,	,,	Do., and eight others, weekly allowance	10	4	9
	,,	,,	Colgan's wife, do. ...	0	15	2
	,,	,,	Hunt and Kiernan, apothecaries, bill from 1 January, 1802, to 21 December, 1803			
38 6 9				38	6	9
£979 5 6				£16,107	10	7

Deduct the amount of the several articles in the margin, in red, received at the Treasury, viz.:

Amount paid for subsistence of prisoners from 30 Sep., 1803, to 31 March, 1804 ...   ... £576 5 0 ⎫
Do., hire of carriages, medical attendance, etc.   403 0 6 ⎬ 979 5 6
                                                              ⎭

Carried forward in another book,   £15,128 5 1

II.
LETTERS, DOCUMENTS, Etc.

II.—LETTERS, DOCUMENTS, ETC.

1. 1795.—DEFENCELESS STATE OF DUBLIN.

Report by Lieutenant-general the Earl of Carhampton in March, 1795, to the Duke of York, on the state of Dublin in case of a coup de main.

PRIVATE.—There is no part of the king's dominions so much exposed to the attempts of the enemy in this war as Ireland; and of all Ireland the part most exposed is its capital. It is high time to understand its situation, to take measures for its safety, and no longer to delay, because its infatuated inhabitants seem lulled into a fatal security. It must be clear to demonstration to those who have considered the subject, and know its relative situation to the ports of Brest, port L'Orient and Rochefort, that a body of 3,000 men and a few field pieces might be equipped unknown to us, from either of those ports, be landed in the vicinity of Dublin, and possess it before the inhabitants were well aware of the attempt. In the space of twenty-four hours a million of money, at least, might be raised in contribution, the city handed over to a municipality formed of the dregs of the people, who, armed with pikes and whiskey, would probably plunder and burn the town, and the whole kingdom then be undone for a century to come. I do assert that an attempt of this nature could not fail of success at this very hour: a wind from west to south, including the eight intermediate points, lasting three days, would serve to bring over and disembark a body of troops sufficient for the attempt; two days more to effect their purpose and re-embark; and were it then to blow from another quarter, they could escape from superior force, by Belfast, without a probability of being overtaken.

The French being now in possession of the Zuyder Zee, and of various ports to the eastward, a great proportion of the British fleet must be stationed in the north sea but were it otherwise, and should a westerly wind prevail for four or five days, no ships of war could come to your assistance from the English channel in time to save your capital. The same wind which shuts in the British fleet wafts over an armament from Brest, and brings them under the Irish land in smooth water; whereas it requires two winds to bring ships from Portsmouth or Plymouth, being obliged to weather Scilly and give it a good offing; from Brest the tract forms a line scarce an angle.—From Portsmouth such an armament would probably be the first messenger of its own approach.

Killiney bay, where frigates may anchor in five fathom water, within a thousand yards of the shore, is the place best calculated for disembarkation; a firm, sandy, dry beach, where fifteen hundred men at least, together with field pieces in proportion, might be landed at once, at any time of tide, not up to their knees in water, and possession of the heights overlooking Dublin taken, before eight hundred soldiers of the garrison could be disentangled from the town, or thrown into any position even half way between the enemy and Dublin.

If the wind should be to the southward the same operation, with very little variation, might be made in the bay of Dublin, at the proper time of tide, at Dalkey, Dunleary and Bullock; or the enemy might distract you, by dividing its force, and forcing a landing at Balscadden, a most excellent landing place, at the back of Howth, where boats may, in perfect safety, land at all times of tide, and frigates anchor within five hundred yards of it to cover the disembarkation, or proceed farther to the northward, and land at Skerries or Balbriggan, and thus keep you under apprehension for all those points at once.

Any officer who may doubt the probability of this attempt, I beg to refer him to the journal of the descent on the coast of France for the purpose of surprising port L'Orient, under admiral Lestock and general Sinclair, in the autumn of 1746. There were three places near together, equally convenient for debarking troops. General Sinclair having delayed landing for two days after his arrival on the coast, two thousand French militia had assembled to oppose his landing, which, however, he effected (six hundred men only being in the first debarkation) without opposition, the militia being harassed by dividing their attention to three several places; and general Sinclair, taking a judicious advantage of the tide, threw his troops on shore without the loss of a man, in the middle of the bay, within the same distance of port L'Orient that Killiney is from Dublin, before a single soldier of the enemy's broken corps could reach that bay to oppose him; and the general, if he had immediately advanced as he might have done, as soon as the second debarkation joined him, might have had possession of port L'Orient in 12 hours, the capitulation being ready drawn up, such was the astonishment of those within the town: as it was, he was visited by a deputation which offered to admit the British forces on conditions which were rejected. After all, the troops re-embarked, having failed in the attempt, which was no wonder, as the ships lay exposed to the weather on an open and dangerous beach for three weeks, at the time of the autumnal equinox, the whole number of troops being scarce three thousand effective men, without guides or tents, scarce any artillery, and no kind of horse.

The difference from Portsmouth to port L'Orient is farther than from Brest to Dublin, the navigation a more dangerous one. Admiral Lestock arrived before it the 4th day; the troops landed in spite of two thousand men collected upon the coast to oppose them, having had two days' time to assemble, for so long had the general delayed the debarkation, they had then ten miles to march to a town not strongly fortified, it is true, but surrounded with ramparts, which it required twelve pounders at least to make a breach in.

With respect to the navigation from Brest to Dublin, it is simple and safe; you are at open sea till you arrive between the Tusker rock and St. David's head, when you have scarce thirty leagues to run before you are abreast of the N.E. point of the Kesh, when you bear down upon Dublin in the packets' track, keeping till then the Welsh coast in sight, steering as the West Indiamen do, when bound to Liverpool, for which fleet it will probably be mistaken. If any person still flatters himself there is danger in the navigation, let me remind him that insurance from Jamaica on large, deep-loaded merchant men to Liverpool, through the gulf of Florida, is done at two and a half per cent.; and there is twice the danger from Dublin to Liverpool than in the whole intermediate passage.

With respect to a landing for the purpose of reaching Dublin in a few hours, no coast can afford such advantages and such a choice of proper places as this coast does. Ships are never out of breath; men and horses are. The troops stationed for the defence of the southern bays can never afford any assistance to those stationed to protect the northern.

Let us consider for a moment the defenceless situation of the metropolis, which holds out a temptation and offers itself a cheap bargain to an enemy. It contains about one hundred and thirty thousand inhabitants within its circuit. I leave to others to calculate what number of those would or could take an active part on such an emergency, what number would be passive and indifferent, and how many would take the opportunity of joining the enemy, or at least do the enemy's business, by breaking loose and plundering the houses of the rich. Well, if they stopped there, but with arms in their hands, which the very iron palisadoes in the town would afford them, together with that additional arm of whiskey, it is impossible to calculate the probable excesses of a Dublin mob in such circumstances.

With respect to the garrison of Dublin, it is scarce equal to furnish such guards as must be stationary in the city, if an enemy appeared on the coast; it consists of about two thousand men; in Chapel Izod there are one hundred and forty artillery men. The following places could not be left unprotected for a moment:

The castle with the ordnance stores.—Banks: National, Finlay's, La Touche's, Newcomen's.—Custom House.—City Prison.—Ordnance stores on the quay.—Public Records, on the Inns' quay.—Battery in the Park.—City Marshalsea.

Besides a strong moving body to occupy the several avenues of the town, bridges, etc., a piquet ready in the barracks, to re-inforce or at least to relieve the former body.

Of the two thousand in garrison, there were to my knowledge but eleven hundred duty men in barracks a few days ago, and scarce equal to the necessary guards now mounted. What a miserable defence for a town in which the journeymen shoemakers alone have in a manner organized (if not disciplined) themselves, so that they can assemble in forty minutes in one body of two thousand men, by concerted signals, from one house of call to another, and have been in the habit of doing so.

Suppose the following preparations to be made in any of the three ports I mentioned, but most probably from Brest:—A body of select troops (about three thousand) to embark on board transports from two hundred and fifty to three hundred tons burthen (allowing one ton to each man); to these will be added a corps of artillerists, consisting of five hundred men, with the proper number of battalion guns, four long eight pounders, six twelve pounders and four howitzers, together with one hundred marksmen; six gun boats of their new construction, carrying one twenty-four pounder in its bow, accompanied by three or four sail of the line, two or three large frigates, besides six small, ships and cutters, of from ten to twenty guns. The ships of war and large frigates having accompanied the armament one half the passage, are destined to cruise off and block up Cork harbour; the smaller vessels of war and transports to proceed to the bay of Dublin. Forty or fifty horses for drawing the heavy guns might be put on board, but no other attirail of an army, not even tents, would be necessary for a coup de main of this nature; one day's bread in the haversack and sixty rounds of cartridges is all that need clog the soldiers' intended rapid movement. The generals conducting the operation would probably be better acquainted with the distances, the positions and avenues of approach to the city than their adversaries; they would not be without a sufficient number of Rush and American pilots. Their manifestoes, calculated to delude the people, would be instantly dispersed; the first debarkation, consisting of from twelve to sixteen hundred men, with light field pieces, would instantly move forward in one or two columns to the town; the second debarkation and heavier guns to support them, and the business be over in four hours from the time of landing.

To those who imagine this coast a dangerous one to lie on for a few days, I beg leave to refer them to the several expeditions on the coast of France in the English channel, amongst the currents of Guernsey and Jersey, and more especially remind them of the bay of St. Lunaire, near St. Malo. The French account states that the ground where the fleet lay at anchor was so foul and rocky, that the people in the neighbourhood came out to see them dash in pieces; they declared they never durst anchor in the bay of St. Lunaire, and were sure our sea officers were very uneasy; yet lord Howe, with the men of war and transports, lay for several days in that bay in September, 1758.

Having shortly stated the danger to which we are at this instant and shall continue to be exposed, during the war, let us enquire how we may make the best use of our means for the defence of the metropolis the first object, so as not to leave the rest of the country unprotected.

An army of forty-one thousand men is voted: suppose thirty-six thousand infantry and five thousand cavalry, together with fourteen hundred artillerists. The most to be expected from this voted number is thirty thousand infantry, four thousand cavalry, and twelve hundred artillerists effective. Those, if to be dispersed through the whole island, may compose a police sufficient for the purpose of protecting you against yourselves, but totally inadequate to repel an attempt of the nature I have described. If several battalions were suddenly brought together, they would be little better than an armed mob, undisciplined for the purpose of military manœuvres, total strangers to each other, though speaking the same language, and incapable of being ranged for defensive or offensive purposes in the face of a disciplined enemy, consisting of half their numbers.

Out of these armed men you must as soon as possible compose one army at least, and let that army be found in the neighbourhood and for the protection of your capital. Suppose it to consist of ten thousand infantry and one thousand cavalry and six hundred artillerists. After what I have said, there can be no doubt I would occupy the position best calculated to defend Killiney and the bay of Dublin; there is ground admirably adapted for it. Here I would station, or encamp or hut five thousand men; three thousand more to the north of Dublin, in a position taken to guard from Balbriggan to Howth. The rest will remain in Dublin as a reserve, from whence re-inforcements may be occasionally afforded to the southern or northern coast, as occasion may demand, or into which may be drawn re-inforcements from these corps.

The new gaol built for the county of Dublin, and which has cost £16,000, is just finished. It would hold 800 men; it is almost a fortress in a position to protect your magazine, to overawe the city, and placed on the Circular Road, leading by several avenues into the Liberty. This should be occupied, and I imagine might be obtained for a twelve-month from the county, upon payment of a compensation—suppose one thousand pounds.

In order to enable you on occasion to draw forth a part of this garrison, and for various other reasons, it might be well done to form in the city, associations for its defence. The several artificers employed by government, both by the Board of works and ordnance, might certainly be formed into an united body; the various bodies of the law, the merchants, wealthy shopkeepers, and even the college. I do not mean to give them either uniform or arms until necessary. Indeed, I always thought a trained band for the protection of the city a more advisable thing for Dublin, than a militia regiment, composed of listed men, to be removed away from it. Alarm posts for assembling the several bodies ought to be fixed on, such as the new buildings on the Inns Quay, old and new Custom House, some of the churches for the infantry. Cavalry associations might readily be formed in Dublin, where so many horses are kept; one of gentlemen, with each a servant; one of shopkeepers; all those have pistols and they can be instantly furnished with swords. Stephen's Green, Merrion Square, several parts of the Circular road, the barracks and the park, the several alarm posts. Dublin would then, by previous arrangement, be occupied, surrounded, overawed and protected, and confidence would ensue. The moment of impending danger is too late to do it—all would be confusion and dismay. The country people would easily be prevented from pouring into the town, and the evil disposed in the town from assembling in numbers. The several associations collected, with a very few regular troops, guns planted to command the avenues and some hand grenadoes ready to throw from the occupied posts and houses, would ensure order and quiet.

The two bodies of hardy labourers, now employed on the two canals, might, by means of the canal companies and the taskers, be hired at half a crown a day, and instantly brought, with their working tools, to join the southern and northern corps and be of good service.

The advantages of assembling a large body of your forces and posting it as I described, are obvious: convenient to its magazines, its hospitals, and to Smithfield market, the better chance of keeping together the militia officers (of which the greater part of the army will be composed) under the eye of government; the opportunity given to your generals and other officers to examine with a soldier's eye the ground they may have to act upon; to make themselves acquainted with the several positions, and enable themselves to form a judgment where to oppose in face or act upon the flank of an enemy, if a landing should be effected by force or surprise; to make the officers and soldiers acquainted with each other, and obtain each other's confidence; to practise a regular system of military movement and manœuvre; to know how to give, convey and execute the necessary orders—in short, to establish discipline and make real soldiers.

I do not mean to enter into a minute military detail of the several positions for temporary or fixed batteries upon a line of forty miles of assailable coast. The small bay of Balscadden must indeed be accurately observed by a skilful engineer, and two or three heavy guns properly placed in battery there. Sutton creek, Malahide and Rush, though bad landing places, must not be neglected. An enemy might use the fishing boats at the very top of the tide, to make a diversion by pushing in a few troops; but the northern corps would be within reach, or probably detachments from Dublin, to take such precautions as to check those attempts. It strikes me that it might be advisable to draw all the fishing boats ashore upon the first alarm.

Care will be taken not to hut or encamp so near the shore as to be within reach of twenty-four pound shot from gunboats, nor within the reach of shells from bomb ketches at anchor; the range of the latter is full two Irish miles.

N.B.—A small corps of enlisted artificers would be a valuable addition to the engineer corps; such are much wanting for making fascines, to attend your guns and carriages, and to throw up temporary earth-works; those raised upon the English establishment have proved a most serviceable corps.

I shall venture to add a very few words in respect to Cork and Belfast. Three thousand men are fully adequate to put that coast in such a state of preparatory defence as would render an attempt from the enemy on Cork not much to be apprehended. The harbour is now sufficiently defended by various batteries, and not to be forced by shipping. To the eastward of the harbour, the small bite under Roche's town and Roche's bay may be easily attended to by the troops stationed at Carlisle fort or near it. Bally Cotton bay is scarcely practicable to land in, when the wind is at all to the southward, and from thence there is a long circuit of twenty miles, through a very strong country to Cork.

To the westward, Rinabelly bay may be easily secured by three or four heavy guns, and attended to by detachments from Ramhead. Some troops should be added to the garrisons of Ramhead and Carlisle for this purpose. Further west again is Robert's cove and Oyster haven: batteries should be there, and small detachments at each. Charles fort you must rely upon to defend the entrance to the harbour of Kinsale. To land and march to Cork, through bad roads, is an operation of two days at least—time would be given to collect your force into one body, to act upon the flank of an invading corps, which must have time to disembark from their ships anchored on dangerous ground, horses for their artillery, provisions, ammunition, cannon, intrenching tools, all the accompaniments of an army, and must keep up a communication with their shipping. In short, such an operation varies much from a coup de main, such as might be undertaken against Dublin, against which, were they to succeed, there would scarce be a corner of the kingdom where a wretched family could escape to for protection, from a commonalty broke loose.

With regard to Belfast, some troops should be placed near Carrick-fergus, and if a fifty-gun ship and some frigates were stationed in the lough of Belfast, it would be the greatest protection against any attempts in St. George's channel, as a westerly wind might bring them in a few hours to Dublin, and would render a hostile attempt, such as I have stated, somewhat precarious.

2.—1796. IRISHMEN IN THE ARMY AND NAVY.

To Duke of York from Right Hon. Thomas Pelham, Chief Secretary, to the Lord Lieutenant of Ireland.

Dublin Castle, November 14, 1796.

Sir,—I did not write to your royal highness at the time I wrote a very long letter to the duke of Portland in answer to a proposal from his majesty's confidential servants in England for raising men in this country, because I wished to furnish your royal highness with some information upon the subject, the details of which I have not been able to complete till now.

By the annexed returns your royal highness will see that the number of men furnished by this country is very short of what it is generally stated to be, and it will appear that the expense is not, as is represented in this country at least, defrayed by Ireland.

I was led to this enquiry partly with a view of meeting the exaggerated statements made by Mr. Grattan and other gentlemen in the House of Commons, and partly with a view of seeing what this country had done, in order the better to judge of its ability to make any exertions now.

From the number furnished one should naturally suppose that the country was not exhausted, and that under proper regulations and encouragement it would not be difficult to procure a great many more.

Your royal highness will observe also that the statement is greatly in favour of Ireland, for I have given her credit for every man who embarked as an Irishman, and consequently all the regiments that were here at the commencement of the war and were chiefly English, are included in the numbers of Irish.

The population of this country is in many parts very great, and the emigration to America has been considerably owing to the population in the north being too great for the land.

Upon all these considerations I confess I was very sanguine in my hopes and expectations of raising men until I was told by people well acquainted with the country that it was impossible; the men who had enlisted were mechanics and inhabitants of towns, and that the peasants could seldom be persuaded under any circumstances to quit their families and place of nativity. I know that rather than quit a farm, or even a cabin, the tenant would give a sum no Englishman under similar circumstances could afford, which was one cause of the rise of estates and the poverty and dissaction of the lower order of people; but I could hardly believe, until I made a minute enquiry, that even in the militia they were chiefly manufacturers and mechanics. To ascertain the fact, I called for a return from the regiments in garrison who happen to come from the different provinces in the kingdom, and I found that two-thirds or three-fourths of each regiment were of that description.

The militia service will certainly induce those who are in it to enter into the army when their militia service expires, but that will be gradual, and afford no immediate resource.

I shall be very happy if the annexed papers afford your royal highness any satisfaction, and I beg leave to assure your royal highness that on this and every other occasion I am, with the most sincere respect, etc. [Thomas Pelham.]

[Enclosure.]

Return of the number of men furnished by Ireland for general service, including army and navy, from the commencement of the war, in 1793, to 1st November, 1796:

Embarked from Ireland, according to the adjutant general's return—rank and file	42334	
To which is to be added: Drafted 104th, 105th, 106th, 111th, 113th, with M. General Whyte, 93rd and 99th	5232	
	47566	
Deduct landed in Ireland ...	30421	
		17145
79 Indl. companies embarked from Duncannon fort	5310	
Deduct 18 of them, which are included in the adjutant general's return	1906	
		3404
Recruits for new corps, 609; for 40 regiments of foot, 1139; for 4 regiments of dragoons, 78 ...		1826
Recruits raised for the marines, 4058; for the navy, 11,457; for the artillery, 763.—Total		38653

3.—STATE OF IRELAND, JANUARY, APRIL, 1797.

i.—To Duke of York from Hon. Thomas Pelham.

Secret and confidential.

Dublin Castle, January 4, 1797.—2 o'clock, p.m.

Sir,—I have the satisfaction of being able to assure your royal highness that the loyalty and spirit of this town remains unshaken, no symptom of disaffection or desire of disturbance in any part of the city; the yeomen drilling every day and undertaking every kind of duty required of them. The merchants' corps furnished fifty infantry and twenty cavalry to escort a train of carriages with arms and ammunition for the north. Upon a false alarm of an intention to attack some stores of flour the night before last, a picket of twenty lawyers was mounted on the spot in fifteen minutes after the notice was given. All our expresses are conveyed by parties of yeomen, stationed on the road, and they convey them so quick that I received an express from lieutenant-general Dalrymple, dated Bandon, 4 o'clock, on Tuesday morning, at 2 o'clock this morning.

General Dalrymple's letter contained nothing material except what is contained in the affidavit which I enclose for your royal highness's perusal.

The conduct of the army in general has been as good as possible. Lieutenant-general Dalrymple and general [Eyre] Coote have, by their prudent and spirited conduct, kept up the spirits both of their troops and of the country, and we have had no complaints of any kind.

Having your royal highness's permission to write in confidence and with freedom, I shall not scruple to say that if the French were to appear again off the western coast I should advise an immediate removal of general [Edward] Smith; his orders are so contradictory and wild, and his letters so extravagant, that I could not risk the fate of that country in his hands.

With regard to the troops that marched from Dublin, every order was given by Hewett[1] that could insure a regular march and the comfort of the soldier. I am sorry to say that the march was extremely irregular; but lord Camden, with a spirit that became him and will, I trust, prevent such misconduct in future, wrote to lord Carhampton, mentioning the reports he had heard from gentlemen who travelled the road and met the troops, and mentioned the names of those generals who had quitted their columns, with a desire that they should be particularly acquainted with his excellency's displeasure.

I have heard nothing directly from general [Ralph] Dundas, who leads the western column. I am sure therefore that all is well.

In the north things are growing better. About Dungannon, Knox's[2]

---

[1] Major-general John Hewett.
[2] Hon. John Knox, brigadier-general.

activity and knowledge of the country have given courage to the loyalty that was kept down by terror, and in his letter of this day he gives me hopes of being able to withdraw part of the troops if it was necessary. I hear nothing from [major-general] Lake or [major-general George] Nugent, who are together at Hillsborough, and I have received an account from the sovereign of Belfast, from which it appears that the principal inhabitants have gained courage, and are coming forward. Lord Cavan[1] is at Derry, and in the town there are some hundreds enrolled to defend it.

If the French have abandoned their expedition it will give us time to reflect on what has passed, and, like mariners after a storm, we should lose no time in examining our vessel, stopping all leaks, and, I believe, putting in some new timbers.

I must beg your royal highness's indulgent consideration of this letter, written in a great hurry, as the messenger going to England is waiting for it, and that your royal highness will be persuaded that my zeal for his majesty's service and my attachment to your royal highness will never abate under any circumstances.

3. ii.—To Right Hon. Thomas Pelham from Lieutenant-General William Dalrymple.

Private.   Cork, April 30, 1797.

My dear Sir,—On Friday Mr. [Arthur] O'Connor was seen going into Cove island. I presume to seek for a passage in some ship. The person who knew him is gone there in search of him.

By the information of captain Canon, of one of the cutters employed in the revenue service, I learn that several persons landed out of the vessel I formerly wrote about. Her appearance and movements on the coast he most amply confirms. I will try every possible means to get on their track.

The people of the country are evidently agitated by some hopes or expectations, and their conduct evinces an assurance of some extraordinary event being on the tapis. Work is abandoned.

I have the honor to be, dear sir, your most humble and faithful servant, W. Dalrymple.

---

[1] Brigadier-general, Richard Lambart, earl of Cavan.

4.—1797. POLITICAL MOVEMENTS IN IRELAND.—STATEMENTS TO SECRET COMMITTEE OF HOUSE OF COMMONS, DUBLIN.

Private memoranda by Right Hon. Thomas Pelham.

House of Commons [Dublin], May 2, 1797.

[Edward John Newell] has been a member of U[nited] I[rish Society] at Belfast about a year; a miniature-painter by profession; lived in Dublin; member of the Philanthropic Society in Dublin; he considered it as a society of Defenders; met at Gallan's, a hair dresser's in Crane-lane [Dublin]. Object of the society:—Parliamentary reform. Books, encouraging Deism, read at the society.—Paine's Rights of Man. Hart belonged to the society. Tom Dry: He left Dublin March twelvemonth and went to Belfast.

Alexander Gordon, a woollen draper, introduced him to Jackson, who had changed his name from Dry. John Gordon, brother to Alexander, swore him as an United Irishman, at the witness' own lodgings. Attended the society the Sunday after; conceived Parliamentary reform to be their object. It was at first the twenty-first, but by splitting it is now become the sixty-ninth. This was their object until about the time of the yeomanry.

Parliamentary reform to be obtained by force. Orders from superior committee to provide army and ammunition made him think they had intended to obtain by force Parliamentary reform. One hundred and eight societies, of from thirty to fifty each, in Belfast about six months ago. Each society chooses a secretary and two committee-men every three months by ballot, and they attend a divisional committee, consisting of delegates from nine societies. Three men out of the twenty-seven or divisional committee form a baronial committee, consisting of nine divisional committees—it may consist of more than nine.

From the baronial committee delegates are sent to a county committee. From a county delegates sent to provincial committee. Provincial sent to a national.

Has heard that the national committee have formed a new code of laws, to take place when this government is overturned—heard this in the report made to his society.

What, have I not dared! and done! have I not, Betray'd my COUNTRY.

[EDWARD JOHN NEWELL, 1798.]

[See pp. ix., xvi.]

STATEMENTS TO SECRET COMMITTEE, IRELAND, 1797.

[Newell] belonged to a baronial committee no. 6. Often attended baronial committee. Has heard reports read from a superior.

First thing: to collect the monthly money which was collected from the members of each society generally, according [to] their ability, and brought up by the delegates to their committee; four pence per month was the stipulated sum; many gave more—has heard of thirty guineas being given by an individual; many voluntary subscriptions. Mrs. Orr, of Cave Hill, near Belfast, gave or sent the thirty guineas.

Then they read the minutes of the last proceedings.

Members proposed, balloted and sworn in. Members proposed and approved and balloted are sent to the county committee for approbation before they are admitted.

Reports and news called for and stated.—Each secretary takes notes of proceedings.

Reports from county committee read.

The reports consist of the number of United Irishmen of each county, the money collected, arms and ammunition.

All rules to be followed; instruction about colours or symbols that may mark them, and about general conduct.

Green colours were ordered, and they forbid cockades, etc., that they might be known at the time of rising.

About five or six weeks ago heard from Gordon that the committees had reported that the societies were ready to follow their leaders into the field at any risk rather than remain in a state of lethargy.

Eighty thousand, the largest number reported in Ulster; divided into companies. —— had the rank of captain. Gordon, a captain also in the same society, no. 69, had made his list and sent it up to county committee. Two captains in his society, lest Gordon should be convicted.

Pikes made after a plan of captain Russell. Each man found his own, or those who could not afford it were furnished out of the national treasury.

Guns concealed in a box with lime to preserve it, buried somewhere about the house.

They were forbid to plunder arms, as they had formed a plan to seize arms of the military.

No discipline but marching. At potato digging marched by

companies, as regularly as soldiers; was present at a potato digging of near three thousand men.—Drilled in the evening or at night in rooms.

Often heard from the reports of the society that the French were expected, and to have a million of money coming.

This society met a few days after the appearance of the French in Bantry bay—great joy expressed; ordered to be ready, and not to be alarmed by the conduct of the south, as they rose only to deceive Government, and would join the French when they landed.

A military committee, composed of the officers, to form plans of discipline, and oaths for officers to administer to the men.

Out of the military committee, consisting of twenty seven officers, twelve chosen to inspect the conduct of suspected men. Power to put them to death belonged to that committee; sentenced persons in their absence. They cast lots among the twelve for those who were to execute the sentence. If occasion required the whole attended.

Trials never reported. The twelve tried and executed at their own discretion; majority decided.

Never knew of this committee till he was chosen. Murder of the informer at Belfast recited. Alexander Gordon, one of the murderers [was] upon coroner's inquest. Burnsides and other members of the military committee attempted to murder him upon suspicion. Knives made at Belfast, for the purpose of close fight and murder.

A book to be opened in every county on the insurrection; the debts of each person to be entered, and the creditor to be paid out of the public fund if the debtor fell.

All the persons in Government to be massacred.

A republic and convention to be established. Neither reform nor Catholic emancipation will satisfy them. They think that they have the power in their hands; if the Defenders join them they need not wait for the French.

Wednesday, May 3 [1797].

Constitution.—Union of power.—New Test.

The seduction of the military their great object; if it succeeds that they will not wait for the French. Their plan to assemble in large towns under pretence of funerals, in order to excite the magistrates to call out the military; not to provoke the military to fire, but engage them to go out of the town, and then throw up a green flag, as a signal for the military to desert their ranks and join them. If the military do not join them to abandon their plan.

Knows from soldiers who were sworn and joined them, that they were promised commissions and farms; these were English soldiers.

At Christmas last a yeoman and a tenant of Mr. S. came to inform him of the mode of swearing and forming committees unasked, with other information already received.

The oath to murder yeomen and join the French, who were expected; the reports came from Belfast; two pence a month paid by every sworn man to defray expenses.

The informer [Newell] had taken the oath of U[nited] I[rishmen], but melted at the oath of assassination of yeomen; the yeomen had upon a former occasion saved the life of the informer. Spears to be bought, and a spear actually brought; the handles to be bought at Cookstown.

The people do not know what Reform meant or what the grievances were;—the Catholicks imagined that they were to have a complete establishment of their persuasion and church; the priest was sworn.

Subscription for prisoners open at Belfast; clandestine in other parts.

Arms had been carried in a coffin, and found by Mr. Lenox Coningham.

Uniformly sworn in Tyrone to join the French.

The body of the Catholicks upon the same plan and principle as the Defenders, and goaded on by the dissaffected Presbyterians to the same acts.

A determination to disarm the yeomanry; take lead wherever they can collect it.

Administration of justice.

Their plan to prevent the due administration of justice. Every witness that came forward on the north-west circuit obliged to fly the country. It is a part of the oath not to give evidence against any brother.

In Tyrone three hundred persons summoned upon juries; not

twenty appeared, from fear; many acknowledged it. Printed papers circulated before the assizes to terrify.

One agent in two counties, Derry and Donegal, employed to defend all the United I[rishmen], of every description for every offence. The same counsel employed for all; Martin and Moody, the agents at Lifford and Derry. Mr. Plunket and Mr. Stokes, the counsel, received their fees in a lump for the United-men.

At Derry a witness afraid to come in. A party of military sent for him, without which he could not have ventured to appear.

At Omagh they could not get a jury to be trusted, until they put upon the grand jury those who were afraid to serve upon petty juries, and the principal gentlemen served upon the petty juries.

The Crown advocates could not venture to indict any man capitally.

'Northern Star'—distributed gratis, in parts of Tyrone.

Thursday, April 4, 1797.

J— S—, connected with many of the leaders of the London Corresponding Society, arrived in Dublin, July, 1795; staid till September, returned to Parkgate, went to Liverpool, from thence to Belfast, where he arrived on the 21st of September,—became acquainted with Samuel Kennedy, talked upon politicks, who introduced him to Neilson, editor of the 'Northern Star'; declined taking the oath necessary to be admitted of their society, thinking it would be a bad example for them to admit strangers. Went to Neilson's house upon Kennedy's invitation, and met a third person, whose name he has never been able to discover; was introduced as an English patriot, and acquainted with the societies in England.

Neilson congratulated him, and lamented that the societies in England were in the minority.

N. observed that an oath had a great effect on the ignorant in binding them to them, for he must be a very bad man who could betray them after taking a volunteer's oath, although he might repent; talked largely on the principles of Godwin's 'Political Justice.'

Talked of the intended separation of Ireland and England as a certain event, but that it would not affect England for a considerable time, and reasoned upon the general effect on manufactures, etc.

Represented the conduct of Government as tyrannical as it could be. That the measures Government was pursuing would forward the cause of liberty. He instanced the confinement of the editor of the Cork gazette, which had not prevented the publication and circulation of that paper, and he carried on a treaty between the Defenders and United I[rishmen] while he was in prison.

They drank several toasts. Mr. N. gave the 'French army, and success to them.'

Kennedy gave 'the French navy.' He gave: 'May liberty take the tour of Europe in a triumphal car.' They drank whiskey; he drank rum; they would not drink anything connected with the slave trade; spoke highly of the French and French generals; all they wanted was a junction with the Defenders, which was retarded by the priests and interested persons on account of religion; wished him to take the oath in order to facilitate a junction with the English societies.

He collected from that conversation that the plan of those societies of U[nited] I[rishmen] was to overturn the English Government and influence, and establish a popular government like that in France. Kennedy and he retired to a tavern. Ken[nedy] spoke highly of Neilson's talents and consequence, and said that the young man whom they had been with at Neilson's had great influence in Ireland, lived on the banks of the lough, and could raise five hundred men on the shortest notice; his opinion is that he was a foreman or clerk in Grimshaw's manufactory.

K[ennedy] introduced him also to Shaunahan, an attorney (a Catholick), a violent man, avowing himself to be a United I[rishman]. He was at his house when his wife laid in. Corporal Burke and a private of the Limerick militia were in the room adjoining the room where the wife was, who came out to drink punch with them, though she had been brought to bed only about forty hours; talked politicks, gave toasts complimentary to the French; the soldier joined in it.

About Christmas he was in great distress from sickness and pecuniary embarrassment; lodged at Parraches, who turned him out of doors; met with ill treatment in different ways, particularly from Kennedy; at last being charged as a spy for Government, he determined to retaliate, and then went to Mr. Skeffington. His distress alone would not have made him impeach him, but the suspicion of being a spy hurt his pride.

Mr. Lake, a watchmaker, who offered to assist, and confirmed the story about Donaldson, viz., Donaldson was to go to Scotland in the character of piper, and go through the country circulating their principles; he was then to go to the south of Ireland, then home to France. Donaldson learnt the language for the purpose.

He actually went to Donaghadee, and was to have been met by M'Cracken, M'Cabe, Neilson, and Cummings, but they failed, and Donaldson, being distressed and neglected, went at last to America, where he now is. Donaldson was an assumed name; Ticklar was his real name. The conduct of the people of Belfast towards this man had also an effect on his mind. M'Cabe told him that he had been in London in order to have an interview with Thellwall. M'Cabe was originally a rigid Presbyterian, adopted Paine's 'Age of reason,' and propagated the principles among the workmen at the Glass House.

He went to Mr. Skeffington in the month of March, came to Dublin in May, returned to Belfast in July.

Went in a sloop, on board of which was one Orr, a tallow chandler, and another man, both of the society. Four days at sea; became intimate with the other man, who was a cotton manufacturer. Orr was very reserved; the cotton manufacturer very communicative; landed at Bangor; as soon as he arrived at Belfast met by Young, Kennedy, Shannahan and Bell. Found a great difference at Belfast. People much elated.

John Young glad to see him, and lamented the manner he had been treated; went with [him] to Mr. Berkley; talked politicks as they walked along. Young had taken the oath since he had been away; told him the soldiers at Blaris camp were become Defenders and United Irishmen; pointing to Strangford lough, [he] said that five thousand men could be collected in that country; that the French were expected in that country the latter end of the summer. Guns firing at the barracks for rejoicing, [he] damned them for wasting the powder;—(conceives that the guns are in the Glass House). Met three persons at Berkley: Coningham, a seaman, Jo. M'Cracken, of Lisburn, and Clarke, a watchmaker; drank freely; three or four bottles of wine mulled before dinner; spoke highly of Teeling, as a leading man. Clarke, M'Cracken and Young acknowledged themselves to be Un[ited] I[rishmen], and spoke with the greatest confidence of success;

said that there were traitors, but Government were afraid to take them up. He declined being of the society, as he was going to America, which was approved of by the party. Young, M'Cracken and Clarke told him that since he had been in Belfast a union had taken place between the leaders of the Defenders and U[nited] I[rishmen]; said that the French would come soon and bring them arms. Commonly talked of guillotining the king in all their meetings.

Kennedy met him at Young's. He paid him a guinea, which he owed him; they dined together. Kennedy talked of the progress of the societies; expressed his concern at Neilson and he having differed; said Neilson was absent on the service of his country; that they had printed above two thousand Constitutions. Spoke of the Limerick and several regiments of militia being gained over; produced an address to the Delegates of Ulster, which was printed. The purport: to state the expense of defending prisoners, particularly Shaw, Richardson, etc., that missionaries had been sent into all parts of Ireland, and their success; that men of confidence had been sent to England and Scotland.

Men of confidence have been sent to parts abroad and had not been sent in vain.

Peace and sobriety recommended; patience under sufferings from Government.

Directed their attention to the success of the arms of liberty, and they must see that their emancipation was not far off.

That the Delegates of Belfast had news to communicate of such importance, that they could not communicate it in writing, but verbally.

Pointed their attention to the corruption of British Government, the state of their finances, etc. That the differences between the societies in Dublin and Belfast had happily terminated, and that Dublin would send delegates.

Delegates from Louth would also attend, from whence none had attended before.

Shannahan talked of the progress of their societies in the same manner as the other, that they increased seventeen in Belfast alone since he had been away.

Militia full of Defenders, but hitherto they could not get them to Unite until lately; that they had constant communication with the town. Said that many arms had been landed from France; that thirteen thousand had arrived, and thirty seven thousand were expected with the fleet; —— told him Dr. M'Donald's brother went to Guernsey, and was met by some of those who had previously gone to France and Amsterdam. He said that the arms which had been sent were of British manufacture, those which had been sent to the royalists in France. The chests of arms carried to the head Delegates or principal men; they were then distributed to individuals according to lists. They were buried in the ground with lime; where they suspected the prudence of any individual they gave a double number to those they could trust.

Endeavoured to ascertain the truth of Shannahan's story by conversation with Bell; talked to him about the ambassadors at Paris or France, and ridiculed the idea. Bell said it was true, but said that it was not known to four people in Belfast, and, at last, he said that he heard it from Shannahan, and it appeared that all that Bell knew of arms, etc., was from Shannahan.

While in company with Shannahan, Potts and Cuthbert went by in a chaise; they were just come from Donaghadee. Shannahan told him they had been inoculating in Scotland, that is, they had been in Scotland, distributing Constitutions, and said that the Scotch were adopting them very fast.

Shannahan shewed him tubes they had got from the soldiers; told him that they were determined to destroy the Orangemen; it would be the first thing they would do after the insurrection. Persons had been sent round Armagh, and the adjoining counties, to get the names of all the king's party, by obliging the societies to make lists of all their neighbours, distinguishing the principles of each—(this was confirmed by many); said that if the royalists had been destroyed in France they would have had no civil war.

Shewed a list of persons at Belfast to be sacrificed: Phillips, butcher, Bolte, of the Glass House, Ch. Skeffington, and about two hundred more. He afterwards saw a printed list, divided into columns, Shannahan told him that about thirty thousand in all.

Shannahan employed to defend the soldiers who killed Dr. M'Murdoch. He and Morrison collected money to pay the counsel, etc. He was playing at shuffle board. Simpson brought corporal Burke, who was genteelly dressed in a blue coat; did not know him at first; recollected him at Shannahan's. Burke told him that he was better off than when he saw him last; told him that all his regiment was up; he was come with dispatches from his regiment; employed as a principal man. Burke told him that he was concerned in throwing the man over the bridge at Belfast. Burke and the man had been drinking together. On the bridge they strangled him and threw him over the bridge. Said what a damned plunge he made in the water.

Met him at Boyd's; he, Shannahan and Rowley Osborn drank together. Osborn and Comins went round on king William's birth-day to see the strength of the party. Osborn had been a Volunteer, had great military knowledge; spoke with inveteracy against the Orangemen, in the same manner that Shannahan had done; had written a new plan of exercise and recommended drills at night.

Talked of arms, the militia joining the French, etc., in the same manner as the others.

They had returns of the arms in gentlemen's houses, and mentioned, as Shannahan had done, that the estates of the nobility were mortgaged for the payment of arms from France; about eleven-twelfths of the estates were to be confiscated

Gordon had more influence among the lower orders than any man in Belfast. He was accused by Faris as a spy. After some investigations by Gordon, ordered to attend a meeting. He was carried up a dark staircase into a room at the Harp, where Gordon, Shannahan and about twelve others were assembled. They congratulated him upon being proved innocent, and told him that it should be communicated to all the societies. The next day he was accosted by many people whom he did not know before, who shook him by the hand. All persons he talked with acknowledged that reform and Cath[olic] emancipation [were] only a mask to cover their designs.

Belfast, Dublin and Dungannon—the principal places. Belfast the first. Thinks Neilson one of the first; M'Cabe, M'Cracken, Sinclair, Captain Russell—active men. Cuthbert—a very active and important man.

Often heard Neilson speak with the same rancour and contempt of Grattan and his party as of the administration. They would never enlist under any man, however popular; general contempt of parliament.

Haislett an active man. Bruce considered a friend.

They expected no assistance from any gentlemen, nor would they have any concern with them though many had offered.

General expectation of success from assistance from Scotland and England and the effect on the English funds.

At Nicols' two artillery-men expressed readiness to join, and said most of the corps were of the same opinion.

At Graham's met others—about seven.

Serjeant M'Donald, of the artillery, kept company with Simpson, Shannahan, etc. Never heard them speak with any respect of any person of property in parliament or others than those of their own description.

Landed property to be applied to the use of the State. The little farmers should have their land.

Thursday night [4 May, 1797].

B. is a U[nited] I[rishman]; had been in the old line or a Defender long ago. Captain Dalton present when he was sworn; afterwards sworn a committee man by Miles Duignan, a grocer in Grafton street. Captain Dalton, Edward Byrne, Dr. Troy and several, near sixty, clergymen present last Sunday sennight, and were all sworn.

Has seen several of the Kilkenny and Kildare militia sworn within this fortnight.—Object to get the army, if possible.

Every man ordered this night to arm and get ready. Willis, the breeches maker, came to his society this night and gave them these orders.

Cane, grocer, in Britain-street, Russell, builder, Circular-road, Flanagan, Summer-hill, George Wimp, lime burner, John Reilly, gardener, Morris Danly, do., Pat. Mahony, do., Sweetmans, do., D. Keines, Robert Low, builder.

Many have engaged through fear. Dublin return six thousand last Saturday. Cork return four thousand the same day.

Funeral on Sunday, to engage the common people by showing numbers. A general plan for swearing servants.

Friday [5 May, 1797].

Sir G. H.—In the neighbourhood of Cumber, in Derry, principal farmers attacked at night, pulled out of their houses, threatened with death, their hair cut, etc., and by such means obliged to Unite. The secretaries used to come the next day and require them to take the oath of secrecy.

Two instances particularly stated.

Mr. Joseph Alexander, a most respectable man in that country, compelled by terror. Many, who had resisted originally, after having been sworn, have been tempted to become as active as any of the more violent.

Mischievous effects of the assizes from Curran's speech.

Friends to order and reform conceive that Government are strong enough to keep down rebellion, and therefore that they may safely push their views of reform. Many have taken the oath of secrecy who have not taken the United oath. Upon this principle they swear women and children; shows a woman who is privy to all the circumstances of Dr. Hamilton's murder, who has been sworn to secrecy. The linen bleachers have declared that in order to secure their property they would not take any part against the U[nited] I[rishmen].

Lions and James Huson, two very active agents, used always begin by praying before they made any speeches or declamations to excite the people; they are Covenanters.

Lieutenant Cockran, a most respectable man, and lieutenant in Mr. Harry Stewart's corps, sworn to secrecy. Those who have taken the oath of secrecy cannot consistently serve on juries.

Thinks the quantity of arms less than is supposed; but says that some were landed in lough Swilly at the time of the French appearing off Bantry. In Derry seven thousand persons registered. Military have not taken above six hundred. They exaggerate their power. Timber for pike handles universally cut down. Sixty men seen at exercise at night with only four firelocks amongst them; but it was supposed that they had more. A scarcity of powder. Seditious and inflammatory publications circulated. Songs given gratis. The suppression of the "Northern Star" gave universal satisfaction.

Saturday, May 6 [1797].

M[arcus] Bere[sford] attended at council for the crown in Armagh, Antrim, and Down. The sheriffs appeared to have exerted themselves to the utmost in procuring respectable juries; sub-sheriff of Antrim equally so.

In Armagh from Tuesday to Saturday not two entire different juries, viz., not twenty-four persons who actually served, and of those several who pressed forward with eagerness to serve upon these juries. Some of them expressed great satisfaction when in the box, and in a very indecent manner, whenever any of the witnesses for the crown spoke doubtfully where he had before spoken positively.

No case, as it was brought forward on the table, so strong as to be able to say that the jury found a wrong verdict. A publication to intimidate the jurors circulated. A committee went round to all the circuit assisting the prisoners. Samuel Turner, of Newry, Patrick Byrne, and Quigly, a Catholick clergyman of Dundalk, and Alexander Lowrie were the principal. They interfered only in the defence of prosecutions on the part of the crown. Constantly in court under the counsel employed by the prisoners, assisted them in challenges, and seemed to give general directions about the trial.

In Antrim a failure of attendance of jurymen at first. The sheriff sent fresh summons in the neighbourhood of Lisburn, and, upon a proper panel appearing, the prisoners put off their trial.

In Antrim he thinks that juries could be procured. In Armagh he thinks that there would be a difficulty. In Down and Antrim juries might be found.

Armagh—Troops to be guarded against. Newry—Samuel Turner, barrister, ruined; Robert Maitland, ruined merchant; John Gordon, merchant; Abraham Walker, merchant; Michael Burn, druggist; — Black, apothecary.

S[amuel] Turner, friend of lord E[dward] Fitzgerald—frequently with him in Dublin.

Yeomanry infantry proscribed as tradesmen.—Quarters allowed, constant pay.

5.—1797. MILITARY EXECUTION.

General Gerard Lake to Right Hon. Thomas Pelham.

Blaris Heath [Co. Down], May 16, 1797.—Three o'clock, p.m.

I have the honour to acquaint you, for the information of the lord lieutenant, that, in consequence of his excellency's warrant for the execution of the four privates of the Monaghan regiment of militia, viz., Daniel Gillan, Owen M'Canna, William M'Canna and Peter M'Carron, they were shot in front of a detachment of the twenty-second light dragoons, a detachment of the royal artillery, sixty-fourth regiment of foot, and third battalion of light infantry, the Monaghan and Carlow militia, the Bredalbane and Argyle Fencibles, in Blaris-Warren, at 1 o'clock, p.m., May 16, 1797.

After the execution the troops marched in divisions, in ordinary time, past the bodies, which were then in the churchyard, upon the ground.

Everything was carried on with great solemnity, and the example appeared to have had the desired effect.

No appearance of any disturbance or an improper word made use of throughout the whole proceeding, although the procession from Belfast to the place of execution was public as possible.

6.—1797. TRANSMISSION OF PUBLIC MONEY.

George Rose to Thomas Pelham.

London, Old Palace Yard, 30th May, 1797.

Agreeably to the promise made to you on Saturday last, the 27th, Mr. Wiffin, one of his majesty's messengers, is now dispatched to you with one hundred thousand pounds in notes of the Bank of England, which, I trust, will relieve you from any immediate pressure.

Mr. Greville told me yesterday that the duke of Portland had received a letter from one of the lords of your treasury, pressing for a further sum of £100,000 beyond the one above mentioned, and saying that if that could be sent you could do without further assistance till the end of the year. There must, I think, have been some mistake about that, as we have now sent all that was asked at present, and I am sure you will want much more in the course of the year.

The Board of Admiralty is returned from Sheerness without having effected anything, at least conclusively. The "Sandwich" and "Inflexible" persist obstinately in the mutiny; the other ships would probably submit. Lord St. Vincent (Jervis) has taken a galleon, and was in expectation of another. The army everywhere behaves as well as possible.

7.—1797. REWARDS FOR DISCOVERIES IN IRELAND.

Thomas Pelham to Lieutenant-General Dalrymple.

PRIVATE. Dublin, 2 June, 1797.

A very unusual press of business prevented me from acknowledging your letter of the 24th sooner. I trust that by a continuance of the activity and vigilance that has been lately shown, and encouraging those who, in consequence of the proclamation, seem disposed to return to their allegiance, we may overcome this spirit of sedition. The military executions in the north have produced the best effects on the military in that part of the kingdom, and I doubt not that your army will experience the same; and I trust that it will teach the officers the necessity of attending to their men for their own personal security, if a sense of duty is not a sufficient reason with them.

I wrote to general Coote about giving rewards for discoveries, and I have only to add that having a perfect reliance on your discretion and discernment, I am unwilling to prescribe any sum, wishing only to be informed from time to time the extent of any promises you may find it necessary to engage in, or of immediate advances which you think it right to make.

We voted the increase of pay to the army yesterday, and I trust that we shall adjourn on Saturday or Monday, and as soon as the bills are returned from England prorogue this dreadfully long session.

8.—1797. APPREHENDED MOVEMENTS IN IRELAND.

i.—To Thomas Pelham from Edward Cooke, Under-Secretary, Civil Department, Ireland.

Dublin, 26 December, 1797.

I learn from my friend that lord E. Fitzgerald received some days since orders from Paris to urge an insurrection here with all speed, in order to draw troops from England. In consequence of it, there was a meeting of the head committee, where he and O'Connor urged immediate measures of vigour. They proposed arming a body of five hundred with short swords; that this body should repair to all the mass houses at midnight mass on Christmas morning, that by false attacks they should persuade the people and raise a cry that the Orangemen were murdering the Catholics; that having raised the uproar they should begin their attack on the Castle, etc. Many priests were anxious for this plan, but Emmet, Chambers, etc., opposed, and in consequence the bishops, who were against outrage, put off mass till seven o'clock in the morning. The moderate party are against insurrection till the French land.

My lord lieutenant has sent for the Speaker and one or two more to consult with to-morrow.

McNevin went for England a few days since in a wherry from Clontarf, and was nearly lost. I suppose he went to Yarmouth. Will you not send after him? He is a neat-made, little man of five feet four.

Our friend received his intelligence from James Tandy, son to Napper, who was alarmed beyond expression at the scheme, and being consulted had opposed it. When I get the written documents I will send them.

8. ii.—To Thomas Pelham from Earl Camden, Lord Lieutenant of Ireland.

Dublin Castle, 27 December, 1797.

The account which J. W. gave in writing fell far short of the verbal communication made to me by Pollock, upon which I sent an express to the Speaker and to the attorney-general to come to town. I am very glad, however, I sent for them, as I had a great deal of general conversation upon the state of this kingdom, and was glad to hear their opinion of the policy of taking steps to seize those whom we know to be the heads of the rebels. The fact, which Cooke mentioned, of an intention to produce an insurrection on Christmas eve is undoubted, and I was in some degree doubtful in my own mind whether it might not be expedient to prevent the possibility of a similar event by confining [Arthur] O'Connor and lord Edward [Fitzgerald], but their opinion agrees with my more mature reflection, that under all the circumstances of our chance of further information, and under the impression of the disadvantage of taking up persons without bringing them to trial, it would be inexpedient to take up the ringleaders of the conspiracy at present. We shall be, if possible, more upon our guard; and, unless I receive some very decided information, I propose that no particular or active steps (of the nature I thought might have been necessary) should take place.

8. iii.—Edward Cooke to Thomas Pelham.

Dublin Castle, 30 December, 1797.

I did not send the document I promised, as it was not so full as I wished, and I have not been able to see my friend; but what I communicated is true. [Arthur] O'Connor has registered himself publisher of the 'Press.' I understand he and the violents pretend to be softened, and no popular insurrection is now to be attempted previous to a landing. A printed order, of which the enclosed is a copy, was circulated on Tuesday night from the head committee in Dublin. Finerty was pilloried to-day; he attempted to speak on coming down; the mob huzzaed, and some of the troops moved forward and a few toes were trod upon.

Mr. Vicars, of the Queen's county, lately wrote to Grattan, desiring him to join in subscriptions in order to detect persons engaged in seditious and treasonable plots. Grattan's answer was: That he was entirely of different politics, that he was determined to overturn the system of the present administration, and he would not subscribe one guinea.

Lawless writes that he has certain information that the French mean to attack Hanover and Bremen, and that they are also making immense marine preparations. I have seen letters from Antrim which give rather a good account.

9.—1798. TITHES AND CLERGY IN IRELAND.—SUGGESTED REGULATIONS.

To Thomas Pelham from Frederick Hervey, Earl of Bristol, Bishop of Derry.[1]

Venice, 16 January, 1798.

You have 'scotched the snake, not killed it,' as Shakespeare says. You have stopped the fever, not cured it, and that you know full well. In all my diocese, the very 'foyer' of rebellion, mutiny and insurrection, the embers are still warm—nay, hot and ready to burst out again, and 'Warm the nations with redoubled rage.' But a good physician like you will not content himself with the blisters and bleedings that have been applied; you will, for the sake of the patient, as well as your own medical reputation, endeavour to extirpate the fever, and finally destroy the seeds of it.

In my time, in the course of thirty years, this is the third great paroxysm we have had—1, 'Hearts of oak'; 2, 'Hearts of steel'; and 3, the 'Defenders,' alias, alias, alias.

All your predecessors having contented themselves with stopping the fever, none have searched the cause or sought to root it out.

After thirty years' experience, and a more intimate acquaintance with the constitution, pulse and habits of your frantic patient than any one of my cloth, after having gained his affections, enjoyed his confidence and merited his esteem, I will venture to assure you in plain terms, and without a metaphor, he is an animal easily led, not to be driven—and that in plain English there are two radical fundamental causes of his discontent and of his savage resentment: tithes, and the nature, quality and pitiful dependence of his teachers on their hearers, who, if they do

---

[1] For notices of this prelate *see* "The Manuscripts and Correspondence of James, first Earl of Charlemont," vol. i., 1745-1783. By J. T. Gilbert, F.S.A. London: Eyre and Spottiswoode, 1891.

not preach what the others like to hear, are sure to be first ill-paid and then dismissed.

I say tithes first, and I beg you to hear me patiently, for you do not know the nature of tithes in Ulster, but here it is:—Besides the general disadvantage it brings to agriculture, by the short, uncertain tenure which a parson can give of the tenth of the land's produce and the tiller's toil, a disadvantage so glaring and so oppressive, it is amazing that any enlightened legislature allows it to outlive the present year; and, in truth, all acts for forty years past to enclose lands do exclude it.

Besides the apparent, or rather seeming injustice of a Presbyterian paying a teacher he does not hear, there is in Ulster a horrid local grievance. The parson either lets his tithes to the farmer during incumbency, or he farms them to a tithe farmer for peace and certainty sake, and then, sir, see the consequence, which for thirty years past has been one of the great and principal causes of our distraction.

He lets his tithe during incumbency, and could he do better? No; but unluckily he does it only to undo it. The farmer, relying on this lease, sets himself to buy lime, marle, and shells at a great expense; he has nothing to fear from his landlord, secured by a lease of twenty-one or thirty-one years, nor from the parson, secured by an incumbency lease. But here comes the rub. In eight or ten years the value of the tithe doubles. The parson then looks out for a brother under similar circumstances with himself; they compare notes, values, increase, &c., and soon obtain from their respective bishops a liberty to exchange, and the farmer remains the dupe of his confidence, and then 'manet alta mente repostum.'

In the case of the tithe farmer it is perhaps more shocking. He begins his reign, as Nero did his quinquennium, all mildness and moderation. Is the farmer unable to pay, he accepts his bond with a moderate interest; the second and third year the same, and when the poor farmer is fairly or foully in the toils, the tithe farmer strips off the mask, raises the price of next year's tithe beyond its value, and then by distress and sale of goods, and backed by the bonds of former years, he makes himself, the parson, and the established religion all equally hated.

My remedy for all this evil is simple. I proposed it in the year 1774, and it was accepted by the bench of bishops, assembled at the late primate's, but, by way of experiment, confined to the diocese of Derry ; but my illness and other circumstances made me drop it.

This was the remedy, grounded on the English statutes for enclosing parishes, and nothing, I believe, can be more simple or more effective : An act to enable every rector and vicar, with consent of patron of the parish and the bishop of the diocese to exchange his tithe or any portion of his tithe for land of the same value, so that the exchange will only be gradual in the parish. And the mode of exchange is equally simple, and grounded also upon the daily practice when a parson wants to build a parsonage, and, having no glebe convenient to his church, he exchanges with a proprietor who has, and the law provides that the sheriff shall summon twelve men to judge of the value, which being usually previously settled and ascertained between the two parties interchanging, the sheriff and jury sign the deeds, and the titles are consecrated for ever after.

I need not descant to you upon the comfort of a parson who has only a glebe or a farm for his sustenance ; how light his heart must feel and how heavy his purse must grow. All this is superfluous to a man of your feelings and of your experience.

I come to the next cause, which requires deeper probing. Is it not a shame that in any civilized country, and where there is an established religion as well as government, there should be teachers professedly paid by their hearers for preaching against both the one and the other ?

Neither Popish nor Presbyterian parson should, in my opinion, be permitted by law to preach or pray, in-doors or out of doors, but under the great seal of Ireland.

The crown should be the patron of all dissenters, seceders and schismatics whatever, and the crown should either pay them or be the cause of their being paid ; and then Government would be certain of the people they appoint and the doctrines they would teach.

I conceive three means of subsisting them, all, in my opinion, equally eligible :—

1. Either for the crown to pay them directly out of the concordatum money, or out of such a fund as parliament should appoint :—

Or—2. Their salary to be raised by a rate upon each separate barony, like the high roads, or upon the county at large, like bridges and hospitals.

Or—3. Upon the vacancy of any living whatever by a portion of the glebe or income at large of that living. Nor could this, in my opinion (and until corrected by yours), be deemed any hardship on the parson, since if every Presbyterian was in a moment, in any parish whatever, to be converted to the established church, the parson's flock would become so numerous he would be obliged to keep a shepherd boy, alias a curate.

This would effectually tear up rebellion by the roots, for where the preacher would be appointed by the proper authority, and then be paid for preaching loyalty instead of disaffection, where the treasure is there would be the heart likewise. And the sour, supercilious, discontented hind could no longer refuse, as he does now, his pitiful mite of a half-crown to the man who would teach him his duty instead of the breach of it.

Anything so anomalous, so incongruous, as a man in a civilized state paid for preaching anarchy, confusion, and rebellion, &c., I do not conceive, but I do conceive that if to this poison your experience, your abilities, and your firmness do not oppose some radical antidote, the diseased body must burst. And so, with every wish for your success, both as a man and as a minister.

10.—1798. AFFAIRS IN DUBLIN, WEXFORD, etc.

Robert Marshall to Thomas Pelham.

Dublin Castle, 2 June, 1798.

I wrote to Aldridge this morning. I do not find that anything very material has occurred since. You will have observed that our militia, even the King's county regiment, have all behaved very well. But there have been many instances of disaffection in the yeomanry—I mean among those in the country. Captain Ormsby's corps at Rathcool had all agreed to desert us, except the captain and two others. The lieutenant, who was a man of some substance, was tried by a court-martial and executed this day at the new gaol. He confessed his guilt, and declared that the priest of Rathcool only was to blame for it. He has made his escape.

A laughable scene happened in the Castle yard [Dublin] about four o'clock to-day, when it was crowded with yeomen and others. A noddy came in with a female in it, and two of the attorneys' corps. They had observed her stepping into that machine in the Liberty [of Dublin], and, thinking there was something unusual in her appearance, they followed her into it and drove her into the Castle yard. Upon pulling up her veil, she proved to be one Bacon, a tailor, who was formerly a major of Volunteers, and is now a general of the rebels. Cooke [under-secretary] had been hunting for him for some days past. He was immediately tried and, I believe, found guilty.

I am sorry to find so very great a proportion of cavalry among the troops which are to be sent to us, because I understand from military men that they are not suited to the nature of this country nor to act against pikemen, as we have found by fatal experience, except in a pursuit, and it is said we have enough already for such a purpose.

I hear that the rebels, with their pikes and some winnowing cloths, are able to make something like tents, which serve them well enough this fine weather.

We expect to hear to-morrow from Wexford, where we have now nearly five thousand men. I am afraid that the rebels have nearly four times that number.

I do not hear anything as yet of the further extension of the mischief, except that a party of about six hundred were met by some yeomen in Leitrim, who killed a few of them.

11.—1798. ORANGE ASSOCIATIONS.—MOVEMENTS IN LEINSTER.—DEATH OF LORD EDWARD FITZGERALD.

To Thomas Pelham from Hon. William Elliot, Under-Secretary, Military Department, Ireland.

PRIVATE.   Sunday, 3 June, 1798.—3 o'clock, p.m.

The letters received in the course of last night and this morning come principally from Wexford and that quarter. They contain, however, little more than a statement of the position of the rebels and of the king's troops. In the skirmish between Arklow and Gorey a priest is said to have been killed on the field of battle in his vestments. The war in that part of the country has certainly assumed a strong religious spirit, and I cannot help suspecting that the Orange associations, which, you will recollect, were formed and promoted by colonel Rochfort and some other gentlemen in the counties of Wexford and Carlow, operated very mischievously. This, however, you will observe, is merely my own suspicion, and I can really give you no particular facts to support my opinion. Lord Fingal and most of the leading persons of the Catholic persuasion have presented a very loyal and spirited address, and, I believe, are perfectly impressed with the danger which is menaced to all religion and to all property. Amongst the lower class of the Catholics there appears to be a very widely extended disaffection, and it will be indubitably the object of the chiefs of the rebellion to fan the flame of religious dissension, which the foolish and acrimonious conversation and conduct of the intemperate part of the Protestants will not tend to abate. The contest is yet by no means decided, but, if the rebels should not have the co-operation of a French army, I trust we shall put them down. If the French should be able to throw a force of five thousand men on any part of our coasts, it would render the result very dubious. Our army is so dispersed that it will be difficult to concentrate it, and I cannot help expressing to you (most privately) my total want of confidence in the ability of the person who must direct its operations. Lake is a brave, cool, collected man, extremely obliging and pleasant in the transaction of business, but he has not resources adequate to the critical situation in which he is placed. The loss of Abercromby will not be easily repaired. I shall keep my letter open in hopes of more news. I send on a separate paper the substance of the intelligence which was received in the course of last night and this morning. Lord Edward Fitzgerald has had several paroxysms of fever, and is thought to be in some danger.

Ten o'clock.—General Lake has had a letter from general Loftus from Arklow, dated early this morning, but it contains nothing of importance, as he had not, at the time he wrote, heard from general Johnson or general Eustace. I have this moment learnt that the messenger who was to have gone this evening is not to go till to-morrow morning. I shall therefore postpone sealing my letter in the hope of having good tidings to communicate to you from Wexford.

Monday, 4 June, [1798,] one o'clock, p.m.

There is no news of importance from the county of Wexford. A detachment of the Meath, the Donegal, and Mid-Lothian received a false alarm on their march from Kilkenny towards New Ross on Saturday night, and, by mistake, fired at each other; but I do not find that the accident was attended with any material mischief.

Lord Edward Fitzgerald is dead. Lady Louisa Conolly supplicated so earnestly for permission to see him last night, that the chancellor [lord Clare] went with her to the prison. Lord Edward, however, was so ill as not to know her. I have just received your letter from Edinburgh, and I hope you will not suffer from fatigue of your journey.

12.—1798. WAR IN WEXFORD.—DEATH OF COLONEL WALPOLE.—PROBABILITY OF GENERAL REVOLT IN IRELAND.

Viscount Castlereagh to Thomas Pelham.

Dublin, 6th June, 1798.

I have chosen an unlucky day for sending you intelligence, knowing how much you will regret Walpole's loss. His detachment, about five hundred strong, was sent by general Loftus from Gorey to drive the rebels from a mountain near Carnew, whilst Loftus himself moved with an equal force nearer the sea, in the direction of Enniscorthy, with a view of cutting off their retreat. Walpole discovered the enemy drawn up on the hill in great force. Part of their body filed and took possession of a wood; the remainder moved down into the plain to receive him. His approach was made in column through a lane with high banks and hedges. Under cover of these the rebels flanked him so as to commence their fire on his entire column, front and rear, at the same moment. They had one or two field-pieces taken from general Fawcit's party between Wexford and Waterford. Thus attacked, where our troops had not room to form with any effect, they were thrown into confusion and obliged to retreat, leaving two six-pounders behind them. Walpole fell early in the action. Major Stark, of the Londonderry, who attended the grenadier company as a volunteer, was wounded in the stomach, I hope not mortally. The loss is not as yet ascertained, but I should suppose about one hundred and fifty men. The remainder of the detachment fell back on Gorey, colonel Cope, with a small party of the

Armagh, covering their retreat, and disputing every inch of ground with the greatest bravery.

The rebellion seems to have taken serious root in Wexford. Their force is very great, the body in question exceeding ten thousand men, a considerable proportion of fire-arms, and conducted with an attention to military principles. Wexford is still in their hands, and a very large force said to be assembled in that side of the county.

This town is quiet, and the yeomanry zealous and numerous. Our regular garrison does not exceed fifteen hundred men, so pressed have we been for reinforcements.

No disturbance has yet appeared in the other provinces, but my information from the north, this day received, makes it extremely to be apprehended that an effort will shortly be made in that quarter. They only wait for a small co-operation from France, or some successes on the part of the southern rebels.

You know how fully prepared every part of Ireland is for revolt. Nothing but a speedy suppression of the mischief can prevent its becoming general. Your information where you now are will enable you to judge whether an invasion of England is likely to happen. Unless it is inevitable and immediate, Great Britain cannot better employ her force than in sending a large force, were it only for a few weeks, into Ireland. Everything depends on the first successes. It will cost much exertion to reconquer the island should the rebellion establish itself in the four provinces. We want officers much; pray press the sending over our brigadiers.

I will keep this open for further intelligence, if any should arrive before the packet sails. I enclose a letter I opened by mistake, also a return of the yeomanry of the metropolis [Dublin] with their stations.

13.—1798. POSSIBLE LOSS OF IRELAND.—DEMAND FOR MORE TROOPS FROM ENGLAND.

To Thomas Pelham from Earl Camden, Lord Lieutenant of Ireland.

Dublin Castle, June 6th, 1798.

The interest you take in the fate of this country and in my character must have made you very uneasy during the dreadful insurrections to which we have been subject, and you, who know the country, its inhabitants, the generals who command, and the troops they have to manage, must feel all the embarrassments of my situation.

I had meant to have written to you yesterday, to have begged you to urge with all the arguments you could use the necessity of an immediate and very strong reinforcement of troops. I have stated this necessity most strongly to the duke of Portland and Pitt, and have been requested by the friends of Government to state it as their decided opinion that unless a very large force is immediately sent from England the country may be lost. General Lake agrees with me in the necessity of such reinforcement, and I hope you will urge it with all your influence.

I remain in the opinion I originally held, that general Lake is not fit for the command in these difficult times, and have written to Pitt in the most serious and impressive manner I am able, to make him master of the actual danger of the country. It is unfortunate that we should have lost the advantage of general Lake's services where he was really well placed, and have brought him to one which is above his capacity. He has no arrangement, is easily led, and no authority. I return to the opinion I had entertained before, that the lord lieutenant ought to be a military man. The whole government of the country is now military, and the power of the chief governor is almost merged in that of the general commanding the troops. I have suggested the propriety of sending over lord Cornwallis, whose name, with some good officers under him, will have great weight; and I have told Pitt that which I really feel, that, without the best military assistance, I conceive the country to be in the most imminent danger, and that my services cannot be useful to the king.

I am sure you must be aware how very unpleasantly circumstanced I am without a commander-in-chief upon whom I have the most perfect reliance, and it is equally unfair to the country and to me to suffer the military business to proceed as it is now conducted.

I even think the scene is sufficiently extensive for the duke of York, whose place may be supplied by the eldest generals during his absence.

The reason I so much press for this relief is the expectation that a landing, even of a small body of French, will set the country in a blaze, and I think neither our force nor our staff equal to the very difficult circumstances they will have to encounter. I should hope you would press the point of some arrangement of this kind; and I cannot avoid thinking the most beneficial one for the public will be that lord Cornwallis should be appointed lord lieutenant.

I hope the spirit of the rebels is broken in the county of Kildare, but the county of Wexford is a terrible example of their fury and licentiousness. There are reports of the troops under general Johnson having been successful in an engagement with the rebels at Ross, but no account has reached us, for which we can only account by the messenger having been intercepted.

Great impatience is entertained from no regiments having arrived from England, and indeed it is mortifying to think that we have not received a man, although the rebellion has lasted for a fortnight; great discontent is already felt upon that subject. From the nature of the war we have been obliged to carry on, small parties are detached under the command of an officer who is to act at his own discretion much more than in any situation in which he could be placed with the rank he may bear, and I therefore think it absolutely necessary they should send us some very excellent officers as brigadiers, in addition to those already meant to be sent here.

P.S.—I am sure you lament, in common with his other friends, poor Walpole's fate. I am afraid he grievously mismanaged the command with which he was entrusted.

14.—1798. AFFAIRS IN WEXFORD AND ULSTER.—FORMIDABLE CHARACTER OF THE IRISH MOVEMENT.

Castlereagh to Thomas Pelham.

Dublin Castle, 8 [June, 1798].

The rebellion in Wexford has assumed a more serious shape than was to be apprehended from a peasantry, however well organized. Their numbers are very great, their enthusiasm excited by their priests, and the face of the country so broken and enclosed that regular formations are impracticable. I send you the copy of a letter from major Vesey, of the county Dublin regiment, an excellent officer, whose account is more detailed than the official despatch from general Johnson. An enemy that only yielded after a struggle of twelve hours is not contemptible. Our militia soldiers have on every occasion manifested the greatest spirit and fidelity, in many instances defective in subordination, but in none have they shown the smallest disposition to fraternize, but, on the contrary, pursue the insurgents with the rancour unfortunately connected with the nature of the struggle.

Had the rebels carried Ross, the insurrection would have immediately pervaded the counties of Waterford and Kilkenny; as it is, the people are in motion on the Kilkenny side of the river.

General Lake has made dispositions for acting with effect against the rebels in that quarter. Needham is posted at Arklow with sixteen hundred men; Dundas will assemble two thousand four hundred at Carnew; Champagné is at Newtown Barry [Co. Wexford] with nine hundred, exclusive of yeomanry; and Johnson has been reinforced since the action with two regiments, making his strength two thousand.

The enemy are in great force at Vinegar Hill, within half a mile of Enniscorthy, and at Carrickburne, near Taghmon. Their numbers consist of the entire male inhabitants of Wexford, and the greatest proportion of those of Wicklow, Kildare, Carlow, and Kilkenny. From Carlow to Dublin, I am told, scarcely an inhabitant is to be seen.

I am sorry to inform you that our fears about the north are too likely to be realized. I have this moment an express from general Knox, at Dungannon, announcing an insurrection at Randalstown, where they have taken captain Jones prisoner, and disarmed the Toome yeomanry. General Nugent had intelligence of this rising, which was fixed for the day on which the Antrim magistrates were to assemble at Antrim to take steps for driving the cattle, etc., in case of invasion, and their plan was to seize as hostages. It was intended to send a force to Antrim from Belfast. I hope it may prove a partial mischief, but I much fear that as the seed has been sown universally, so it will be productive. You know the country so well, and can estimate from the affair at Ross what the intelligence of the north may effect, that it is unnecessary to add any observations of mine.

I understand from Marshall you are rather inclined to hold the insurrection cheap. Rely upon it there never was in any country so formidable an effort on the part of the people. It may not disclose itself in the full extent of its preparation if it is early met with vigour and success; but our force cannot cope in a variety of distant points with an enemy that can elude an attack where it is inexpedient to risk a contest.

15.—1798. DANGER OF IRELAND BEING LOST TO GREAT BRITAIN.

Lord Camden to Thomas Pelham.

Dublin Castle, 11 June, 1798.

Elliot will deliver this letter to you. I write to you as one who is better acquainted with the situation of this kingdom than any other person in England, and possibly, in Ireland. I consider you as still attached to my embassy here, and therefore address you officially upon the perilous state of this kingdom. The correspondence I have held with the duke of Portland, the enclosures I have sent to him, and Elliot's communications, will make you master of the subject, and you may be assured that the complexion this rebellion wears is the most serious it is possible to conceive. Unless Great Britain pours an immense force into Ireland the country is lost. Unless she sends her most able generals those troops may be sacrificed. The organization of this treason is universal, and the formidable numbers in which the rebels assemble oblige all those who have not the good fortune to escape to join them.

The rebels have possessed themselves of Wexford and of that whole county. They have possessed themselves of Newtownards, and the whole neck of land on that side the lough of Strangford is evacuated. The force from Wexford is so great that it is not thought proper to advance against them, particularly as very large assemblages are making in various parts of the neighbourhood of Dublin, and there is no doubt of an intention to attempt a rising within the city.

I have to request you will in my name request that his majesty's ministers may be assembled, that you would represent to them that, from the delay in sending the reinforcements which were promised, the rebellion has much extended itself; that it now assumes so formidable a shape that I think it my duty to state through you to those ministers that the country is lost, unless a very large reinforcement of troops is landed; that every sacrifice ought to be made to preserve this country, and that nothing would so effectively secure it as the exchange of militia regiments.

You will have the goodness to impress this opinion, which is universal, upon the duke of Portland and the rest of his majesty's confidential servants. In thus laying before them the perilous situation of Ireland, I have done my duty. I cannot suffer my character and my peace of mind to be trifled with, and I therefore trust my representation of the necessity of troops will be as public as it is urgent.

16.—1798. WEXFORD.—ULSTER.—MILITIA ARRANGEMENTS.

Castlereagh to Thomas Pelham.

Dublin Castle, 13 [June, 1798.]

I did not write to you yesterday, as lord Camden undertook to inform you of what had occurred subsequent to Mr. Elliot's departure, from whom, of course, you have received a much more intelligible account than it is possible to convey by letter.

Although your exertions with the ministers had already obtained for us very powerful succours, yet I am happy Elliot went, as he can explain many points in respect to our situation, which might not suggest themselves even to one so well acquainted with the country and the treason as you are. The rebellion in Wexford has disappointed all my speculations. I had not a conception that insurgents could remain together and act in such numbers. It will be yet four days (owing to Sir James Stewart's disobedience of orders) before the troops will be in their places to act. General Moore, in addition to the first disposition, will pass from Waterford to Duncannon fort, which will strengthen Johnson's column, moving from Ross. It was first intended to unite Needham's, Dundas's and Loftus's columns at Carnew, and proceed from thence against Enniscorthy, but the rebels have since assembled their principal force near Gorey, which will render it necessary for Dundas to move to Carnew before Needham leaves Arklow, and to co-operate in dispositing them from their position near Gorey, which is said to be strong.

The northern rebellion is as yet in an unascertained state. Only two counties have moved. This circumstance I should consider as encouraging, if it had not been arranged, to our knowledge, by the leaders that the rising in Down and Antrim should precede that of the other counties, where the disaffection is less general. In Antrim the rebels are for the present dispersed. In Down they are posted on the high hill called Scrabo, above the town of Newtownards, and at Creevy, near Saintfield. Nugent was to act against them to-day from Down, Ballynahinch, Blaris and Belfast. Much will depend on the result of this expedition.

Lord Clanrickard writes in considerable alarm about Connaught, his force having been weakened; and Sir James Stewart seems equally apprehensive of a rising in Munster. There can be no doubt the organization is universal, and in the loyal county of Galway, Trench admits they are all sworn, as appeared the other day when lord Clanrickard offered pardon upon certain conditions. The people almost universally acknowledged they had taken the oath.

I hope Mr. Pitt will not let slip this opportunity of making the militia of both countries what it ought to be, an imperial force, for the defence of the empire at home. Whether the militia of one country should be liable to serve in the other except in the case of actual rebellion or invasion, may be a question, but there can be none that when either [of the] countries is visited by one or both of these calamities, that the service of every soldier should be at the king's disposal. I think the measure would in appearance as well as in fact strengthen our connection, and the experience we have already had of the Irish militia has completely dispelled all our apprehensions as to their fidelity and must remove every jealousy on the part of England in employing them in Great Britain, should the occasion call for their service. It might be sufficient to legalize the employing such regiments out of their own kingdom as shall voluntarily offer their services until the expiration of the present term of service of the men, but hereafter every militia-man to be attested to serve in Great Britain or Ireland, under such restrictions as may be thought consistent with the main object. We should gain security by the measure at present, but the day may come when the plague may have spent itself here, and when England may experience the same struggle.

17.—1798. APPREHENSIONS OF THE FRENCH.—CONSIDERATION OF
MEASURES FOR PACIFICATION IN IRELAND.

Edward Cooke to Thomas Pelham.

[Dublin Castle] 14 June, 1798.—Ten at night.

No troops yet. Some say the French [are] in the offing.

Sir J. Stewart's disobedience of orders has delayed the operations against Wexford disgracefully, if not dangerously. I do not expect that our attack will commence before the 18th or 19th.

We have not at present troops to disperse little plundering bodies, hanging over the neighbourhood. Nugent's business is clever. We wait for its effect.

I have no alarm, nor have I had any, except the French come.

You know Ireland better than most men. You have leisure, you have documents, you have no prejudices, and you are a Whig. Can you bend your mind to the consideration of what ought to be the measure to pacify after victory, and what the measure of settlement to secure peace, tranquillity and loyalty hereafter. Three contending religions, two independent legislatures under the same crown. How are you to work on such data?

18.—1798. "DETERMINED BRAVERY" OF THE IRISH.—ULSTER, WEXFORD.
ARRANGEMENT OF BRITISH TROOPS.

Castlereagh to William Elliot.

Dublin Castle, 15 [June, 1798].

I have postponed writing, in hopes that the events of the two days that have elapsed since you sailed, might have enabled me to alter in some degree the impression under which you left us.

The operations in the north have so far been very favorable; we have succeeded in giving the rebels, both in Down and Antrim, a severe check, which, considering the reduced state of Nugent's force, and the serious consequences that might have resulted from any reverse in that quarter (where troops were not immediately at hand to repair a disaster), is in itself an important advantage, though it by no means ensures the suppression of the rebellion, nor can it be looked to as securing us against its extension to the other counties of the provinces.

The rebels fought at Ballynahinch [Co. Down], as in Wexford, with determined bravery, but without the fanaticism of the southerns. They made the attack and used some wretched ship guns mounted on cars with considerable address. The body there assembled was entirely dispersed; in their ranks were found two of my father's servants, a footman and postilion. The rebels are in possession of the Ards, and their force considerable on the mountain above Newtownards.

Upon the whole the north is divided in sentiment. We have numerous adherents, and I am inclined to hope that the effort there will prove rather a diversion than the main attack. In Wexford things remain stationary. The forces will not be at their destination till the 18th, when Lake will proceed in person to attack the rebels. Since the attack on Arklow, except in a small excursion against Borris, they have remained inactive; however, they now avow themselves as a party, exercising the powers of government, and have issued proclamations, which put persons and property in requisition under pain of death, and are signed by Bagenal Harvey, as commander-in-chief. I understand from captain Hay, of the third foot, who has been in their hands for some days and has just made his escape, that they have little ammunition and still continue, though in immense numbers, in a very irregular and undisciplined state. The force collected at the different points of assembly, exclusive of yeomanry, is near ten thousand men, viz., Ross:—Johnson: 3,084. Duncannon:—Moore: 1,200. Newtownbarry:—Duff: 1,630. Tallow: Loftus: and Baltinglass:—Dundas: 2,385. Arklow:—Needham: 1,479.

Lake only waits the arrival of the hundredth regiment to strengthen Dublin. It is off Arklow and may be expected to-night: he will probably leave town to-morrow. The delay attending the arrival of the reinforcements from England is unfortunate, not merely as cramping our operations, but as affording a moral, which the disaffected do not fail to reason from, that with French assistance the people could have carried the country before a regiment from the other side found its way to our assistance. This circumstance, which will hereafter weigh both in France and here, makes it of the last importance that strongholds should be established in the north and south, as well as in the neighbourhood of Dublin, on which the army might fall back if not in force to contend against the enemy, and through which Great Britain might act. Until this is accomplished, we shall either require such an army as cannot without much injury to the service be allotted to the defence of Ireland, or be exposed suddenly to be overpowered by a very insignificant foreign attack, assisted by our own insurgents. We have not heard that any troops are landed either in the north or south. The calmness of the weather has been very unfavourable to their passage. When they do arrive our force will be fully equal to every internal difficulty, if the French leave us to ourselves. You may easily conceive how much I long for your return. Watson has taken post in your office. I shall write to Mr. Pelham by to-morrow's post, to which I refer you for any intelligence I may have to send, in case you should remain in London so long. Lord Camden has sent Crawford's letter. I am sorry to tell you general Johnson has put him under an arrest. They are both warn in their tempers, and I see by a letter from Crawford this day to Lake, that he does not consider himself as under Johnson's orders, and demands a court-martial.

19.—1798. LETTERS FROM EARL CAMDEN, LORD LIEUTENANT OF IRELAND.

i.—To William Elliot, London.

Dublin Castle, 15 June, 1798.

You recollect the letter I wrote to Pitt upon the necessity of an efficient military character being placed here, and the opinion I gave, that if such a one could not be found to act with me, that the two functions should be entrusted to the same person. Pitt writes me word that under the present circumstances he sees no other alternative than appointing lord Cornwallis, and I have this day received his intimation that he had mentioned the subject to the king. I am so convinced of the necessity of the appointment of an efficient military character being essential to the well-being of the country, that I am ready to sacrifice every personal consideration to an object which is so extremely material to the salvation of the empire. Your friendship towards me has frequently suggested that you thought some cabinet office ought to be given to me when I retired from Ireland. If I relinquish my situation, as I do now, merely for the public good at the risk of a false construction, it becomes doubly necessary that I should receive some mark of confidence, that it may not be supposed I am recalled from any opinion on the part of the ministers that I have not acted as became me. I have mentioned this impression upon my mind to Pitt, to lord Chatham, and to Pelham, and I venture also to suggest it to you, as I am conscious your friendship towards me will dictate to you the propriety of urging this object to your friends in confidential situations. General Nugent has been successful at Ballynahinch and Saintfield, but I believe we shall have a tough business both in the north and at Wexford.—I have not time to add more.

19. ii.—Camden to Thomas Pelham, London.

Dublin Castle, 15th June, 1798.

I thought it my duty to represent very strongly to Pitt the necessity of having the most efficient military man as commander-in-chief in Ireland, and if such a man could not be found the two functions of lord lieutenant and commander-in-chief should be united in the same person.

From the consideration he has given this subject, both he and lord Chatham agree in the propriety of entrusting the government and the command to lord Cornwallis, and I understand he is willing to undertake the task. General Lake is certainly perfectly inadequate to the situation he now fills, and it is impossible that the Government could go on as at present it is constituted—I mean the military part of it—the very great danger of the country, unless it is placed on a proper military footing, at this moment induces me to think the measure which I understand (in consequence of my suggestion) is adopted, a very advantageous one for the country, and I trust my friends will take care it is not understood that the alteration takes place in consequence of any want of confidence in me, but entirely as a military arrangement.

I should have been very glad to have seen this storm quelled during my residence here, but personal feelings ought to yield to public duties, and I feel I have performed mine in openly and candidly stating my opinions, and as I look upon myself as the servant of the public, I am ready to devote myself to its service, should any alteration in the position of affairs take place which should make necessary the alteration of the measure now proposed.

Elliot will have explained to you the danger of the country, and I commissioned him to say I was ready to devote myself here or elsewhere in whatever manner it was judged I might be the most usefully employed.

I cannot look upon the rebellion as nearly at an end, and therefore I am sure a military man ought to be in Ireland. Was it not so, my knowledge of the country might enable me to be of some use towards the settlement of it. We shall now probably meet in England much sooner than we had expected. Let me know if you have any commands for me here.

20.—1798. ULSTER.—WEXFORD.—KILDARE.—EARL CAMDEN.—
PROTECTION OF DUBLIN.

Viscount Castlereagh to Thomas Pelham, London.

Dublin, 16 June, 1798.

The accounts from the north to-day are more satisfactory. The affair at Ballynahinch, which was well fought, and in which the rebels lost in killed full five hundred men, has discouraged the party in Down. The rout was complete, and the fugitives have shown rather a disposition to submit than to re-assemble. Nugent, with the exception of a few leaders, has offered them pardon and protection upon condition of surrendering their arms and returning peaceably home. I understand they have evacuated Newtownards. My father, at the head of his yeomanry, was proceeding with general Champagnè into the Ards. Numbers of prisoners have been taken, amongst others their general, Munro, and his aid-de-camp, Kean, formerly a clerk in the 'Star' office, Belfast. Sir George Hill writes from Derry that the assemblage at Maghera, never formidable, had retired to the mountains; the rest of the county quiet, but some agitation observable amongst the people.

The twentieth is the day named for a general rising in the north. It certainly has been a measure decided on, and the general effort was to be preceded by the rising which has actually taken place in Down and Antrim. Although our information has generally proved but too true, yet I am not without hopes, particularly if the brigade from Scotland should arrive speedily, that the other counties, warned by the failure of their neighbours, may remain quiet.

General Lake sets out to-morrow morning for Wexford. I suppose his columns cannot be in motion before Tuesday. Much will depend on the event of this operation. In Kildare the rebellion has degenerated into a plundering banditti. They have left the gentlemen and rich farmers neither furniture or stock of any kind. Your friend, Griffith, last night lost eight hundred sheep, and everything of value he possessed.

The conduct of the troops is everything we could wish in point of spirit; their discipline not much improved by free quarters. Nugent writes in the highest praise of the northern yeomanry; he describes them for this particular service as equal to the best troops. The force in this town is very considerably increased, and has shown the best disposition; their numbers not less than five thousand on paper.

I have seen letters from Mr. Pitt and lord Chatham on a subject deeply interesting to us both. Connected and attached as we feel to lord Camden, the considerations, as well with reference to the individual as to the public, arising out of the event in question, are too extensive for a letter. With relation to myself, I can only say (having also seen your last letter to lord Camden) that, circumstanced as the country is, I can have no other feeling than readiness to obey any commands I may receive; and in the present instance, although I cannot feel indifferent to the change, yet I shall have very particular pleasure in doing anything in my power which may give this country again the advantage of your services.

I shall communicate with general Lake in respect to the cantonment of the English troops. The hundredth regiment has been landed here to secure Dublin, during the operations against Wexford. When that service is performed it can proceed to join its brigade. The lord lieutenant has written to obviate, if possible, Nugent's being superseded in the north by general Campbell. It is of the last importance that the command should remain with him. General Lake has settled the cantonments as suggested in your letter.

21.—1798. CHANGES OF VICEROY OF IRELAND AND CHIEF SECRETARY.

Edward Cooke to Thomas Pelham.

Dublin Castle, 16 June, 1798.

I do not like this manœuvre of a change at all, nor can I possibly see what good can result from it except loss of reputation to my lord lieutenant. Let us explain and explain and explain till we tire ourselves, we shall never persuade others of the real motive.

I conceive, of course, we shall finally lose you, which for your own sake, I rejoice in, for I do declare it to be my sincere opinion that your health will not admit the fatigue and vexation of your present situation, and I sincerely recommend it to you to clear yourself of the subject. You cannot have a friend who values your life (and I must profess myself one of that number) who does not think with me.

Surely the decision on a change has been rapid. Our struggle may probably be over next week, and if the events hoped for from the Mediterranean and the Continent turn out well, surely all our difficulties will be more of a civil than military complexion.

It is singular that during this struggle I have not been at all uneasy ; yet I will admit that the battles of New Ross and Arklow were critical. As the north stands secure, I feel certain all will do right, unless other parts of the south burst forth this week, which I do not expect.

22.—MARQUIS CORNWALLIS, VICEROY.—RETIREMENT OF EARL CAMDEN.

Camden to Thomas Pelham.

Dublin Castle, 19 June, 1798.

I understand lord Cornwallis will be here to-morrow. I shall stay a day or two after his arrival, and then proceed to London as quickly as

I can. I am desirous of seeing my friends as soon as possible, and of stating to them my way of thinking about this strange proceeding, which, though right in principle, is most disadvantageous in the mode of carrying it into execution.

It is probable I shall be in town before Wednesday, and wish to meet you there on my arrival.

P.S.—We have given the rebels a licking at Kilcock this morning.

23.—1798. MARQUIS CORNWALLIS AND HIS CHIEF SECRETARY.—TRIALS.—PARLIAMENT IN IRELAND.

Edward Cooke to Pelham.

Dublin, 19 June, 1798.

I did not like, and I do not like, this sudden change. It is taken, however, not unfavourably, and I think credit is done to lord Camden's motives and feelings.

Elliot gives me no flattering account of your strength and health. I should advise you to go to Portugal, if possible, at least to the best climate in England, and away from all business.

I trust the actual rebellion will be over this week; consequently, trials will come on and parliamentary proceedings commence. These ought not to commence without the tableau of the country being well considered; and all parliamentary measures should be pointed to the final settlement of the kingdom, whatever that is to be.

In such a situation there can be no sense in lord Cornwallis's coming over unless he is to settle the country; and I think it is necessary that his chief secretary should know his situation, and feel his ground, and be able to make his arrangements early, and to form the line of conversation to be adopted, and to hint the system to be pursued.

The parliament is untried, is very wild, very independent; no one can at present foresee what turn it will take or what parties will arise; and I am sure much management, discretion and exertion will be wanting.

I send you our bulletin—the rebels mentioned in the two actions are the same body. The north is nearly subdued. The operations against Wexford commence to-day.

24.—1798. REDUCTION OF INSURGENTS.—TRIALS.—THOMAS REYNOLDS. —STATE PRISONERS. — EXECUTION. — ATTAINDERS. — UNION WITH ENGLAND.—CORNWALLIS.—CASTLEREAGH.—CHIEF SECRETARYSHIP IN IRELAND.

William Elliot to Thomas Pelham.

Private.   Dublin, 28 July, 1798.

I have been sadly remiss in my correspondence, and you have been very kind in giving me so unequivocal a proof of your forgiveness in your letter of the 16th.

Though I by no means think the country in a state of security, the aspect of its affairs is much improved since I saw you. The rebellion is completely broken. Several thousands of the lower description of rebels have come in under the proclamation and taken the oaths of allegiance, and most of the leaders have either been seized and executed, or have availed themselves of the clemency of Government, and surrendered on condition of banishment. There are still bodies of banditti in the county of Wicklow, who rob and burn, and in the neighbourhood of the bogs and mountains it is difficult to prevent such depredations. It is to be hoped, however, that the approach of harvest may revive in the people the habits of industry, and that their minds may be gradually quieted and composed, if the gentlemen of the country will use their victory with moderation.

The success of the late trials must have been a source of infinite satisfaction to you. Reynolds's testimony has risen in estimation on every trial.

The conviction of [Oliver] Bond seems likely to lead to very important consequences. On Tuesday a memorial was presented to Government, with the signatures of the State prisoners (I believe all except Sampson and O'Connor), offering to communicate the whole extent of their information relative to the conspiracy, provided the punishment of [William] Byrne and Bond was commuted for banishment, and provided the persons who signed the proposition should be permitted to transport themselves, and also provided that their information should not be used for the prosecution of any individuals who might be involved in it. I did not see the paper, and therefore I ought, perhaps, to add that I am not quite sure that the proposition was so specific and precise as I have represented it; but it was to that effect. On Wednesday (the day appointed for Byrne's execution) there was a meeting of the two chief justices [Kilwarden and Carleton] and the crown lawyers at the Castle. The leaning of lord Castlereagh's mind was strongly for respiting Byrne, in order that the subject might be more fully considered and the detail of the proposition more explained and understood: but even lord Kilwarden and lord Carleton, who are in general moderate and temperate in their opinions, were so decisively against a respite, that Byrne was executed. On Thursday (the day appointed for Bond's execution) the proposition was renewed, with the signatures of [William] Sampson and O'Connor. Another meeting was held at the Castle, and after much discussion it was determined to respite Bond till Monday next. I confess I thought the decision of Wednesday was much too precipitate. The proposition certainly deserves mature deliberation. If the persons who made it are sincere, and will communicate with Government freely and without reserve, their information may prove of the utmost importance. It would be a complete justification of all the measures of Government, by developing the conspiracy in all its parts, and proving beyond all possibility of controversy the guilt of those persons whom the opposition in England have represented as so immaculate and injured. A faithful narrative of the communication with the Directory by MacNeven would also be of inestimable value. The chancellor [lord Clare] has had a cold, and is now at Mount Shannon, but comes to town early to-morrow. The Speaker [Foster], who was not consulted, is, I hear, quite outrageous. The tone of the rest of the Orange party is also very violent.

Cooke will communicate with the prisoners more fully than he has hitherto done in the course of to-day and to-morrow, and if it should appear that their proposal has been made with sincerity, I presume a further respite will be granted to Bond.

If it should prove that it was an expedient devised merely to delude the Government into the pardon of Bond, the law will be suffered to take its course. A motion was yesterday made by the attorney-general for leave to bring in a bill for attainting lord Edward Fitzgerald, Bagenal Harvey and Grogan, and leave was granted without any opposition.

This is, I think, all the news I have at present to communicate.

Lord Cornwallis's attention is principally directed to military business, but on all the political points which have been brought before him he has, I believe, formed a sound judgment. He is very firm, and, I am happy to tell you, has the most implicit confidence in lord Castlereagh, of whom he frequently speaks to me in terms of the strongest commendation. The army is, I fear, still in a sad state of disorder and want of discipline, and the troops have been guilty of great outrages in the course of the rebellion.

You, I suppose, are apprised that general Knox is removed from this establishment, and is appointed to the government of St. Domingo. The loss to us is incalculable.

I now must touch on that part of your letter which relates to the possibility of your return to this country. You are well acquainted with my sentiments on that subject as far as it concerns the public interest; but in considering it I cannot help looking to your health, and I really should feel myself guilty of a great breach, not only of friendship, but of duty, if I were not to state to you that the detail of the business of the country daily increases; that as the military arrangements occupy almost the whole of lord Cornwallis's time, the civil department of the State would chiefly devolve upon you; that, as far as I can form a judgment, the next session of parliament is likely to be long and probably troublesome, and that there must be considerable pecuniary embarrassments of which you will be obliged to take the management. All these circumstances must expose you to incessant fatigue and anxiety, which you ought not to encounter unless you feel yourself much stronger in point of health and constitution than you did last year.

With regard to an Union, it is really a subject of such magnitude that my mind cannot even approach to an opinion on it. I can only say that if there was any chance of my being even in the most subordinate degree concerned in the execution of such a measure, I should wish to hear the topic frequently and fully discussed before I

T

embarked in it. Besides the many previous difficulties which are to be surmounted, I cannot help doubting whether, if the object were accomplished, the advantages resulting from it would answer the sanguine expectations that many persons entertain. I believe also that my scepticism on this point has the sanction of your opinion. Lord Cornwallis's mind appears to have a strong preponderance on the side of an Union.

I perceive no chance of my going to England for some time, as the session, in consequence of the bills of attainder, is likely to be protracted to a great length. Lord Castlereagh does not wish you to come to Ireland until you are strong enough in point of health to resume your office, if that should be your ultimate decision, as he is apprehensive that notwithstanding you both accord in the measures and system which are pursued, your residence here out of office would occasion embarrassing speculations, and in the present fluctuating state of the public mind I think you would find inconvenience from it. This is, however, a most disinterested opinion that I am giving you, as I assure you it would afford me inexpressible satisfaction to talk with you on topics I am now obliged to write on. I forget whether in a former letter I mentioned that a few days after lord Camden's departure, I took an opportunity of explaining to lord Cornwallis the precariousness of my tenure here, and that your determination would include mine. In case you should not return, I trust the ministers will not think of sending a new man here. It is absolutely necessary that in the present circumstances of the country the person who is to be associated with the lord lieutenant in the government of it should be perfectly conversant with the measures which are carrying on, and lord Castlereagh has displayed such ability in parliament, and such sound discretion and judgment in council, that the administration would act injuriously for the country and unjustly both towards you and towards him, if they were to appoint any other person as your successor.

Farewell. I will not fail to write when any further intelligence reaches me respecting the proposal from the prisoners.

I have written from the War Office, and in such haste, and with so many interruptions, that I can scarcely, in reading my letter, decipher my own hand, and I am afraid you will experience still greater difficulty. I assure you in these times it is seldom I can catch an hour for private correspondence.

25.—1798. ORIGIN AND PROGRESS OF "UNITED IRISH" MOVEMENTS.

Memoir or detailed statement of the origin and progress of the Irish Union: Delivered to the Irish Government by Messrs. Thomas Addis Emmet, Arthur O'Connor, and William James M'Neven, August the 4th, 1798.

The disunion that had long existed between the Catholics and Protestants of Ireland, particularly those of the Presbyterian religion, was found by experience to be so great an obstacle to the obtaining a reform in parliament, on any thing of just and popular principles, that some persons, equally friendly to that measure and to religious toleration, conceived the idea of uniting both sects in pursuance of the same object—a repeal of the penal laws, and a reform, including in itself an extension of the right of suffrage to the Catholic.

From this originated the societies of the United Irishmen in the end of the year 1791; even then it was clearly perceived that the chief support of the borough interest in Ireland was the weight of English influence; but as yet that obvious remark had not led the minds of the reformers towards a separation from England. Some individuals, perhaps, had convinced themselves that benefit would result to this country from such a measure; but during the whole existence of the society of United Irishmen of Dublin, we may safely aver, to the best of our knowledge and recollections, that no such object was ever agitated by its members, either in public debate or private conversation; nor until the society had lasted a considerable time, were any traces of republicanism to be met with there; its views were purely, and in good faith, what the test of the society avows. Those, however, were sufficient to excite the most lively uneasiness in the friends of Protestant ascendancy and unequal representation; insomuch that the difficulty of their attainment, notwithstanding the beginning union of sects, became manifest. But with the difficulty, the necessity of the measure was still more obvious; and the disposition of the people to run greater risks, for what they conceived both difficult and necessary to be had, was increased. This will sufficiently account for the violent expressions and extraordinary proposals that are attributed to that society. One of the latter was, that of endeavouring, at some future, but undetermined time, to procure the meeting of a convention which should take into consideration the best mode of effecting a reform in parliament, as had been done in the year 1784. It was thought the weight and power of such a body, backed, as it was hoped it would be, with the support of Catholic and Protestant, and the increased spirit towards liberty which arose from the French revolution, would procure a more favourable issue to the efforts of that convention than had attended those of the former; but the object, as yet, went no further than a reform in parliament, only on more broad and liberal principles.

The discussion, however, of political questions, both foreign and domestic, and the enacting of several unpopular laws, had advanced the minds of many people, even before they were aware of it, towards republicanism and revolution; they began to reason on the subject, and to think a republican form of government was preferable to our own; but they still considered it as impossible to be obtained, in consequence of the English power and connection. This, together with its being constantly perceived that the weight of English was thrown into the scale of borough interest, gradually rendered the connection itself an object of discussion, and its advantages somewhat problematical. While the minds of men were taking this turn, the society of United Irishmen in Dublin was in the year 1794 forcibly dissolved, but the principles by which it was actuated were as strong as ever; as hypocrisy was not of the vices of that society, it brought its destruction on itself by the openness of its discussion and publicity of its proceeding. Its fate was a warning to that of Belfast, and suggested the idea of forming societies with the same object, but whose secrecy should be their protection. The first of these societies was, as we best recollect, in the year 1795. In order to secure co-operation and uniformity of action, they organized a system of committees, baronial, county, and provincial, and even national; but it was long before the skeleton of this organization was filled up. While the formation of these societies was in agitation, the friends of liberty were gradually, but with a timid step, advancing towards republicanism, they began to be convinced that it would be as easy to obtain a revolution as a reform, so obstinately was the latter resisted, and as the conviction impressed itself on their minds, they were inclined not to give up the struggle, but to extend their views; it was for this reason that in their test the words are, 'an equal representation of all the people of Ireland,' without inserting the word 'parliament.' The test embraced both the republican and the reformer, and left to future circumstances to decide to which the common strength should be directed; but still the whole body, we are convinced, would stop short at reform. Another consideration, however, led the minds of the reflecting United Irishmen to look towards a republic and separation from England—this was the war with France; they clearly perceived that their strength was not likely to become speedily equal to wresting from the English and the borough interest in Ireland even a reform; foreign assistance would, therefore, perhaps become necessary; but foreign assistance could only be hoped for in proportion as the object to which it would be applied was important to the party giving it. A reform in the Irish Parliament was no object to the French—a separation of Ireland from England was a mighty one indeed. Thus, they reasoned: shall we, between two objects, confine ourselves to the least valuable, even though it is equally difficult to be obtained, if we consider the relation of Ireland with the rest of Europe.

Whatever progress the United system had made among the Catholics throughout the kingdom, until after the recall of lord Fitzwilliam (notwithstanding many resolutions which had appeared from them, manifesting a growing spirit), they were considered as not only entertaining an habitual predilection for monarchy, but also as being less attached than the Presbyterians to political liberty. There were, however, certain men among them who rejoiced at the rejection of their claims, because it gave them an opportunity of pointing out that the adversaries of reform were their adversaries; and that these two objects could never be separated with any chance of success to either. They used the recall of that nobleman, and the rejection of his measures, to cement together in political union the Catholic and Presbyterian masses.

The modern societies, for their protection against informers and persecution, had introduced into their test a clause of secrecy. They did more—they changed the engagements of their predecessors into an oath; and mutual confidence increased when religion was called in aid of mutual security.

While they were almost entirely confined to the north, but increasing rapidly there, the Insurrection bill was passed in the beginning of the year 1796, augmenting the penalties upon administering unlawful oaths, or solemn obligations, even to death ; but death had ceased to alarm men who began to think it was to be encountered in their country's cause. The statute remained an absolute dead letter, and the numbers of the body augmented beyond belief.

To the Armagh persecution is the Union of Irishmen most exceedingly indebted. The persons and properties of the wretched Catholics of that county were exposed to the merciless attacks of an Orange faction, which was certainly in many instances uncontrolled by the justices of peace, and claimed to be in all supported by Government. When these men found that illegal acts of magistrates were indemnified by occasional statutes, and the courts of justice shut against them by parliamentary barriers, they began to think they had no refuge but in joining the Union. Their dispositions so to do were increased by finding the Presbyterians, of Belfast especially, step forward to espouse their cause and succour their distress. We will here remark, once for all, what we most solemnly aver, that wherever the Orange system was introduced, particularly in Catholic counties, it was uniformly observed that the numbers of United Irishmen increased most astonishingly. The alarm which an Orange lodge excited among the Catholics made them look for refuge by joining together in the United system ; and as their numbers were always greater than that of bigoted Protestants, our harvest was ten-fold. At the same time that we mention this circumstance, we must confess, and most deeply regret, that it excited a mutual acrimony and vindictive spirit, which was peculiarly opposite to the interest, and abhorrent to the feelings of the United Irishmen, and has lately manifested itself, we hear, in outrages of so much horror.

Defenderism has been supposed to be the origin of the modern societies of United Irishmen ; this is undoubtedly either a mistake or a misrepresentation ; we solemnly declare that there was no connection between them and the United Irish, as far as we know, except what follows :

After the Defenders had spread into different counties, they manifested a rooted but unenlightened aversion, among other things, to the same grievances that were complained of by the Union. They were composed almost entirely of Catholics, and those of the lowest order, who, through a false confidence, were risking themselves, and the attainment of redress, by premature and unsystematic insurrection. In the north they were also engaged in an acrimonious and bloody struggle with an opposite faction, called Peep-of-day boys. The advantage of reconciling these two misguided parties, of joining them in the Union, and so turning them from any views they might have exclusively religious, and of restraining them from employing a mutually destructive exertion of force, most powerfully struck the minds of several United Irishmen. For that purpose, many of them in the northern counties went among both, but particularly the Defenders, joined with them, showed the superiority of the Union system, and gradually, while Government was endeavouring to quell them by force, melted them down into the United Irish body. This rendered their conduct infinitely more orderly, and less suspicious to Government.

It has been alleged against the United Irishmen that they established a system of assassination. Nothing that has ever been imputed to them, that we feel more pleasure in being able to disavow. In such immense numbers as were to be found in that body, although uniformity of system may have given a wonderful uniformity of action, yet it is unfair and unjust to charge the whole body with the vices of a few of its members: individual grievances produced individual resentment, and the meeting of many sufferers in the same way, frequently caused them to concur in the same resolutions. It appears, indeed, by some trials, that a baronial once took that subject into consideration, but it was manifest it was taken up by them as individuals, whose principles, as it afterwards appeared, were not repugnant to the act. A committee of assassination has been much talked of—we have heard persons mentioned as members of it, whom we know, from the most private and confidential conversations, to be utterly abhorrent from the crime. We solemnly declare, we believe that such a committee never existed. We most positively aver, it never was with the cognizance of any part of the Union. We also declare, that in no communication from those who were placed at the head of the United Irishmen, to the rest of that body, and in no official paper, was assassination ever inculcated, but frequently and fervently reprobated. It was considered by them with horror, on account of its criminality—and with personal dread, because it would render ferocious the minds of men in whose hands their lives were placed, most particularly placed; inasmuch as between them and the rest of that body they were out of the protection of the law. In proof of this assertion, we would beg leave to refer to a sketch of a publication which we believe was seized among the papers of one of us, at the time of his arrest, and which it was intended should appear if the paper to which it alluded had not been discontinued.— One other consideration, which we entreat may not offend, will, we hope, be decisive. If such committee had existed, and if the men at the head of the United Irishmen had thought assassination a justifiable mode of obtaining their ends, and had been capable of encouraging such atrocity, possessed as they were of wide-spread means of acting, and powerful control over men, who, it is now manifest, held the loss of life in utter contempt, the poniard would have been directed, not against such petty objects as an obnoxious country magistrate or an informer.

We were none of us members of the United system until September or October in the year 1796; at that time, it must be confessed, the reasons already alleged, and the irritations of the preceding summer in the north, had disposed us to a separation and republic, principally because we were hopeless that a reform would ever be yielded to any peaceable exertions of the people. We cannot be accurate as to the progress either of the numbers or organization of the United Irishmen, it having been an invariable rule to burn all the returns or other papers after they ceased to be useful. We have no documents wherewith to refresh our memories; but we apprehend the report of the secret committee to be, in that case, sufficiently accurate, except that the numbers were always much greater than appeared by those reports. The documents on which they rely only noticed those who went regularly into societies; but great numbers, perhaps, at a rough guess, half as many were sworn to the test, who were prevented by private motives and local circumstances from committing themselves in that way: we are, however, convinced that the numbers of the whole body could not latterly be less than 500,000.

The return from the different societies and committees upwards, specified, among other things, arms and ammunition; they were not originally included in them, nor were they introduced until after the passing the Insurrection and Indemnity acts, when the people began to be more than ever carried towards resistance, and were extremely irritated by the indemnified violations of law in the north. The returns also stated, sums of money having been collected; those sums were always very small, and applied towards the support of persons imprisoned on charges connected with the Union, and in conducting of their defences; any other expenses were defrayed by occasional private subscriptions.

The printed constitution mentions a national committee: none such, strictly speaking, was ever formed at first, because to its appointment two provincials at least were necessary; and before the organization in any other part of the kingdom could reach to a provincial, the immense number in Ulster required a supreme head. Some persons were then chosen by the northern provincial, with powers to associate to themselves such others as they should think fit. They were commonly called the executive. When the organization began in Leinster, and shortly after the French left Bantry bay, some persons resident in this province were associated to that body; things continued thus until many began to think that elections should take place pursuant to the constitution. The fidelity of the people had by that time been so abundantly proved, that men did not hesitate to submit themselves to a guarded election by the Leinster provincial. National delegates were therefore chosen by it, who acted for their own province, and occasionally consulted with the executive of the north on subjects of general importance. The election of national delegates first took place, as we best recollect, about the latter end of November or December, 1797.

The military organization had no existence until towards the latter end of 1796, and was as near as could be engrafted on the civil: in order to avoid giving alarm, it continued to conceal itself as much as possible under the usual denominations. The secretary of a society of twelve was commonly the petty officer; the delegate of five societies to a lower baronial, when the population required such an intermediate step, was usually the captain, and the delegate from the lower to the upper baronial elected by those they were to command, but at that point the interference of the societies ceased, and every higher commission was in the was usually the colonel. All officers to colonels up were indispensably appointment of the executive; only as soon as sufficient numbers of regiments were organized in any county, the colonels were directed to transmit to the executive the names of three persons fit, in their opinion, to act as adjutants-general for that county; of those the executive choose one; and through this organ all military communications were made to the several counties. In consequence of such arrangements, not more than one of the executive need ever be committed with any county, and that only to a person of his own choice from among three. It so happened that the same member was entitled to hold communication with several adjutants-general, which still further diminished the risk to the executive: we refer to the amended printed constitution, where the military organization, without being named, is more correctly set forth than we can give it from memory. As to the manner in which these men were to be provided with arms and ammunition, every man who could afford it was directed to provide himself with a musket, bayonet, and as much ammunition as he could; every other man with a pike, and, if he was able, a case of pistols; but this, we apprehend, was not strictly adhered to. We have heard it said, that treasurers were appointed for raising money to purchase arms, but no such appointment was ever made, at least by the executive. Perhaps some private societies might have adopted such a measure.

In many instances the lower orders went about to private houses to search for arms; this the executive constantly endeavoured to prevent, because they were unwilling to raise alarm in their adversaries, or let the members of their body acquire habits of plunder, and be confounded with robbers. They endeavoured to dissuade them from these acts, by representing to the people that the arms would always be kept in better condition by the gentlemen than by them, and could be easily seized whenever necessary. In other respects our stores were in the arsenal in the castle, and the military depots throughout the country; our supplies were in the treasury.

A military committee was appointed by the executive in February, 1798, for the principal purpose of preparing plans of operations, either in case of a premature insurrection, if we should be unfortunately and unwillingly forced into one, or of the invasion from France. As a committee it did nothing; but some of its members took up the consideration of the latter subject, and framed instructions how to act in case of a landing of a foreign force. These were sent by the executive to such adjutants-general as had received their appointments; they generally went to use every effort in favour of the French.

Attempts were made with as much zeal as the necessary caution would permit, to introduce the system among the military, the militia especially; but the reports of the agents were mostly confused and unsatisfactory, so that the success of the measure could never be ascertained with any tolerable accuracy.

We have read in some evidence lately given, that a person was appointed colonel by a commission from a general in the rebel army. We must beg leave to doubt, if not deny, the truth of that assertion. No general was ever chosen for Leinster, and colonels were always appointed by their captains; they derived their authority from this appointment, not from any commission of a general.

If Irish officers in foreign service had joined in our cause, they would have been gladly received, and rapidly promoted. Indeed an attempt to procure that was actually set on foot; we counted on their attachment to the native soil, and hatred to England, as a substitute for republicanism; and when they should be convinced that such a form of government was the best security for the permanent separation of the two countries, we were sure of their fidelity. It so happened, however, from the delay of peace on the Continent, or because our agent was over-cautious in conducting the negotiation lest it should become known to the respective potentates, and communicated to the British court, that nothing in consequence of it has hitherto been effected.

We can aver, that no general plan of insurrection existed before the 12th of March, 1798; but some individuals had perhaps formed local ones, adapted to taking Dublin, and a few other places. When the north was on the point of rising, after the celebrated proclamation of general Lake, a plan of operations had been suggested for that occasion, which was destroyed as soon as the people were dissuaded from the enterprize, of which we cannot now speak with any degree of precision.

Several recommendations were occasionally handed down from the executive, through the committees, the dates or contents of which we cannot undertake to detail, unless they should be called to our recollection. The most remarkable, as they now occur to us, was a recommendation to abstain from spirituous and exciseable articles, not so much to destroy the resources of Government, as for the purpose of preserving sobriety, which was so necessary to secrecy; and morality, which was so necessary to good order. It may be right to remark, that the recommendation was, however painful to the people and contrary to their former habits, most astonishingly complied with. The executive also directed to discourage the circulation of bank notes, and published a hand-bill cautioning against the purchasing of quit-rents, pursuant to a scheme then in agitation, declaring that, as such a sale was an anticipation of the future resources of the country, it should not be allowed to stand good in the event of a revolution. The reasons for these publications are obvious. We must here remark, that many things were entrusted by the executive to some one of its members; it having been an invariable rule, that no more than one of them should, on any occasion, be committed with persons not of its body. For this reason, many things here stated are set forth on the credit of one individual, but believed by the remainder.

About the middle of 1796, a meeting of the executive took place, more important in its discussions and its consequences, than any that had preceded it; as such we have thought ourselves bound to give an account of it with the most perfect frankness, and more than ordinary precision. This meeting took place in consequence of a letter from one of the society, who had emigrated on account of political opinions: it mentioned that the state of the country had been represented to the Government of France in so favourable a point of view, as to induce them to resolve upon invading Ireland, for the purpose of enabling it to separate itself from Great Britain. On this solemn and important occasion a serious review was taken of the state of the Irish nation at that period: it was observed that a desperate ferment existed in the public mind. A resolution in favour of a parliamentary reform had indeed been passed in 1795 by the House of Commons; but after it had been frustrated by several successive adjournments, all hope of its attainment vanished, and its friends were everywhere proscribed; the Volunteers were put down; all power of meeting by delegation for any political purpose, the mode in which it was most usual and expedient to co-operate on any subject of importance, was taken away at the same time. The provocations of the year 1794, the recall of lord Fitzwilliam, and the re-assumption of coercive measures that followed it, were strongly dwelt on: the county of Armagh had been long desolated by two contending factions, agreeing only in one thing, an opinion that most of the active magistrates in that county treated one party with the most fostering kindness, and the other with the most rigorous persecution. It was stated that so marked a partiality exasperated the sufferers, and those who sympathized in their misfortunes. It was urged with indignation, that notwithstanding the greatness of the military establishment in Ireland, and its having been able to suppress the Defenders in various counties, it was not able, or was not employed, to suppress these outrages in that county, which drove 7,000 persons from their native dwellings. The magistrates, who took no steps against the Orangemen, were said to have overleaped the boundaries of law to pursue and punish the Defenders. The Government seemed to take upon themselves those injuries by the Indemnity act, and even honoured the violators; and by the Insurrection act, which enabled the same magistrates, if they choose, under colour of law, to act anew the same abominations. Nothing, it was contended, could more justly excite the spirit of resistance, and determine men to appeal to arms, than the Insurrection act; it punished with death the administering of oaths, which in their opinion were calculated for the most virtuous and honourable purposes. The power of proclaiming counties, and quieting them by breaking open the cabins of the peasants between sunset and sunrise, by seizing the inmates, and sending them on board tenders, without the ordinary interposition of a trial by jury, had, it was alleged, irritated beyond endurance the minds of the reflecting, and the feelings of the unthinking inhabitants of that province. It was contended that even according to the constitution and example of 1688, when the protection of the constituted authorities was drawn from the subject, allegiance, the reciprocal duty ceased, to bind; when the people were not redressed, they had a right to resist, and were free to seek for allies wherever they were to be found. The English revolutionists of 1688 called in the aid of a foreign republic to overthrow their oppressors. There had sprung up in our own time a much more mighty republic, which, by its offers of assistance to break the chains of slavery, had drawn on itself a war with the enemies of our freedom, and now particularly tendered us its aid. These arguments prevailed, and it was resolved to employ the proffered assistance for the purpose of separation. We are aware it is suspected that negotiations between the United Irishmen and the French were carried on at an earlier period than that now alluded to, but we solemnly declare such suspicion is ill-founded. In consequence of this determination of the executive, an agent was dispatched to the French directory, who acquainted them with it, stated the dispositions of the people, and the measures which caused them. He received fresh assurances that the succours should be sent as soon as the armament could be got ready.

About October, 1796, a messenger from the republic arrived, who, after authenticating himself, said he came to be informed of the state of the country, and to tell the leaders of the United Irishmen of the intention of the French to invade it speedily with 15,000 men, and a great quantity of arms and ammunition; but neither mentioned the precise time nor the place, doubting, we suppose, our caution or our secrecy. Shortly after his departure, a letter arrived from a quarter which there was reason to look on as confidential, stating that they would invade England in the spring, and positively - Ireland. The reason of this contradiction has never been explained; but the consequence of it, and the messenger not having specified the place of landing, were, that when the armament arrived in December, 1796, at Bantry bay, they came at a time and in a port we had not foreknown.

After the intended descent had failed, it occurred to some of the members of the association, and their friends in the city, and to some of the most considerate of the United Irishmen, that one more attempt should be made in favour of parliamentary reform They hoped that the terrible warning which had been given by the facility of reaching our coasts, and, if the armament had landed, the possibility at least of its succeeding, would have shown the borough proprietors the necessity of conceding to the popular wish. The storm had dispersed a cloud big with danger, but it might again collect, and the thunder of republic and revolution again roll, and burst over their heads. This was then judged the best moment to persuade them, in the midst of their fears, to a measure strictly counter-revolutionary.

We think it but right to state, that no greater connection ever subsisted between any of the members of the opposition and the United Irishmen, except in this instance, and for the accomplishment of this purpose. In consequence of these joint efforts a meeting was held at the exchange, which declared in favour of reform, and a proposal of that nature was submitted to parliament. If in the course of that effort for reform it had not become evident that success was hopeless, it was the wish of many among us, and we believe the executive would have gladly embraced the occasion of declining to hold any further intercourse with France, except sending a messenger there to tell them that the difference between government and the people had been adjusted, and that they would have no business a second time to attempt a landing. In fact, no attempt or advance was made to renew the negotiation till April, 1797, when an agent was sent. In the May following, the well-known proclamation of general Lake appeared. This very much increased the ferment of the public mind, and the wish for the return of the French, to get rid of the severities of martial law. It did more—it goaded many people of the north to press the executive to an insurrection, independent of foreign aid.

About this time a letter arrived, which assured us the French would come again, and requesting that a person should be sent over to make previous arrangements. The eagerness of those in the north, who were urgent for insurrection, was checked by making known this communication to them, and entreating for delay; it was resisted likewise by some of the most sober and reflecting among themselves, who were of opinion they were not yet sufficiently prepared for the attempt. Those considerations prevailed, particularly as, in order to enforce them, an advantage was taken of the wish expressed by their enemies that the people might rise.

The impatience, however, which was manifested on this occasion, and the knowledge that it was only controlled by the expectation of speedy and foreign assistance, determined the executive to send an agent speedily to France in answer to the letter. This person departed in the latter end of June, 1797. By both these agents, rather a small number of men, with a great quantity of arms, ammunition, artillery and officers were required; a small force only was asked for, because the executive, faithful to the principle of Irish independence, wished for what they deemed just sufficient to liberate their country, but incompetent to subdue it. Their most determined resolution, and that of the whole body, being collected as far as its opinions could be taken, always has been in no event to let Ireland come under the dominion of France; but it was offered to pay the expenses of the expedition. The number required was 10,000 men at the most, and at the least 5,000. The executive inclined to the larger number; but even with the smaller the general opinion among them was, there could be no doubt of success. As to the quantity of arms, by the first messenger 40,000 stand were specified, but by the second, as much more as could be sent. The difference arose from the disarming that had gone on in the north, and the increasing numbers who were ready to use them. The executive also instructed its agents to negotiate for a loan of money, if it could be had in France; if not, to negotiate with Spain—the sum was half a million. Our second agent, on his arrival at Hamburg, wrote a memorial containing those and other details, a copy of which some way or other, we perceive the Government has obtained, and therefore refer to it. He then proceeded to Paris, to treat further on the business, where he presented a second memorial; the object of this was to urge motives arising out of the state of affairs, which would induce the Directory not to postpone the invasion. We cannot precisely state the whole of its contents, as, according to the practice already mentioned, no copy of it has been preserved; but it went to demonstrate that the disposition which then existed in the Irish mind was in no future contingency to be expected, nor in any subsequent rupture between Great Britain and the French republic; that his majesty's ministers must see Ireland would infallibly become the seat of war, if they did not previously remove those grievances, the existence of which would naturally invite, and prove a powerful auxiliary to the enemy. Such a rupture, it was observed, must be in the contemplation of the British cabinet, as several of its most leading members declared that they considered the existence of the British monarchy incompatible with that of the republic. Conciliation, then, according to every rule of policy and common sense, would be ultimately adopted; and though it should fall short of the wishes of the people, it was asserted, if once possessed of a reasonable share of liberty, they would not be brought to run the chance of a revolution in order to obtain a more perfect system of freedom.

Our second agent, while at Paris, and pending the negotiation at Lisle, was told by some of the persons in power in France, that if certain terms, not specified to him, were offered by the English, peace would certainly be made. However, after the negotiation was broken off, he received positive assurance that the Irish never should be abandoned until a separation was effected, and that they should be left entirely at their own option to choose their own form of government.

About this time a person came over, informing us that a considerable army was ready, and embarked at the Texel, destined for Ireland, and only waiting for a wind. The troops afterwards disembarked, but we are ignorant of the reason why they never sailed, except, perhaps, that the wind continued so long adverse that the provisions were exhausted, and that in the meantime disturbances broke out in the French Government. It may be proper to remark, that in none of the communications or negotiations with France, did the Government of that country ever intimate the place they would land, or, except in the first, the force they would bring.

Sometime in the beginning of the year a letter was received from France, stating that the succours might be expected in April. Why the promise was not fulfilled we have never learned. We know nothing of further communications from any foreign State, nor of the future plan of operations of the French; but we are convinced they will not abandon the plan of separating this country from England, so long as the discontents of the people would induce them to support an invasion.

Let us, then, while Ireland is yet our country, be indulged in a few remarks, which we deem extremely important to its future prosperity; now that we have given these full and faithful details of the past, we cannot be suspected of any but pure and disinterested motives in what we are about to say, ere we leave it for ever. The parts we have acted have enabled us to gain the most intimate knowledge of the dispositions and hearts of our countrymen. From that knowledge we speak, when we declare our deepest conviction that the penal laws, which have followed in such doleful and rapid succession—the house-burnings, arbitrary imprisonments, free quarters, and, above all, the tortures to extort confessions—neither have had, or can have, any other effect but exciting the most lively rancour in the hearts of almost all the people of Ireland against those of their countrymen who have had recourse to such measures for maintaining their power, and against the connection with Great Britain, whose men and whose aid have been poured in to assist them.

The matchless fidelity which has marked the Union—the unexampled firmness and contempt of death displayed by so many thousands at the halbert, in the field, in the goal, and at the gibbet—exempt us from claiming any belief on our personal credit. If the hearts of the people be not attached by some future measures, this nation will be again and more violently disturbed, on the coming of a foreign force. If a reform be adopted founded upon the abolition of corporations and boroughs, as constituent bodies, and the equal division of the representatives among those who may be entitled to the elective suffrage, the best possible step will be taken for preserving the monarchial constitution and British connection. For the success of this measure we would not now answer; but of this we are sure—you must either extirpate or reform.

The hurry and still agitated minds with which we write, will, we hope, not only apologize for any inaccuracy of style, but likewise serve the much more important purpose of excusing any expressions that may not be deemed sufficiently circumspect. Much as we wish to stop the effusion of blood, and the present scene of useless horrors, we have not affected a change of principles which would only bring on us the imputation of hypocrisy, when it is our most anxious wish to evince perfect sincerity and good faith. We, however, entreat Government to be assured that while it is so much our interest to conciliate, it is far from our intention to offend.

ARTHUR O'CONNOR, THOMAS ADDIS EMMET, WILLIAM JAMES MAC NEVEN.

26.—1798. NEGOTIATIONS WITH PRISONERS.—SECRET COMMITTEE.— MOVEMENTS IN CARLOW.—ORANGE SOCIETIES.—WICKLOW.

William Elliot to Thomas Pelham.

Dublin, 7 August, 1798.

Since I wrote to you last week Government has received a paper drawn up and signed by O'Connor, Emmet and Mac Neven, containing the substance of all the information which they state it is in their power to give. Lord Castlereagh is in possession of the memoir, and Marshall has promised to send you either a copy or an abstract of it. There is not much new matter in it, but it is a complete confirmation of the intelligence which has been hitherto received, and you will perceive that Mac Neven recognizes his memoir on the subject of invasion. Mac Neven is to be examined to-day before the secret committee. I should conceive that further information of importance may be obtained from some of the other prisoners. Cooke had a few days ago a long conversation with a man of the name of Ivers, who is confined at Kilmainham. Though he was not above the condition of a mat-maker, he was the principal agitator of the county of Carlow, and Cooke represents him to be a man of extraordinary talents. He told Cooke that lord Fitzwilliam's departure had a considerable influence on the minds of the people in the county of Carlow and the parts of the country adjacent. He said also that the conviction had been obtained under the Insurrection act by perjury, which had exasperated the people; but the principal cause which he assigned for the rapid progress of the system of the United Irishmen in that part of the kingdom, was the institution of Orange societies there. These associations have certainly been mischievous in their effects in all quarters of the kingdom, and I cannot divest myself of the belief that their influence was peculiarly injurious in the county of Wexford previous to the rebellion. All parts of the country are now quiet except the county of Wicklow, which still continues to be infested with banditti.

27.—1798. EXAMINATION OF WILLIAM JAMES MAC NEVEN BEFORE THE SECRET COMMITTEE OF THE HOUSE OF LORDS, DUBLIN, AUGUST 7, 1798.

I took the following minute of my examinations before the secret committees of the lords and commons, being convinced that they would not publish the entire of my answers, and that I should possibly find it necessary, in vindication of truth, to publish them myself. The garbled, disingenuous report of these committees has appeared, and when I had an opportunity of complaining to the lord chancellor [Clare] of the unfairness with which my examinations are set forth in the appendix to it, he did not deny the fact, but declared very roundly, I must not expect they would publish more of them than would answer their purpose. This, to be sure, was candid, and I will not conceal one of the very few merits I can allow his lordship.

The lord chancellor had before him extracts from the memoir which we sent to lord Castlereagh on the 4th of August, in fulfilment of our agreement with Government. They related to the facts detailed in our paper concerning the history and progress of the Union, detached from an account of the motives and abuses which were stated by us to have given rise to the resolutions we adopted. The examination was altogether conducted in a manner to obtain for such parts of the memoir a certain authenticity for publication without publishing the memoir itself. He went into a minute examination of the civil and military organization, and the various communications with France. When he came to that part which mentions a memoir given to the French minister at Hamburg, he turned to an extract of a copy of it which he had before him. Upon some subsequent occasion he said that no copy of the entire was ever sent from England, and in this I can readily believe him. He asked how that memoir happened to be given to the French minister? I answered that the Irish agent applied to the French minister for a passport to go into France, which the minister made some difficulty in granting, but called for a memoir, and offered to transmit it to his Government. The memoir was accordingly written, and soon after the person got a passport. This tedious examination took up several hours.

Lord Chancellor. Pray, Dr. Mac Neven, what number of troops did the Irish directory require from the French Government for the invasion of Ireland?

Mac Neven. The *minimum* force was 5,000 men, the *maximum* 10,000; with that number, and a large quantity of arms and ammunition, we knew that an Irish army could be formed and disciplined; this, aided by the universal wish of the people to shake off the yoke, we had no doubt would succeed; and we were always solicitous that no foreign force should be able to dictate in our country: Liberty and national independence being our object, we never meant to engage in a struggle for a change of masters.

Lord Chancellor. Was not your object a separation from England?

Mac Neven. It certainly became our object when we were convinced that liberty was not otherwise attainable; our reasons for this determination are given in the memoir; it was a measure we were forced into, inasmuch as I am now, and always have been of opinion, that if we were an independent republic, and Britain ceased to be formidable to us, our interest would require an intimate connexion with her.

Lord Chancellor. Such as subsists between England and America?

Mac Neven. Something like it, my Lord.

Archbishop of Cashel. In plain English, that Ireland should stand on her own bottom, and trade with every other country, just according as she found it would be her interest?

Mac Neven. Precisely, my lord; I have not, I own, any idea of sacrificing the interests of Ireland to those of any other country; nor why we should not, in that and in every respect, be as free as the English themselves.

Archbishop of Cashel. Ireland could not support herself alone.

Mac Neven. In my opinion she could; and if once her own mistress, would be invincible against England and France together; but this, my lord, is a combination never to be expected. If necessary, I could bring as many proofs in support of this opinion as a thing admits of which may be only supported or opposed by probabilities.

Lord Kilwarden. Had the north any intention of rising in rebellion in the summer of 1797?

Mac Neven. It had an intention of rising in arms after general Lake's proclamation.

Lord Kilwarden. What prevented it?

Mac Neven. The people of the north were made acquainted with assurances received about this time from France, that the expected succours would be shortly sent to us; and it was represented to them that we would be giving the English a great advantage by beginning before they arrived. For this, as well as other reasons, I was always averse to our beginning by ourselves.

Lord Kilwarden. Then, if you thought you would have succeeded, you would have begun?

Mac Neven. Most probably we should; at the same time I am bound to declare that it was our wish to act with French aid, because that would tend to make the revolution less bloody, by determining many to join in it early, who, while the balance of success was doubtful, would either retain an injurious neutrality, or even perhaps oppose it.

Lord Kilwarden. The Union held to the poor an assurance that their condition would be ameliorated: how was this to be accomplished?

Mac Neven. In the first place, by an abolition of tithes; and in the next, by establishing such an order of things as would give more free scope to their industry, and secure to them a better recompense for it.

Archbishop of Cashel. You know very well if tithes were abolished the landlords would raise the rents, and the tenant would not be benefited.

Mac Neven. I know, my lord, that during the period of the lease, at least, there would be no such rise; but that now, year after year, there is not a single improvement made by the tenant without the parson's getting a proportion of the profits; it is a tax which increases in proportion to the tenant's industry, and encroaches on his capital in order to form an income for a man to whom he is not indebted for any service; and in general there is the loss of the full tenth between the incumbent and his proctor.

Archbishop of Cashel. Can you account for the massacres committed upon the Protestants by the Papists in the county of Wexford?

Mac Neven. My lord, I am far from being the apologist of massacres, however provoked; but if I am rightly informed as to the conduct of the magistrates of that county, the massacres you allude to were acts of retaliation upon enemies, much more than of fanaticism Moreover, my lord, it has been the misfortune of this country scarcely ever to have known the English natives or settlers otherwise than as enemies; and in his language the Irish peasant has but one name for Protestant and Englishman, and confounds them; he calls both by the name of *Sasanagh;* his indignation, therefore, is *less against a religionist* than against a *foe;* his prejudice is the effect of the ignorance he is kept in, and the treatment he receives. How can we be surprised at it, when so much pains are taken to brutalize him?

Lord Chancellor. I agree with Dr. Mac Neven; the Irish peasant considers the two words as synonymous; he calls the Protestant and Englishman, indifferently, *Sasanagh.*

Lord Kilwarden. I suppose the religious establishment would be abolished with the tithes?

Mac Neven. I suppose it would.

Lord Kilwarden. Would you not set up another?

Mac Neven. No, indeed.

Lord Kilwarden. Not the Roman Catholic?

Mac Neven. I would no more consent to that than I would to the establishment of Mahometanism.

Lord Kilwarden. What would you do then?

Mac Neven. That which they do in America? let each man profess the religion of his conscience, and pay his own pastor.

Lord Chancellor. Do you think the mass of the people in the provinces of Leinster, Munster and Connaught, care the value of this pen, or the drop of ink it contains, for parliamentary reform or Catholic emancipation.

Mac Neven. I am sure they do not [if by the mass of the people your lordship means the common illiterate people; they do not understand it]. What they very well understand is, that it would be a very great advantage to them to be relieved from the payment of tithes [and not to be fleeced by their landlords; but there is not a man who can read a newspaper, who has not considered the question of reform, and was not once at least attached to that measure; the people of the least education understand it; and why the common people, whose opinion on every other occasion is so little valued, should be made the criterion of public opinion on this, I do not know].*

Lord Chancellor. I dare say they all understand it better than I do?

Mac Neven. As to Catholic emancipation, the importance of that question has passed away long since; it really is not worth a moment's thought at the present period.

Lord Dillon. Has the Union extended much into Connaught?

Mac Neven. It has, very considerably.

Lord Dillon. I did not think so. What is the extent of the organization?

Mac Neven. Less, perhaps, than in other places; it got later into Connaught, but very great numbers have taken the test. From the misery of the poor people, and the oppressiveness of landlords in many parts of that province, we have no doubt but if the French ever land in force there, they will be joined by thousands, probably by the whole of its population.

---

* "All that part of the answer inclosed within brackets, has been purposely omitted in the published report of the secret committee of the House of Lords. Here, where the entire answer is set down, the effect of the suppression in altering the sense is manifest. But long before, Sydney was forced to observe to another corrupt judge, that if he took the Scripture by pieces, he would make all the penmen of the Scripture blasphemers. He might accuse David of saying there was no God; and accuse the Evangelists of saying Christ was a blasphemer and a seducer; and the Apostles that they were drunk."

Archbishop of Cashel. If the French had made peace at Lisle, as you say they were willing to do, they would have left you in the lurch; and may they not do so again?

Mac Neven. The French Government declared that it would not deceive the Irish; and that it must make peace if England offered such terms as France had a right to expect; but that if the insincerity of the cabinet of St. James's should frustrate the negotiation, the Irish should never be abandoned; and I now consider the directory as bound by every tie of honour never to make peace until we are an independent nation.

Archbishop of Cashel. What security have you that the French would not keep this country as a conquest?

Mac Neven. Their interest and our power: If they attempted any such thing, they must know that England would not fail to take advantage of it; that she would then begin to get a sense of justice towards Ireland, and make us any offer short of separation, as she did to America, when by a like assistance America was enabled to shake off her yoke; moreover, it is not possible for the French to send any force into this country which would not be at the mercy of its inhabitants; but the example which was held out to them and to which they promised to conform, was that of Rochambeau in America.

A member of the Committee. To what number do you think the United Irishmen amounted all over the kingdom.

Mac Neven. Those who have taken the test, do not, I am convinced, fall short of 500,000, without reckoning women and old men. The number regularly organized is not less than 300,000; and I have no doubt all these will be ready to fight for the liberties of Ireland when they get a fair opportunity

Lord Chancellor. We shall not trouble you with any more questions.

28.—1798. EXAMINATION OF WILLIAM JAMES MAC NEVEN, BEFORE THE SECRET COMMITTEE OF THE HOUSE OF COMMONS, DUBLIN, AUGUST 8, 1798.

Lord Castlereagh. Dr. Mac Neven, the lords have sent us the minutes of your examination before them, and we only wish to trouble you with some questions relative to the interior state of the country.

Speaker [John Foster.] Pray, sir, what do you think occasioned the insurrection?

Mac Neven. The insurrection was occasioned by the house burnings, the whippings to extort confessions, the torture of various kinds, the free quarters, and the murders committed upon the people by the magistrates and the army.

Speaker. This only took place since the insurrection.

Mac Neven. It is more than twelve months (looking at Mr. Corry) since these horrors were perpetrated by the ancient Britons about Newry; and long before the insurrection they were quite common through the counties of Kildare and Carlow, and began to be practised with very great activity in the counties of Wicklow and Wexford.

Corry and Latouche. Yes, a few houses were burned.

Mac Neven. Gentlemen, there were a great deal more than a few houses burned.

Speaker. Would not the organization have gone on, and the Union become much stronger, but that the insurrection was brought forward too soon?

Mac Neven. The organization would have proceeded, and the Union have acquired that strength which arises from order; organization would at the same time have given a control over the people, capable of restraining their excesses; and you see scarcely any have been committed in those counties where it was well established.

Lord Castlereagh. You acknowledge the Union would have become stronger, *but for the means taken to make it explode.*

Mac Neven. It would every day have become more perfect, but I do not see anything in what has happened to deter the people from persevering in the Union and its object; on the contrary, if I am rightly informed, the trial of force must tend to give the people confidence in their own power—as I understand, it is now admitted that if the insurrection was general and well conducted, it would have been successful.

Sir J. Parnel. Do you know the population of Wexford county?

Mac Neven. Not exactly; but people agree that if the insurrection of a few counties in Leinster, unskilfully as it was directed, was so near overthrowing the Government, a general rising would have freed Ireland.

Lord Castlereagh. Were not the different measures of the Government, which are complained of, subsequent to various proceedings of the United Irishmen?

Mac Neven. Prior, my lord, to most of them; if your lordship desires it, I will prove, by comparison of dates, that Government throughout has been the aggressor.—*(His lordship was not curious.)*

Speaker (looking at the minutes from the lords). You say that you wished to keep back the insurrection; how do you reconcile that with the general plan of arming?

Mac Neven. From the time we had given up reform as hopeless, and determined to receive the French, we adopted a military organization, and prepared to be in a condition to co-operate with them; but it was always our wish to wait, if possible, their arrival. We wished to see liberty established in our country with the least possible expense of private happiness, and in such a way that no honest man of either party should have cause to regret it. We had before our eyes the revolution of 1688, in which a popular general, with only a small army, gave the friends of liberty an opportunity of declaring themselves; accordingly, upon that celebrated occasion, the junction of the people of England with king William was so extensive, that war and its concomitant evils were entirely precluded. I know the case would be the same here if there was a French landing.

Mr. Alexander. Although talents and education are to be found in the Union, yet there is no comparison in point of property between those who invited the French and those who brought in king William.

Mac Neven. Pardon me, sir; I know very many who possess probably much larger properties than did lord Danby, who signed the invitation to the prince of Orange, or than did lord Somers, who was the great champion of the revolution. The property in the Union is immense; but persons in a situation to be more easily watched, were not required to render themselves particularly conspicuous.

Speaker. But in case of a revolution, would not many persons be banished or destroyed, and their properties forfeited—for instance, the gentlemen here?

Mac Neven. We never had a doubt but in such an event many of those who profess to be the warmest friends of the British connection, would very quickly join us; and the readiness with which we have seen them support different other administrations, led us to suppose they might possibly do us the HONOUR of supporting our own. I am confident, sir, that in case of a revolution, the United Irishmen would behave better to their enemies than their enemies to them.

Speaker. Was not the 'Olive Branch,' and the arms she had on board, destined for this country?

Mac Neven. I never heard they were; arms have been frequently offered, but we always refused to accept them without troops; for we knew that insurrection would be the immediate consequence of a landing of arms, and we constantly declared to the French Government that we never meant to make our country a La Vendée, or the seat of Chouannerie.

Speaker. Do you think Catholic emancipation or parliamentary reform are objects of any importance with the common people?

Mac Neven. Catholic emancipation, as it is called, the people do not care about; I am sure they ought not now; they know, I believe, very generally, that it would be attended with no other effect than to admit into the House of Peers a few individuals who profess the Catholic religion, and enable some others to speculate in seats in the House of Commons. No man is so ignorant as to think this would be a national benefit. When lord Fitzwilliam was here, I considered the measure a good one, as it would have removed the pretext of those feuds and animosities which have desolated Ireland for two centuries, and have been lately so unhappily exacerbated; but now that those evils have occurred, which the stay of that nobleman would have prevented, they are not little measures which can remedy the grievances of this country.

[*Speaker*, looking over at somebody: See that.]

Speaker. But are you not satisfied that reform would go as little way to content the people as Catholic emancipation?

Mac Neven. Sir, I can best answer that question by declaring what the sentiments of the United Irishmen were at different periods. When Mr. Ponsonby brought in his first bill of reform, I remembered having conversed with some of the most confidential men in the north on that subject; and they declared to me they would think the country happy, and likely to think itself so, by getting that bill. When he brought in his last bill, I am sure the country at large would have been satisfied with the same.

Lord Castlereagh. They would have been satisfied to effect a revolution through a reform?

Mac Neven. If a change of system be one way or other inevitable, of which I have no doubt, and which you yourselves cannot but think highly probable, who can be so much interested in its occurring peaceably as you are. In any tranquil change you will retain your properties, and the immense influence which attaches to property; in such a situation, you would necessarily have a considerable share in the management of affairs; and I cannot conceive how a revolution, effected in such a manner, would much confound the order of society, or give any considerable shock to private happinesss.

Speaker. Don't you think the people would be dissatisfied with any reformed parliament which would not abolish the church establishment and tithes?

Mac Neven. I have no idea of a reformed parliament that would not act according to the interest and known wishes of the people. I am clear that tithes ought to be suppressed, and have no doubt the church establishment would follow.

A member. Would you not set up another?

Mac Neven. Most certainly not; I consider all church establishments as injurious to liberty and religion.

Mr. J. C. Beresford. Will you tell me what you understand by a free House of Commons?

Mac Neven. One which should be annually and freely returned by the people, and in which their interests, for the most part, should direct the decisions.

Mr. J. C. Beresford. What do you think of Potwollopping boroughs —they afford a specimen of universal suffrage?

Mac Neven. I know some adversaries of reform who have less reason to be displeased with them than I have, but they are a proof how useless would be any partial reform, and that a thing may be noxious in a detached state, which would form a valuable part of a good system.

A member. It seems we are reduced to the unfortunate situation of not being able to content the people without a reform which would overthrow the church establishment and break the connection with England?

Mac Neven. If you be in that situation, give me leave to tell you it was brought on by the perseverance with which every species of reform has always been refused, and the contumely manifested towards those who petitioned for it. Discussion was provoked by this treatment, and resentment excited: the consequences of which are now, that the people would probably exercise to its full extent whatever privilege they acquired, though if timely granted they would stop far short of the length to which it might be carried: this is the nature of man; but, sir, I see no necessary connection between the fall of the establishment and a separation from England.

Speaker. Sure if the head of the church was removed, the connection would be broken?

Mac Neven. It might be preserved through the king, if the Irish thought proper to retain it. As the parliament now exists, with two-thirds of it (if I may be allowed to speak frankly) the property of individuals in the pay of the British cabinet, the connection is indeed injurious to Ireland, and it is rendered so by the parliament; but if we had a free parliament, there might be a federal connection advantageous to both countries.

Sir J. Parnel. Under the federal connection, Ireland would not go to war when England pleased.

Mac Neven. I hope not. Were the connection of this nature, it would probably have preserved England from the present war, and rendered her the same kind of service which might be expected from a free House of Commons if she had one.

A member. What has hitherto prevented the French from invading this country?

Mac Neven. Nothing, I am sure, but inability; this, however, will not always last; and I have not the least doubt but, when it passes off, they will invade it, unless by a change of system you content the nation, and arm it against them; it will then defend itself, as it did before, by its Volunteers.

Speaker. What system?

Mac Neven. A system of coercion, and a system of injustice; to be replaced by a system of freedom.

Sir J. Parnel. Would you not be disposed, as well as other gentlemen who may have influence with the people, to exert it, in order to induce them to give up their arms, without the intervention of force?

Mac Neven. I cannot answer that question, unless I am told what equivalent is meant to be given them for such a surrender.

Sir J. Parnel. Pardon.

Mac Neven. They never considered it a crime to have arms, nor do I; on the contrary, they have been taught, and know it is a right of theirs, to possess them. If any attempt is made to take from them their arms, they will mistrust the motive, and think, not without reason, that it is intended by such conduct to leave them naked, at the mercy of their enemies.

Sir J. Parnel. Pikes are horrible weapons, and I don't know but a law might be passed against them.

Mac Neven. I am sure I have seen as strange laws passed without any difficulty; but one might equally as well be made against muskets and bayonets.

Sir J. Parnel. But pikes are not in the contemplation of the law which gives the subject the right of possessing arms.

Mac Neven. I believe, Sir John, the law which declares that right to belong to every freeman, was partly obtained by the pike.

Speaker. It was Magna Charta.

Lord Castlereagh. What is likely to be the effect of the insurrection that has been just put down?

Mac Neven. It will teach the people that caution which some of their friends less successfully endeavoured to inculcate; and I am afraid it will make them retaliate with a dreadful revenge the cruelties they suffered, whenever they have an opportunity.

Lord Castlereagh. Will they, do you think, raise again.

Mac Neven. Not, I believe, till the French come; but then most assuredly, wherever they can join them.

Speaker. Will the people consider themselves bound hereafter by the oaths of the Union?

Mac Neven. I suppose they will.

Speaker. Would you?

Mac Neven. I, who am going to become an emigrant from my country, am dispensed from answering that question; yet I acknowledge, were I to stay, I would think myself bound by them; nor can I discover anything in what has passed to make it less my duty.

Speaker. Aye, you consider a republican government more economical.

Mac Neven. Corruption is not necessary to it.

Speaker. How did you mean to pay the loan from Spain; I suppose from our forfeited estates?

Mac Neven. Rather, sir, from your places and pensions. If I only take the pension list at £100,000 (it has been considerably higher, and I believe is so still), that alone would be sufficient to pay the interest of four times the half million we meant to borrow. I need not tell you that money can be got when the interest can be regularly paid. We conceive also there are several places with large salaries, for which the present possessors do no other service than giving votes in parliament; another considerable fund would, we imagine, be found by giving these sums a different application.

Speaker. Do you remember Mr. Grattan's motion about tithes—was not that a short cut towards putting down the established church?

Mac Neven. If the stability of the established church depends on the payment of tithes, the church stands on a weaker foundation than in civility I would have said of it; but sure I am, sir, that if tithes had been commuted according to Mr. Grattan's plan, a very powerful engine would have been taken out of our hands.

A member. Is not the Union much indebted to the Roman Catholic clergy?

Mac Neven. The principle of burying all religious differences in oblivion was warmly embraced by the Catholic clergy; some of them became more active members of the Union, and I make no doubt but they are in general well affected to the liberties of their country.

Speaker. Have not the priests a great influence over the people?

Mac Neven. When they espouse the interests of the people they are readily obeyed by them, from the reliance that is placed on their better sense and education; when they oppose these interests they are certainly found to have neither authority nor influence; of this I can give you two important examples. At the time the Catholic committee was opposed by the *sixty-eight*, together with Lord Kenmare and his *marksmen*, a priest, between Kilbeggan and Moate, who endeavoured to seduce his flock to support the slavish principles of that party, was well nigh *hanged* by his own parishioners, for what they deemed treachery to their interests. The other, a priest in the north, who thought fit to preach against the Union: the flock immediately left the chapel, and sent him word they would for that Sunday go to the meeting-house ; and that if he did not desist from such politics in future, they would come near him no more. Of such a nature, gentlemen, is the influence of the Catholic clergy.

Speaker. Are the bishops much looked up to ?

Mac Neven. They are not, as far as I can learn, so well beloved, nor so much confided in by the people as the inferior clergy.

Speaker. Can you assign any reason for that?

Mac Neven. I am inclined to believe it is because they are seen so much about the Castle, and because some acts coming from that body have manifested an over-extraordinary complaisance for the supposed wishes of Government.

Speaker. Did you see Dr. Hussey's letter—what do you think of that ?

Mac Neven. I have seen it, and disapprove of it. As one name and paper is mentioned, I cannot help saying that I have seen another letter, with the name of Dr. Moylan, which contained a remarkable falsehood in favour of the administration ; but as this was only a pious fraud perhaps, I could never hear that they complained of it.

Lord Castlereagh. We will detain you no longer.

29.—1798. SUBSTANCE OF THOMAS ADDIS EMMET'S EXAMINATION, BEFORE THE SECRET COMMITTEE OF THE HOUSE OF LORDS, DUBLIN, AUGUST 10, 1798.

Committee. Were you an United Irishman ?

Emmet. My Lords, I AM one.

Com. Were you a member of the executive ?

Emmet. I was of the executive from the month of January to the month of May, 1797, and afterwards from December, 1797, till I was arrested.

[I was then asked as to the military organization, which I detailed.—They then asked when the returns included fire-arms and ammunition.]

Emmet. After the Insurrection and Indemnity acts had been passed, when the people were led to think on resistance, and after 4,000 persons had been driven from the county of Armagh by the Orangemen.

Com. Was not the name of Orangeman used to terrify the people into the United system?

Emmet. I do not know what groundless fears may have been propagated by ignorant people; but I am sure no unfair advantage was taken by the executive. The Orange principles were fairly discussed, as far as they were known, and we always found that wherever it was attempted to establish a lodge the United Irish increased very much.

Lord Dillon. Why, where was it endeavoured to introduce them, except in the north and the city of Dublin?

Emmet. My lord, I can't tell you all the places in which it was endeavoured, but I will name one, in the county of Roscommon, where I am told it made many United Irishmen.

Lord Dillon. Well, that was but very lately, and I endeavoured to resist it.

Com. When were the first communications with France?

Emmet. The first I heard of were after the Insurrection and Indemnity acts had been carried; the first I knew of was after the French fleet had left Bantry bay, and after it was manifest the effort for reform would not succeed; and permit me to add, on my oath, it was my intention to propose to, and from conversations I had with some of the executive Directory, I am sure it would have been carried there, that if there had been any reasonable hope of reform being adopted, to send one more messenger to France, and he should have told them the difference between the people and the Government was adjusted, and not to attempt a second invasion.

[They then took me into detail through the whole of the negotiations and message. I stated that the demand on our part was from five to ten thousand men, and forty thousand stand of arms, by the first agent; that the instructions to the second agent differed by requesting more arms in consequence of the disarming of the north, which had intervened, and that the French had promised we should be at perfect liberty to choose our own form of government. It was expressly stipulated with them that they should conduct themselves so.]

Lord Chancellor. As they did in Holland.

Emmet. As Rochambeau did in America, my lords.

They then entered on the subject of separation.

Lord Chancellor. How is it possible, Mr. Emmet; just look on the map, and tell me how you can suppose that Ireland could exist independent of England or France?

Emmet. My lords, if I had any doubt on that subject I should never have attempted to effect a separation; but I have given it as much consideration as my faculties would permit, and I have not a shadow of doubt that if Ireland was once independent, she might defy the combined efforts of France and England.

Archbishop of Cashel. My God! her trade would be destroyed!

Emmet. Pardon me, my lord; her trade would be infinitely increased: 150 years ago, when Ireland contained not more than one million and a half of men, and America was nothing, the connection might be said to be necessary to Ireland; but now that she contains five millions, and America is the best market in the world, and Ireland the best situated country in Europe to trade with that market, she has outgrown the connection.

Lord Chancellor. Yes, I remember talking to a gentleman of your acquaintance, and I believe one of your body and way of thinking, who told me that Ireland had nothing to complain of from England; but that she was strong enough to set up for herself.

Emmet. I beg, my lords, that may not be considered as my opinion: I think Ireland has a great many things to complain of against England; I am sure she is strong enough to set up for herself; and give me leave to tell you, my lords, that if the government of this country be not regulated so as that the control may be wholly Irish, and that the commercial arrangements between the two countries be not put on the footing of perfect equality, the connection cannot last.

Lord Chancellor. What would you do for coals?

Emmet. In every revolution, and in every war, the people must submit to some privations; but I must observe to your lordships, there is a reciprocity between the buyer and the seller, and that England would suffer as much as Ireland if we did not buy her coals. However,

I will grant our fuel would become dearer for a time; but by paying a higher price we could have a full sufficient abundance from our own coal mines, and from bogs, by means of our canals.

Archbishop of Cashel. Why, twelve frigates would stop up all our ports.

Emmet. My lord, you must have taken a very imperfect survey of the ports on the western coast of this kingdom, if you suppose that twelve frigates would block them up; and I must observe to you, that if Ireland was for three months separated from England, the latter would cease to be such a formidable naval power.

Lord Chancellor. Well, I conceive the separation could not last twelve hours.

Emmet. I declare it to God, I think that if Ireland was separated from England she would be the happiest spot on the face of the globe.

[At which they all seemed much astonished.]

Lord Chancellor. But how could you rely on France that she would keep her promise of not interfering with your government?

Emmet. My reliance, my lords, was more on Irish prowess than on French promises; for I was convinced that though she could not easily set up the standard herself, yet, when it was once raised, a very powerful army would flock to it, which, organized under its own officers, would have no reason to dread 100,000 Frenchmen, and we only stipulated for a tenth part of that number.

Lord Kilwarden. You seem averse to insurrection; I suppose it was because you thought it impolitic?

Emmet. Unquestionably; for if I imagined an insurrection could have succeeded without a great waste of blood and time, I should have preferred it to invasion, as it would not have exposed us to the chance of contributions being required by a foreign force; but as I did not think so, and as I was certain an invasion would succeed speedily, and without much struggle, I preferred it, even at the hazard of that inconvenience which we took every pains to prevent.

Lord Dillon. Mr. Emmet, you have stated the views of the executive to be very liberal and very enlightened, and I believe yours were so; but let me ask you, whether it was not intended to cut off (in the beginning of the contest) the leaders of the opposition party by a summary mode, such as assassination? my reason for asking you is,

John Sheares's proclamation, the most terrible paper that ever appeared in any country: it says, that "many of your tyrants have bled, and others must bleed," &c.

Emmet. My lords, as to Mr. Sheares's proclamation, he was not of the executive when I was.

Lord Chancellor. He was of the new executive.

Emmet. I do not know he was of any executive, except from what your lordship says; but I believe he was joined with some others in framing a particular plan of insurrection for Dublin and its neighbourhood—neither do I know what value he annexed to those words in his proclamation; but I can answer, that while I was of the executive, there was no such design, but the contrary, for we conceived when one of you lost your lives, we lost an hostage. Our intention was to seize you all, and keep you as hostages for the conduct of England; and after the revolution was over, if you could not live under the new Government, to send you out of the country. I will add one thing more, which, though it is not an answer to your question, you may have a curiosity to hear. In such a struggle, it was natural to expect confiscations; our intention was, that every wife who had not instigated her husband to resistance should be provided for out of the property, notwithstanding confiscations; and every child who was too young to be his own master, or form his own opinion, was to have a child's portion. Your lordships will now judge how far we intended to be cruel.

Lord Chancellor. Pray, Mr. Emmet, what caused the late insurrection?

Emmet. The free quarters, the house-burnings, the tortures, and the military executions, in the counties of Kildare, Carlow and Wicklow.

Lord Chancellor. Don't you think the arrests of the 12th of March caused it?

Emmet. No; but I believe if it had not been for these arrests, it would not have taken place; for the people, irritated by what they suffered, had been long pressing the executive to consent to an insurrection; but they had resisted or eluded it, and even determined to persevere in the same line; after these arrests, however, other persons came forward, who were irritated, and thought differently, who consented to let that partial insurrection take place.

Lord Chancellor. Were all the executive arrested or put to flight by the arrests of the 12th of March?

Emmet. Your lordships will excuse my answering to that question, as it would point out individuals.

Lord Chancellor. Did you not think the Government very foolish to let you proceed so long as they did?

Emmet. No, my lord; whatever I imputed to Government, I did not accuse them of folly. I knew we were very attentively watched, but I thought they were right in letting us proceed. I have often said, laughing among ourselves, that if they did right, they would pay us for conducting the revolution, conceiving, as I then did, and now do, that a revolution is inevitable, unless speedily prevented by very large measures of conciliation. It seemed to me an object with them, that it should be conducted by moderate men, of good moral characters, liberal education, and some talents, rather than by intemperate men of bad characters, ignorant, and foolish; and into the hands of one or other of those classes it undoubtedly will fall. I also imagined the members of Government might be sensible of the difference between the change of their situation being effected by a sudden and violent convulsion, or by the more gradual measures of a well conducted revolution, if it were effected suddenly by an insurrection—and I need not tell your lordships, that had there been a general plan of acting, and the north had co-operated with Leinster, the last insurrection would have infallibly and rapidly succeeded; in such case, you would be tumbled at once from your pinnacle; but if a revolution were gradually accomplished, you would have had time to accommodate and habituate yourselves to your new situation. For these reasons, I imagined Government did not wish to irritate and push things forward.

Lord Chancellor. Pray, do you think Catholic emancipation and parliamentary reform any objects with the common people?

Emmet. As to Catholic emancipation, I don't think it matters a feather, or that the poor think of it. As to parliamentary reform, I don't think the common people ever thought of it, until it was inculcated to them that a reform would cause a removal of those grievances which they actually do feel. From that time, I believe, they have become very much attached to the measure.

Lord Chancellor. And do you think that idea has been successfully inculcated into the common people?

Emmet. It has not been my fortune to communicate much with them on that subject, so that I cannot undertake to say how far it has been successfully inculcated into them; but of this I am certain, that since the establishment of the United Irish system, it has been inculcated into all the middling classes, and much more among the common people, than ever it was before.

Lord Chancellor. And what grievances would such a reformed legislature remove?

Emmet. In the first place, it would cause a complete abolition of tithes; in the next, by giving the common people an increased value in the democracy, it would better their situation, and make them more respected by their superiors; the condition of the poor would be ameliorated; and what is perhaps of more consequence than all the rest, a system of national education would be established.

Lord Dillon. The abolition of tithes would be a very good thing; but don't you think it would be more beneficial to the landlords than the tenants?

Archbishop of Cashel. Aye, it is they would benefit by it.

Emmet. My lords I am ready to grant that if tithes were now abolished, without a reform, there are landlords who would raise the rent on their tenants, when they were making new leases, the full value of the tithes, and, if they could, more; but if a reform succeeded the abolition of tithes, such a reformed legislature would very badly know, or very badly perform its duty, if it did not establish such a system of landed tenures as would prevent landlords from doing so; and let me tell your lordships, that if a revolution ever takes place, a very different system of political economy will be established from what has hitherto prevailed here.

Lord Glentworth. Then your intention was to destroy the church?

Emmet. Pardon me, my lord, my intention never was to destroy the church. My wish decidedly was to overturn the establishment.

Lord Dillon. I understand you—and have it as it is in France?

Emmet. As it is in America, my lords.

Lord Kilwarden. Pray, Mr. Emmet, do you know of any communications with France since your arrest.

Emmet. I do, my lord; Mr. Cooke told me of one.

Lord Kilwarden. But don't you know in any other way, whether communications are still going on between this country and France?

Emmet. No; but I have no doubt that even after we shall have left this country, there will remain among the 500,000 and upwards which compose the Union, many persons of sufficient talents, enterprise, enthusiasm and opportunity, who will continue the old, or open a new communication with France, if it shall be necessary; and in looking over, in my own mind, the persons whom I know of most talents and enterprise, I cannot help suggesting to myself the persons I think most likely to do so; but I must be excused pointing at them.

30.—1798. THE EXAMINATION OF THOMAS ADDIS EMMET, BEFORE THE SECRET COMMITTEE OF THE HOUSE OF COMMONS, AUGUST 14, 1798.

Lord Castlereagh mentioned that the minutes of my examination before the lords had been transmitted to them, and that they only wanted to ask me a few questions in explanation of those minutes. The general turn of the examination was therefore the same as that before the Upper House; but I could observe much more manifestly this time than before, a design out of my answers to draw the conclusion that nothing would content the people but such changes as would be a departure from what they choose to call the English constitution and the English system; and therefore I presume they meant to infer that the popular claims must be resisted at all hazards.—The Speaker seemed to me to take the lead in conducting the investigation to this point.

Lord Castlereagh. Mr. Emmet, you said in your examination before the lords, that the French had not made known the place where they intended landing; how then will you explain an address which we have here, stating that the French were shortly expected in Bantry bay?

Emmet. My lord, I know nothing at present of that address; but I suppose on farther enquiry it will be found to be some mistake, as I am positive they never mentioned Bantry bay in any communication; I know, on the contrary, Galway bay was looked on as the probable place of their landing.

N.B. *I find, upon enquiry, that address is without a date, and was written after the French had disappeared from Bantry bay, and were generally expected to return.*

Mr. Alexander. I have here some resolutions (*which he read, and which, among other things, spoke of the extent of the confiscations that would be made in the event of a revolution, and how they should be applied*)—do you know anything of them?

Emmet. I have a recollection of having read them before; and if that recollection be right, they are resolutions that have been passed by an individual society at Belfast, and were seized at the arrests of Barrett, Burnside, and others.

Mr. Alexander. They are the same.

Emmet. Then I hope the committee will draw no inference from them as to the views of the executive or of the whole body. You know the north well, and that every man there turns his mind more or less on speculative politics; but certainly the opinion of a few of the least informed among them cannot be considered as influencing the whole.

Mr. J. C. Beresford. Aye, but would you be able to make such people give up their own opinion to follow yours?

Emmet. I am convinced we should; because I know we have done it before, on points where their opinions and wishes were very strong.

Mr. Alexander. How did you hope to hold the people in order and good conduct when the reins of government were loosened?

Emmet. By other equally powerful reins. It was for this purpose that I considered the promoting of organization to be a moral duty. Having no doubt that a revolution would, and will take place, unless prevented by removing the national grievances, I saw in the organization the only way of preventing its being such as would give the nation lasting causes of grief and shame. Whether there be organization or not, the revolution will take place; but if the people be classed and arranged for the purpose, the control which heads of their own appointment will have over them, by means of the different degrees of representation and organs of communication, will, I hope, prevent them from committing those acts of outrage and cruelty which may be expected from a justly irritated, but ignorant and uncontrolled populace.

Mr. Alexander. But do you think there were in the Union such organs of communication as had an influence over the lower orders, and were at the same time fit to communicate and do business with persons of a better condition?

Emmet. I am sure there were multitudes of extremely shrewd and sensible men, whose habits of living were with the lower orders, but who were perfectly well qualified for doing business with persons of any condition.

Speaker. You say the number of United Irishmen is five hundred thousand—do you look upon them all as fighting men?

Emmet. There are undoubtedly some old men and some young lads among them; but I am sure I speak within bounds when I say the number of fighting men in the Union cannot be less than three hundred thousand.

Speaker. I understand, according to you, the views of the United Irish went to a republic and separation from England; but they would probably have compounded for a reform in parliament. Am I not right, however, in understanding that *the object next their hearts* was a separation and a republic?

Emmet. Pardon me: *the object next their hearts* was a redress of their grievances; two modes of accomplishing that object presented themselves to their view—one was a reform by peaceable means, the other was a revolution and republic. I have no doubt but that if they could have flattered themselves that *the object next their hearts* would be accomplished peaceably by a reform, they would prefer it infinitely to a revolution and republic, which must be more bloody in their operation; but I am also convinced, when they saw they could not accomplish the object next their hearts, a redress of their grievances, by a reform, they determined in despair to procure it by a revolution, which I am persuaded is inevitable, unless a reform be granted.

Speaker. You say that a revolution is inevitable, unless a reform be granted: what would be the consequence of such a reform in redressing what you call the grievances of the people?

Emmet. In the first place, I look to the abolition of tithes. I think such a reformed legislature would also produce an amelioration of the state of the poor, and a diminution of the rents of lands, would establish a system of national education, would regulate the commercial intercourse between Great Britain and Ireland on the footing of perfect equality, and correct the bloody nature of your criminal code.

Speaker. You speak of the abolition of tithes; do you include in that the destruction of the establishment?

Emmet. I have myself no doubt of the establishment's being injurious, and I look to its destruction; but I cannot undertake to say how far the whole of that measure is contemplated by the body of the people, because I have frequently heard an acreable tax proposed as a substitute, which necessarily supposes the preservation of the establishment.

Speaker. Don't you think the Catholics peculiarly object to tithes?

Emmet. They certainly have the best reason to complain, but I rather think they object as tenants more than as Catholics, and in common with the rest of the tenantry of the kingdom; and if any other way of paying even a Protestant establishment, which did not bear so sensibly on their industry, were to take place, I believe it would go a great way to content them; though I confess it would not content me; but I must add, that I would (and I am sure so would many others who think of establishments like me) consent to give the present incumbents equivalent pensions.

Lord Castlereagh. Don't you think the Catholics look to accomplishing the destruction of the establishment?

Emmet. From the declaration they made in 1792, or 1793, I am sure they did not then;- I cannot say how far their opinions may have altered since, but from many among them proposing a substitute for tithes, I am led to believe they may not yet be gone so far.

Lord Castlereagh. But don't you think they will look to its destruction?

Emmet. I cannot pay so bad a compliment to the reasons which have convinced myself, as not to suppose they will convince others. As the human mind grows *philosophic*, it will, I think, wish for the destruction of all religious establishments, and therefore, in proportion as the Catholic mind becomes *philosophic*, it will, of course, entertain the same wishes—but I consider that as the result of its *philosophy*, and not of its religion.

Lord Castlereagh. Don't you think the Catholics would wish to set up a Catholic establishment in lieu of the Protestant one?

Emmet. Indeed I don't, even at the present day. Perhaps some old priests, who have long groaned under the penal laws, might wish for a retribution to themselves; but I don't think the young priests wish for it, and I am convinced the laity would not submit to it, and that the objections to it will be every day gaining strength.

Speaker. You also mention that a reform would diminish the rents of lands; how do you think that would be done?

Emmet. I am convinced rack rents can only take place in a country otherwise essentially oppressed; if the value of the people was raised in the state, their importance would influence the landlords to consult their interests, and therefore to better their condition. Thus I think it would take place, even without any law bearing upon the matter.

Mr. Alexander. Mr. Emmet, you have gone circuit for many years; now, have you not observed that the condition of the people has been gradually bettering?

Emmet. Admitting that the face of the country has assumed a better appearance; if you attribute it to the operation of any laws you have passed, I must only declare my opinion, it is *post hoc sed non ex hoc*. As far as the situation of the lower orders has been bettered in Ireland, it results from the increased knowledge, commerce and intercourse of the different States of Europe with one another, and is enjoyed in this country only in common with the rest of civilized Europe and America. I believe the lower orders in all those countries have been improved in their condition within these twenty years, but I doubt whether the poor of this kingdom have been bettered in a greater portion than the poor in the despotic States of Germany.

Speaker. You mention an improved system of national education; are there not as many schools in Ireland as in England?

Emmet. I believe there are, and that there is in proportion as great a fund in Ireland as in England, if it were fairly applied; but there is this great difference: the schools are Protestant schools, which answer very well in England, but do little good among the Catholic peasantry in Ireland. Another thing to be considered is, that stronger measures are necessary for educating the Irish people than are necessary in England; in the latter country no steps were taken to counteract the progress of knowledge; it had fair play, and was gradually advancing; but in Ireland you have brutalized the vulgar mind, by long continued operation of the popery laws, which, though they are repealed, have left an effect that will not cease these fifty years. It is incumbent, then, on you to counteract that effect by measures which are not equally necessary in England.

Speaker. You mentioned the criminal code; in what does that differ from the English?

Emmet. It seems to me that it would be more advisable, in reviewing our criminal law, to compare the crime with the punishment, than the Irish code with the English; there is, however, one difference that occurs to me on the instant—administering unlawful oaths is in Ireland punished with death.

Lord Castlereagh. That is a law connected with the security of the State.

Emmet. If it is intended to keep up the ferment of the public mind, such laws may be necessary; but if it be intended to allay the ferment, they are perfectly useless.

Speaker. Would putting the commercial intercourse on the footing of equality, satisfy the people?

Emmet. I think that equality of situations would go nearer satisfying the people than any of the other equalities that have been alluded to.

Speaker. Then your opinion is, that we cannot avoid a revolution unless we abandon the English constitution and the English system in our establishment, education and criminal laws?

Emmet. I have already touched on the latter subjects; as to the English constitution, I cannot conceive how a reform in parliament can be said to destroy that.

Speaker. Why, in what does the representation differ in Ireland from that in England? are there not in England close boroughs, and is not the right of suffrage there confined to 40s. freeholders?

Emmet. If I were an Englishman, I should be discontented, and therefore cannot suppose that putting Ireland on a footing with England would content the people of this country. If, however, you have a mind to try a partial experiment, for the success of which I would not answer, you must consider how many are the close boroughs and large towns which contribute to the appointment of their 558, and diminish in the same proportion the number of the close boroughs and towns which contribute to the appointment of our 300—even that would be a gain to Ireland; but that there should be no mistake, or confusion of terms, let us drop the equivocal words of *English constitution,* and then I answer, I would not be understood to say that the government, of king, lords and commons, would be destroyed by a reform of the lower house.

Lord Castlereagh. And don't you think that such a house could not co-exist with the government of king and lords?

Emmet. If it would not, my lord, the eulogies that have been passed on the British constitution are very much misplaced; but I think they could all exist together, if the king and lords meant fairly by the people; if they should persist in designs hostile to the people, I do believe they would be overthrown.

[It was then intimated that they had got into a theoretical discussion, and that what they wished to enquire into was facts.]

Sir J. Parnel. Mr. Emmet, while you and the executive were philosophizing, lord Edward Fitzgerald was arming and disciplining the people.

Emmet. Lord Edward was a military man, and if he was doing so he probably thought that was the way in which he could be most useful to the country; but I am sure that if those with whom he acted were convinced that the grievances of the people were redressed, and that force was become unnecessary, he would have been persuaded to drop all arming and disciplining.

Mr. J. C. Beresford. I knew Lord Edward well, and always found him very obstinate.

Emmet. I knew Lord Edward right well, and have done a great deal of business with him, and have always found, when he had a reliance on the integrity and talents of the person he acted with, he was one of the most persuadable men alive; but if he thought a man meant dishonestly or unfairly by him, he was as obstinate as a mule.

[Many questions were then put to me relative to different papers and proceedings of the United Irish; among the rest, John Sheares's proclamation was mentioned with considerable severity. I took that opportunity of declaring, that neither the execution of John Sheares, or the obloquy that was endeavoured to be cast on his memory, should prevent my declaring that I considered John Sheares a very honourable and humane man.]

Mr. French. Mr. Emmet, can you point out any way of inducing the people to give up their arms?

Emmet. Redressing their grievance, and no other.

Lord Castlereagh. Mr. Emmet, we are unwillingly obliged to close this examination by the sitting of the house.

Emmet. My lord, if it be the wish of the committee, I will attend it any other time.

Lord Castlereagh. If we want you, then we shall send for you.

After the regular examination was closed, I was asked by many of the members whether there were many persons of property in the Union. I answered that there was immense property in it. They acknowledged there was great personal property in it, but wished to know was there much landed property; I answered there was. They asked me was it feesimple; to that I could give no answer. The attorney-general said there was in it many landholders who had large tracts of land, and felt *their* landlords to be great grievances. I admitted that to be the fact. They asked me had we provided any form of government. I told them we had a provisional government for the instant, which we retained in memory; but as to any permanent form of government, we thought that, and many other matters relating to the changes which would become necessary, were not proper objects for our discussion, but should be referred to a committee chosen by the people.

They did not ask what the provisional Government was.

31.—1798. FRENCH SOLDIERY AT KILLALA.

i.—Memorandum by John Knox of Bartera.

1798, August 22.—On this evening twelve hundred French invaded Ireland by landing at Killcommon, near Killala, in the county of Mayo. Stock, the bishop of Killala, with his family, were made prisoners, and the French took possession of his house, but allowed the family the upper part of the house for their accommodation. I remained at my residence, Bartera, close to Killala, was made a prisoner twice by the people under the countenance of the French, and received the annexed protection or passport on the last occasion from colonel Charost, who commanded the party left behind to guard some ammunition, the greater part having gone to Castlebar. They afterwards surrendered to the king's troops at Ballina, much about the middle of September in the same year.

IV.
Passport from M. Charost, French Commander at Killala, 1798.

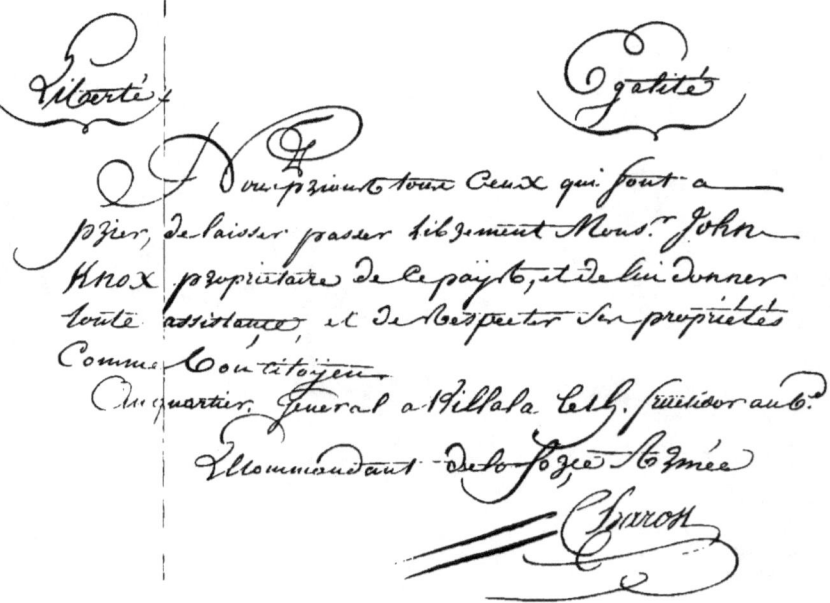

Original in collection of the Editor.

31. ii.—Liberté. Egalité.

Nous prions tous ceux qui sont a prier de laisser passer librement Monsieur John Knox, proprietaire de ce pays et de lui donner toute assistance et de respecter ses propriétés comme bon citoyen.

Au quartier general a Killala, le 19 fructidor au sixieme.

Le commandant de la force armée.—Charost.

32.—1798. VICEROYALTY OF MARQUIS CORNWALLIS.—PROJECT OF PROVISIONAL GOVERNMENT FOR ENGLAND IN IRELAND.—PELHAM.—LORD CLARE.

Duke of Portland to Thomas Pelham.

Private and confidential. London, Friday, 7 September, 1798.

As I am sure you will agree with me in the propriety of every precaution being taken to obviate as much as possible the consequences which would arise from lord Cornwallis being deprived either of his natural existence or of the means of administering his government, you will also concur in opinion with me and the rest of the king's servants that it is expedient that a provisional government should be appointed to take place in either of those cases ; and that if you were in Ireland, that trust could not be so properly vested in any hands as in your own. Convinced, therefore, as I am of the indisputableness of this fact, and indulging, as I have done, the idea of your being impressed with the importance of your presence in Ireland at this crisis, I express with confidence the hope I entertain, that your health is sufficiently re-established to permit you to return there for the purpose of your being ready to assume the reins of government, should either of those misfortunes take place. Considering your absence, it has occurred to us that it might be more agreeable to you, and remove some of the difficulties which you might feel in acceding to this proposal, if another person was joined in the commission with you, and that the chancellor [lord Clare] was of all others (I mean in Ireland) the person with whom you would prefer to be associated. I therefore submitted the idea to the king, who immediately expressed his entire approbation of it, and commanded me to lose no time in acquainting you with his anxious wish and hope that your health will permit you to accede to this proposal, which, from what I have told you on the subject of lord Cornwallis' appointment, you must yourself be sensible he thinks of the utmost importance to his service and to the existence of his Government in Ireland. In order, therefore, to meet this view, it has been submitted to his majesty that the best mode that could be adopted would be that of appointing provisionally a lord deputy, or two lords deputies, and he has accordingly directed me to order such a commission to be made out, constituting you and lord Clare, or either of you, to exercise that office in case of a vacancy of the present Government by the death or other deprivation of lord Cornwallis from the functions of the lieutenancy; and as partly out of tenderness to lord Cornwallis, and principally to prevent those speculations to which every Irish mind is addicted, his majesty thinks that this provisional appointment should not become a subject of conversation, I am to desire you not to communicate this application or the intention with which I have acquainted you, until you receive his majesty's leave to that effect. Considering that this is Friday, I send this by a messenger, that I may not have to wait two days for your answer.

33.—1798.   BISHOPRIC OF CLONFERT.—STATE OF IRELAND.—UNION.—
           MEASURE FOR PERMANENT TRANQUILLITY.

Marquis Cornwallis to Thomas Pelham.

Phœnix Park [Dublin], 15 October, 1798.

I received your letter with greater pleasure, from my having previously named Dr. [Matthew] Young for the vacant bishopric [of Clonfert], and it was a matter of no small satisfaction to me to find that I had done exactly what you thought I should do.

We have as yet no distinct accounts from the northern coast, but on the whole we have reason to suppose that our squadron has gained a considerable advantage.

The state of this country is, I am afraid, every day growing worse, and I am apprehensive that an Union between Great Britain and the Protestants in Ireland is not likely to do us much good.

I am sensible that it is the easiest point to carry; but I begin to have great doubts whether it will not prove an insuperable bar, instead of being a step towards the admission of Catholics, which is the only measure that can give permanent tranquillity to this wretched country.

34.—1798. GEORGE III.—DUKE OF PORTLAND.—PELHAM.— PROTESTANT BISHOPRICS IN IRELAND.

Duke of Portland to Thomas Pelham.

Private and confidential.

London, Thursday, 1 November, 1798.

Had other more urgent occupations permitted me, I should have told you yesterday that I performed the sad task of acquainting the king with your finding it necessary to decline returning to Ireland, upon which he expressed his sincere concern, and observed that you were too much a man of honour for him to urge you to do what he was sure your want of health alone would have suffered you to decline; and again repeated that 'he was most extremely sorry for it.' After some time he resumed the subject, and added, 'with the views you (meaning myself) know I had, and in the present circumstances, it is the greatest loss and the greatest disappointment I could have experienced.' I thought, in justice to his majesty and to you, I ought to make this report to you of what passed in the closet relative to yourself, and I certainly have not added one word—though I may have omitted many—expressive of the same sentiments.

I shall write to the lord lieutenant to acquaint him with this event, and to say that I suppose he will hear it from you as soon as he receives my information of it.

The recommendations to the bishoprics came yesterday: Ossory [Thomas Lewis O'Beirne] to Meath; Clonfert [Hugh Hamilton] to Ossory; Dr. [Matthew] Young, to Clonfert.

1 B

35.—1799. To THOMAS PELHAM, FROM FRANCIS MOYLAN, D.D., ROMAN CATHOLIC BISHOP OF CORK.

Cork, 4th January, 1799.

Allow me to take the liberty of requesting your interference in favour of an object of justice, charity, and humanity. A Mr. William Kelly, native of this city, died in the year 1793, at Trinidad, then under the Spanish Government. In his last will and testament he ordered that, after deducting the different legacies bequeathed by him, the residue of his property should be, as soon as possible, remitted to me *in trust*, to be placed out on good securities, the annual produce to be given to a nephew and four nieces during their lives; and on their death to be disposed of in the support and education of twenty- poor orphans, if adequate to the purpose. The acting executor, a Mr. John Nugent of that island, was so backward in complying with the testator's instructions, that I was advised to send out a power of attorney to two gentlemen, in order to engage him to discharge the trust reposed in him, Those gentlemen, to succeed the more effectually in their commission, applied to the governor, lieutenant-colonel Picton, for his protection. The executor in consequence gave in to them a statement of the effects, and settled matters amicably to their satisfaction; but the governor, to their great astonishment, ordered them to retain in their hands, and by no means to remit to Ireland, the sums they may receive from the executors of the late Mr. Kelly; and gave them at the same time to understand that he thought himself warranted to invalidate the will, as being made in favour of Popish education. How he could invalidate a will made under the sanction of the laws of that country, according to which it was valid, and which laws are still in force, seems to me rather an over-stretch of power than conformable to the rules of justice and equity. Besides, as far as I can learn, there is no existing law at present in this kingdom which prohibits legacies being left for the support and education of poor orphans of the Roman Catholic persuasion. Permit me then, dear sir, to request you will have the goodness to procure from the Secretary of State, in whose department the island lies, directions to governor Picton, not only to withdraw his prohibition, but to have the kindness to assist by his influence my attorneys to make the remittances as speedily as possible. This will be an act of justice in favour of the nephew and nieces of the late Mr. Kelly who suffer by the delay; it will also be an act of charity and humanity in favour of the poor orphans, who hereafter are to benefit by the legacy. I trust you will be so good as to excuse the trouble I presume to give you on this occasion.

The incorporation of this country with England is the great subject of political talk and discussion here, as it is in every part of this kingdom. Various are the opinions on it, as people are variously affected by self-interested or political views. It is a question of great magnitude, on which I certainly am not competent to judge, how far it may eventually tend to the advantage or disadvantage of this country. But I am strongly of opinion that whatever might effectually contribute to re-establish and consolidate peace and good order in this ill-fated kingdom; to remove and suppress those odious party distinctions which so shamefully disgrace its inhabitants; to support the constitution in its vigour, and strengthen the empire at large against French principles and French machinations—this would be a measure most desirable, and should have the approbation of every real friend to both kingdoms.

I shall be happy to hear that your health, which was rather weak on your leaving this country, is perfectly re-established. The obligations we are under to you and to Lord Camden for the active part you were both pleased to take in the erection and support of the college at Maynooth, can never be forgotten by the Roman Catholick prelates and by all the real Roman Catholicks of this kingdom.

36.—1799. SUGGESTIONS BY ROMAN CATHOLIC PRELATES IN IRELAND FOR GOVERNMENTAL PROVISION.

At a meeting of the Roman Catholick prelates held in Dublin, the 17, 18, and 19 January, 1799, to deliberate on a proposal from Government of an independent provision for the Roman Catholick clergy of Ireland under certain regulations not incompatible with their doctrines, discipline or just influence:

It was admitted that a provision through Government for the Roman Catholick clergy of this kingdom, competent and secured, ought to be thankfully accepted.

That in the appointment of the prelates of the Roman Catholick religion to vacant sees within the kingdom, such interference of the Government as may enable it to be satisfied of the loyalty of the person to be appointed, is just, and ought to be agreed to.

That, to give this principle its full operation without infringing the discipline of the Roman Catholick Church, or diminishing the religious influence which prelates of that Church ought justly to possess over their respective flocks, the following regulations appear necessary:

i.—In the vacancy of a see, the clergy of the diocese recommend as usual a candidate to the prelates of the ecclesiastical province, who elect him or any other they may think more worthy by a majority of suffrages; in the case of equality of suffrages, the metropolitan or senior prelate to have a casting vote.

ii.—In the election of a metropolitan, if the provincial prelates do not agree within two months from the vacancy, the senior prelate shall forthwith invite the surviving metropolitans to the election, in which each will then have a vote: in the equality of suffrages the presiding metropolitan to have the casting vote.

iii.—In these elections the majority of suffrages must be ultra medietatem, as the canons require, or must consist of the suffrages of more than half the electors.

iv.—The candidate so elected will be presented by the president of the election to Government, which, within one month after such presentation, will transmit the name of said candidate (if no objection lie against him), to the Holy See for appointment; or return said name to the president of election for such transmission as may be agreed on.

v.—If Government have any proper objection to such candidate, the president of the election will be informed thereof within one month after presentation, who in that case will convene the electors, and proceed to the election of another candidate.

Agreeably to the discipline of the Roman Catholick Church, these regulations can have no effect without the sanction of the Holy See, which sanction the Roman Catholick prelates of this kingdom shall, as soon as may be, use their endeavours to procure.

The prelates are satisfied that the nomination of parish priests, with a certificate of their having taken the oath of allegiance, be notified to Government. [See page 206.]

37.—1799. LETTERS ON DEBATE IN PARLIAMENT AT DUBLIN ON LEGISLATIVE UNION WITH GREAT BRITAIN.

i.—To Thomas Pelham from Henry Alexander, M.P. for Londonderry.

Dublin, January 22 [1799], Tuesday night,
10 minutes before 11 o'clock.

Your letter made me extremely happy, as I was apprehensive misapprehension or misrepresentation might have changed your favourable sentiments of me, and I really felt an interest more than common that they should be not destroyed.

I snatch a moment from the debate to let you know as warm a debate is going on as ever took place. [Sir John] Parnell, with good sense and moderation, intermingling some desperate insinuations, only argued the question as diminishing imperial strength. His argument is specious, but not lastingly formidable. He made no motion, but his tendency was to procure an avowal that legislative Union was the measure of consolidation alluded to in the king's speech. Lord Castlereagh avowed it to be his opinion that was the only means of continuing the Union. I wish he had said the best.

Tighe, as usual. George Ponsonby, a long speech, concluding with a recapitulation of the Declaration of 1782, that a resident legislature was necessary to the prosperity of Ireland. The question is now at issue, and in a speech of near an hour, that ought to have been a preface to a motion for separation, recapitulated all grievances for seven hundred years. His tendency was to prove that we must commence supple slaves to Ireland to continue domestic tyrants. He is seconded by Parsons, without a speech, followed by Conolly, who has recapitulated all his prophecies that our government would not work; called it a monster with two heads and recited the really shameful profusion of offices given to members of parliament.

I have time, before the post goes, to add, the business of the country was postponed by an ill-natured motion of George Ponsonby, that lord C[astlereagh] had vacated his seat. He was followed in terms personally disrespectful by Plunkett and by O'Donnell, the trumpeter, with an invocation of 'O Ireland, hear' as if he was praying to one of his saints.

I wish you had answered my letters only, as I think I might have been useful to the country, as I would have waited on you. At any rate I would have remonstrated most strenuously against your carrying over any man to England whose sentiments you could not ascertain.

Money has charms only to certain minds. The Speaker's [Foster's] is above its influence, as I believe. He feels for power and if his own and the public interests, in his opinion, lead one way, he is immovable.

I have to add, if I did not feel as I do, that Ireland and England depend upon the measure, I would scarce oppose his opinion; but, from an attentive perusal of every circumstance, I feel it my decided duty to support an Union of the legislatures, and shall act con amore; at the same time, I am afraid with less effect than if I had previous preparation.

They have offered me the chairmanship of the committee of ways and means, and to retain my present situation. I have accepted the chairmanship with gratitude, but will relinquish my present trust, as I dislike its responsibility, and income I never cared about, except to guard against a contested election.

Rely upon it, my brother is a man of much inferior learning, but of infinitely superior reflection and powers to your most valuable friend, doctor Young, and would be the highest acquisition a government could make, from his coolness, decision and habits of enquiry.

P.S.—Ponsonsby's language was only to do every thing by our parliament also.

I will possibly write you the occurrences of the week on Sunday. Much pains taken to terrify and intimidate.

37. ii.—Richard Griffith to Thomas Pelham.

Dublin, Molesworth-street, 24 January, 1799.
Wednesday, 2 o'clock, afternoon.

I am this moment returned from the gallery of the House of Commons, where I have sat above twenty-one hours. Immediately on the

Speaker's taking the chair, about 4 o'clock yesterday afternoon, George
Ponsonby moved that the Speaker do issue his warrant, etc., to elect a
knight for the county of Down in the room of lord Castlereagh, who
had accepted an office of emolument under the crown and had thereby
vacated his seat, etc. This produced a warm debate for upwards of two
hours, which was at length ended by George Ponsonby withdrawing his
motion. Lord Tyrone then moved the address, to which Sir John
Parnell moved an amendment, and George Ponsonby a second amendment, both pledging the House against an Union with Great Britain. I
hope to send you the votes by this night's post. The debate on these
amendments lasted till half-past one o'clock this morning, and on the
division there appeared for the amendments 105, against them 106.
The question was then put upon the address as originally moved, when
there appeared for the address 107, against it 105. I understand that
there was some mistake in reckoning the House, and that Government
had 107 on the first division as well as on the last. Immediately after
the report of the tellers on the second division, George Ponsonby asked
lord Castlereagh whether he intended to persist in the measure of an
Union? To which no decisive answer being made, he was again asked
whether he intended to bring it forward again this session? Upon
which Sir John Parnell interfered, and said he did not think it fair to
press the noble lord to an immediate answer upon a subject of such
importance; at the same time he took the liberty of strenuously advising the noble lord not to think of the measure any more, at least while
the sentiments both of people and parliament appeared so decisively
against it; and concluded with saying that he relied so much on the
goodness of the noble lord, as to be perfectly satisfied that he had no
wish or intention of forcing the measure on the House, and that consequently he would not bring it forward again. Lord Castlereagh
acquiesced in this kind of half promise made on his part, but said that
he was so well convinced of the beneficial effects of a legislative Union
with Great Britain, that whenever the House and the nation appeared
to understand its merits he should think it his duty to bring it forward.
After appointing a committee to draw up the address, the House
adjourned till to-morrow. Lord Castlereagh made a good speech, but
had no one to give him any real support except the Knight of Kerry,
who made a long and able speech; and William Smith, the baron's son,

whom I like and admire very much, notwithstanding his peculiarities of character. Smith's was an excellent defence of the competency of parliament to enact the Union. I firmly believe that if he had not spoken Government would have been left in a minority of six or seven, and if he had spoken earlier in the debate they would have had as many more majority. Toler made a wretched figure, and it is said of Corry that he borrowed his name-sake's, Isaac's dulcimer. George Ponsonby made a great display of ability, but was outshone by Plunkett, who, notwithstanding his very bad voice, made a very powerful impression on the House, and, I may say, decided the question. I never witnessed a debate in which the votes of so many members were decided by the eloquence of the speakers.

Do you remember that Mr. Plunkett was one of the rising young men at the bar whom I took the liberty once, in a letter, of recommending to your notice. I cannot help thinking that a very different issue might have been had to the business if you had remained here.

Many very high compliments were paid you in the debate, and among others an involuntary tribute to your talents by Plunkett, who, among his other congratulations on the prospect of success against the measure, thanked God that you were gone, and had left the business in the hands of such an insufficient boy.

In the House of Lords I understand that a similar amendment was made to the address; and on a division, 17 were for the amendment and 53 against it. The 17 were as follows: duke of Leinster, lord Mountnorris, bishop of Down, Enniskillen, Granard, Bellamount, Charlemont, Belmore, Farnham, Mountcashell, Clanwilliam, Powerscourt, Chetwynd, Kilmaine, Dunsany, Pery, and one proxy.

It is most probable, I think, that the measure of an Union will now be laid aside, at least for the present session of parliament; and as it is not likely that I shall have any material matter to communicate to you for some time, I must entreat a line to inform me how you are, and at the same time remind you of your promise to send me a good engraving of your picture. Indeed, I think I am entitled to a proof print for sitting down to write this letter instead of going to sleep.

37. iii.—To Thomas Pelham from Hugh Carleton, Chief Justice of the Common Pleas, Ireland.

At seven o'clock this morning, on the report of the address to the king, Government was beaten in the House of Commons by a majority of five, and, in consequence thereof, the clauses in that address, and also in the address to the lord lieutenant, 'promising to take the subject of union into consideration,' were expunged. Then some motion was made by George Ponsonby, but afterwards abandoned, tending to express a determination 'never at any period to take the subject into consideration.' Thus, the peculiar circumstances of this kingdom at this time, have failed of producing the proposed effect upon the deliberations of parliament, and I am unable to surmise what limits may be put to the pernicious and dangerous consequences likely to result from the ferment and the exasperation of the public mind occasioned by bringing the subject forward to discussion at so inauspicious a period. On the first day of the session, in the House of Lords we had a long debate, very ill supported on the part of the opposition by lords Farnham, Bellamont, Powerscourt and Dunsany; but ably maintained on the side of Government by the chancellor and lords Glandore, Glentworth, Yelverton and Carysfort. I took a decided part for the measure at considerable length and with no inconsiderable zeal, and my friends (perhaps misled by their partiality for me) have expressed themselves very handsomely as to the merit of the performance. I took an extensive view of the subject, as it involved the competence of parliament, and as it was connected with the relative situations of the two kingdoms; the power, stability and prosperity of the empire at large; the particular difficulties under which this country labours; the questions of reform and Catholick representation; the probable effects of an incorporation of the two kingdoms upon the trade, wealth and tranquillity of Ireland; and the security which the interest of Great Britain in our prosperity, connected with a reasonable and moderate ratio of contribution to the general exigencies of the State, varying with the increase or diminution of our ability, would afford of our receiving at all times just and liberal treatment from the parliament of the united kingdoms. The majority in the House of Lords was (as you already know) large. But many of those who supported the question for considering a proposition for incorporation, could not be depended upon if the question came directly under consideration, whether a Union ought to be acceded to.

A resolution was yesterday entered into by the bar to give such precedence to James Fitzgerald as he had held when he was prime sergeant. But the chancellor and all the judges resolved that although the bar might by compact amongst themselves regulate the precedency of outer barristers, we were not authorized to take away such precedence and pre-audience as his majesty's grant had conferred.

What determination lord Cornwallis has come to as to any further proceedings on the subject of Union, I know not. I did not intend to have spoken until the merits had come directly before us; but it having been rumoured that I continued hostile to the measure, and Glentworth having called on those who at any time took a part in debate, to declare their sentiments, I thought it not honourable or manly to decline disclosing mine. Probably much unpopularity will be bestowed on me, in company with those who have taken the same part with me. It is beyond my comprehension that the calculation of forces on the different sides should have been so erroneous, or so misstated. In the present critical situation of affairs, I hope no idea may be entertained of continuing that ferment, which I am heartily sorry was raised.—25 January, 1799.

37. iv.—To Thomas Pelham from Sir George Shee, Bart., M.P. for Knocktopher.

Dublin, 25 January, 1799.

The report of the committee appointed to prepare the address was read yesterday, paragraph by paragraph, and the last, which recapitulated what the speech contained touching the Union, having been objected to, a motion was made by Sir Laurence Parsons for expunging it. The debate that ensued was acrimonious and violent, and it lasted until six o'clock in the morning, when there was a majority of five against us. Ponsonby immediately attempted to follow his blow by moving a resolution that the measure should be relinquished for ever; but Fortescue, lord Cole, French of Roscommon, and one or two others, having declared that they would not support the motion, it was, with great reluctance, given up, a piece of good fortune that could scarcely have been expected, considering that it was almost verbatim the same as the amendment that had been supported the day before by a minority of a hundred and five, in which the gentlemen I mention were included. Time is, at all events, gained by this business, which in all political contests is of great use, and I think the opposition is so constituted that it cannot become systematic or remain united; indeed, several of the independent men who composed it, have already declared that in every other question they would support Government as usual. Lord Castlereagh made a highly animated and able speech in the beginning of the debate, and he threw out a personal defiance that was quite necessary, considering what had passed when the address was first moved. I believe there is little doubt but that the Speaker [Foster], Parnell and Ponsonby have formed a connection, and if the latter had abstained from appearing as the head of the party he might perhaps have carried the motion.

An indirect hint from Lord Castlereagh of a probable necessity for a dissolution of parliament seemed to have had great effect. The majority against us was owing to Conolly, old Beresford and Sir Hercules Langrishe having been absent, and three new members having arrived from the country. If Beresford had been sincerely with us, he might, I think, have paired off with his son, who voted against us yesterday.

38.—1799. VIEWS ON LEGISLATIVE UNION OF IRELAND WITH GREAT BRITAIN.

To Thomas Pelham from Matthew Young, Protestant Bishop of Clonfert.

[Dublin,] 2 February, 1799.

I have been wishing for an excuse of again writing to you, which I think my consecration, which is to take place to-morrow, gives me—an event which, though so gratifying in itself, and by the manner in which it has been effected by the lord lieutenant and lord Castlereagh, still comes in a very particular manner to me, by finding that I was not mistaken in attributing this promotion, entirely in intention and in a great measure in fact, also to you. It is a pleasure of that kind which few that have been so promoted have to reflect on, and I hope I shall convert it to its proper use, which is in making your wishes, as signified in the letter I had the satisfaction of receiving from you, the rule of my conduct, when I shall be able to have the happiness of residing at my see. I am thoroughly persuaded of the truth of your opinions relative to our discontents here, that they would at least have been much abated, if not substantially removed, by a diligent discharge of duty in the clergy; and, I trust, I shall be able ere long to bring this conjecture, even now, in some degree to the test of experiment. I am sorry to tell you, sir, that our disturbances are by no means at an end. Perhaps I might say with truth that they are as violent as ever; yet, as so many of the men of talents and principal leaders of the rebellion have been cut off, I cannot think their designs equally formidable. The question of the Union, which, no doubt was brought forward with the best intentions, for no others could lord Castlereagh entertain, which is in itself, I do verily believe, the best measure that could be adopted by this country, has unfortunately been made an instrument to stir up the spirit of disaffection once more. And they who work the machine have been very active indeed, and too successful. A great question has, for the present, been unfortunately lost. Yet how could it well be otherwise? An incorporating Union is certainly a degrading measure to a nation in possession of its own parliament, and in appearance entirely independent. Many evils naturally suggest themselves as springing from such a Union. The good consequences are more remote from view, and are to be derived from topics not popular in their nature. It must, therefore, require time to remove the general dislike, and to silence the foolish but natural suggestions of national pride. We cannot, therefore, be surprised that a question of such a nature, so suddenly proposed to the decision of the country, should be rejected. It is curious to observe what lord Rochford says, who once meditated a legislative Union. He says, first, that it should be proposed in a time of peace, as it would be insanity to attempt it in a time of war; secondly, that the best writers should be employed on the question, so that it should be fully, fairly and argumentatively discussed before it should be proposed; and, thirdly, that there should be an army ready to restrain the madmen, or such as from absurd notions of national dignity might be induced to oppose a measure of such great national advantage. But this army, he says, must be Irish, in order to show them that there was no intention in England of using force. All these precautions, wise in themselves and naturally resulting from a consciousness of the virtue of the proposition, were in the present instance neglected. Yet though such has been the fate of the question, I cannot but think that the objections to it will by degrees appear to [be] either exaggerated or unfounded: that the prejudices of the gentry, as well as of the mass of the people against it, will progressively abate; so that at a future day perhaps we may have the good fortune to see the union effected, which, I think, is the only thing which can secure the Protestant interest in this country, and with it the connection of the two kingdoms. But I fear that another attempt of this kind immediately would be attended with some danger, as a great number of the most loyal gentlemen have taken a decided and even a most violent part in opposing the measure; and their enthusiasm has spread itself widely indeed, so that I am inclined to think that we should now begin where, I think, we should have begun before, to discuss this question in private companies, where our opinions will not be disturbed by any vanity arising from a public display of patriotism.

Though I have the vanity to think that I have lost the pleasure of many delightful evenings by your absence from this country, yet it is a source of perpetual satisfaction to me that you did not again plunge yourself into the waves of Irish politics, and with heartfelt pleasure indeed I learn, that while you are pursuing the arts of peace, you are establishing that health for which no person living can be more solicitous.

39.—1799. CONSIDERATIONS IN RELATION TO LEGISLATIVE UNION OF IRELAND WITH GREAT BRITAIN.—GOVERNMENTAL ARRANGEMENTS SUGGESTED FOR ROMAN CATHOLIC CLERGY IN IRELAND.

To Thomas Pelham from Francis Moylan, D.D., Roman Catholic Bishop of Cork.

Cork, 9 March, 1799.

Accept of my most grateful thanks for your very kind attention to the affair I took the liberty of recommending to you [see p. 194]. The orders sent out to governor Picton are completely satisfactory, and I can have no doubt but they will have the desired effect.

The great opposition made in our House of Commons to the legislative Union of this kingdom with Great Britain was unexpected. It proves how strongly party spirit and faction prevail in this ill-fated country. Among the many who so violently exclaimed against that measure, few, very few, I am persuaded, ever considered it under any other point of view but as it affected their private interest or ambition. The real interests of the nation they had little regard to; happy that the excess of violence with which they debated on that important question, has not caused the irritation it should naturally make in England.

Nothing, surely, can be fairer than the open and liberal manner in which the question has been proposed and discussed with you. And I trust that the heat of passion will soon subside here, and that our representatives will in cooler moments consider the measure with more temperance, and in a more favourable light, than they have hitherto.

I am perfectly satisfied of the truth of the assertion that it is impossible to extinguish the feuds and animosities which disgrace this kingdom, nor give it the advantages of its natural and local situation without an Union with Great Britain. This is the opinion also of a great many respectable characters whom I conversed with on the subject, both here and in Dublin, and I doubt not but the majority in our parliament will, on reflection, be convinced of it. God grant it may soon take place! The tranquillity and future welfare of this poor distracted country rest in a great degree thereon. The earlier it is accomplished the better. May God give a blessing to it!

Lord Castlereagh intimated to the Roman Catholick prelates who lately met in Dublin on the affairs of the college at Maynooth, that it was the intention of Government to make a provision for the decent support of the Roman Catholick clergy of this kingdom under certain regulations, and wished to know our sentiments thereon.

Doctor Troy and I waited on his lordship with the resolutions agreed to, a copy of which I beg leave to transmit [see p. 195], for your perusal, and shall be thankful for your thoughts thereon. As we are satisfied that nothing will be required of us incompatible with our principles and the duties of our state, so may Government be well assured of the readiness of the Roman Catholick prelates of this kingdom to give every proof in their power of our unfeigned allegiance and attachment to our most gracious sovereign and to his Government.

40.—1799. IDEAS AS TO ARRANGEMENTS BETWEEN ENGLISH GOVERNMENT AND ROMAN CATHOLIC CLERGY IN IRELAND.

Duke of Portland to Thomas Pelham.

Bulstrode, Tuesday, 26 March, 1799.

I am unwilling to detain Dr. Moylan's letter any longer, though I am as unable as I was a week ago to satisfy the enquiry you have been so good as to make respecting the opinion of Government upon the plan which has been given in by the Roman Catholick prelates. Until I received yours I did not know that any conversation had passed upon the subject between them and lord Castlereagh—I mean in so official a form as to have produced such a deliberation as you have sent me the result of, and consequently without any knowledge of the sentiments of the Government or bishops in Ireland; and of course being, as you see, in the same state of ignorance with regard to those of my colleagues in administration, and the great lights of the English church, it would not only be imprudent, but is really impossible for me to state anything upon this question that ought to be considered as an opinion, or is really more than the outline of my own ideas, which I must desire you to understand are by no means settled, and neither can nor ought to be so, until I am better informed of the sentiments of the heads of our church in both kingdoms. It has always seemed to me that the establishment of the Gallican church was likely to be the best model we could follow, but that the Roman Catholick religion, after all, could only be tolerated. The provision to be given to the clergy of that persuasion could not be put upon a more permanent footing than that which is applied to the use of the Dissenting clergy; and that, moreover, the established religion of the country being Protestant, the making this provision would afford an occasion which should not be lost, of rendering the Roman Catholick clergy amenable to the common law of the land in the same cases to which those of our own church are subject to it, and that the judgments and sentences of the Catholick prelates or church against the lay members of their communion should be as open to the superintendence and control of the courts of law, as those of our own ecclesiastical courts. What I particularly allude to is the power the Roman Catholicks exercise of excommunication, which, I know, is grievously complained of by the Protestant bishops, and, if I am rightly informed, with great reason, and is a power which, in the manner and for the purpose for which I understand it to be exercised, is not to be endured, and could not have been suffered in any well-ordered Catholick country. I must now have convinced you of the correctness of my first position, viz., my inability to give an opinion upon the Roman Catholick plan, and also have given you wherewithal to employ your thoughts, which I shall be very glad to receive from you, and shall thankfully attend to any suggestions of any kind which you will be so good as to supply me with, either for the solution of this or any other of the difficulties which are likely to occur in the arrangement of our final settlement, concerning which I am much gratified by having my opinion so fully confirmed in almost every respect by so high an authority as that of Dr. Moylan.

I return you the letter and plan enclosed.

You will have received before this time an account from lord Sheffield, of the East Grinsted, etc., clubs. I think it would be very desirable to introduce into them some false brother, whose judgment and accuracy can be depended upon, and that there can hardly be two opinions on the necessity of putting them down effectually.

41.—AN ACCOUNT OF THE TREATY BETWEEN THE UNITED IRISHMEN AND THE ANGLO-IRISH GOVERNMENT IN 1798.—BY WILLIAM J. MAC NEVEN.

The object of the United Irishmen was at first like that of the Americans, a redress of grievances. When not only that redress was refused, but they who demanded it were subjected to persecution, instead of desisting with the submissive resignation of slaves, they manfully arraigned the injustice of their oppressors, enlarged their views, and sought for independence. When compelled to pay the largest price that a nation can give for its happiness, they were not such pusillanimous fools as to content themselves with a condition which would not afford a reasonable expectation of for ever excluding the return of their calamities. A reform in the Commons House of parliament, comprehending the emancipation of the Catholics, was what the United Irishmen earnestly desired; but when they found the whole force of English influence exerted to defeat their object, they easily perceived that the master grievance of their country was its dependence on England. Then, and not before, they resolved to sever the enslaving connection.

The English cabinet on their side, judged that the moment was now arrived for bringing that treason to issue which lord Clare, according to his own confession,[1] had been plotting during several years, for annihilating the parliament of Ireland, and vesting the whole dominion of the country in a foreign legislature.

Joined with him in this conspiracy were some others, and in the number lord Castlereagh; all of whom, with cold-blooded artifice, stirred up an insurrection that was to supply the necessary pretext for effecting their nefarious design.

In former times resort was had to similar acts of outrage, for the purpose of driving the natives into a resistance that should be followed by a forfeiture of their estates. Now a rebellion was intentionally produced by the chief agents of the British ministry, in order to give an opportunity for confiscating the whole political power, and the independent character of the country, by an act of Union.

The confidential friends of the British Government were known to boast of having plunged the nation into this scene of horrors. Nor was the executive committee of the Union unacquainted with the intention of reducing Ireland to depend on the will of a foreign power,[2] and that power an ambitious rival. They exerted themselves therefore, and for some time with effect, in restraining the impatience of their

---

[1] 'In debates in the Irish House of Lords on the Union.'

[2] 'So little was the policy of the British cabinet on the subject, a secret even out of Ireland, that the director, Carnot, told Dr. Mac Neven, in August, 1797, that a Union was Mr. Pitt's object in his vexatious treatment of Ireland, and that it behoved the United Irishmen to be aware of his schemes.'

irritated countrymen. Although a recourse to arms might become necessary for the attainment of one of their objects—separation, yet this itself was contemplated by them as the alternative only of an unrelenting refusal to reform; and the executive in that, the last extremity, wished, through the co-operation of a respectable French force, to exclude the barbarity of a purely civil war. This, when excited by the provocation daily given to it, was the convulsive effort of despair; and but for the systematic atrocities of the conspirators against the legislative independence of Ireland, no *civil war* would have occurred there to the present moment. We have the authority of the American Congress, that the colonies were driven designedly into resistance, for the purpose of giving an opportunity to impose on them a standing army, illegal taxes, and to establish among them a system of despotism. This arbitrary project, after miscarrying in America, was transferred by the same monarch to Ireland, and unhappily succeeded there. Before assistance could be obtained against his schemes from the natural ally of his persecuted subjects, an enlarged scope was given to the intolerable practice of house-burnings, free quarters, tortures and summary executions, which, as the ministry intended, exploded in rebellion. After this manner they facilitated the Union; but neither the recollection of the means, nor the nature of the measure, could have any other effect than to strengthen the desire of separation.

When the contest began, its vigour greatly exceeded the calculations of those who provoked it. For some time it carried with it the justest terrors; and partial as it was, it almost shook the Government to its centre. Of the progress of this insurrection, of the valour it developed, or of its unfortunate issue, I shall not speak at present. Let me, however, observe, that the prowess manifested by men untutored in scenes of death, except by their own sufferings, has convinced every thinking mind, that if they had then received even the small co-operation which arrived too late under Humbert, or if they had been possessed of more military skill and military stores, their success would have been certain. But at the end of two months from the commencement of the insurrection, the enemy had acquired a decided superiority, in consequence of being incomparably better provided with the means of warfare. Most of the insurgent chiefs had fallen or surrendered, their forces had capitulated or were dispersed. Before the 22nd of July, the actions of New Ross, Arklow and Vinegar Hill were lost. Messrs. Aylmer and Fitzgerald, with the remaining forces in the county of Kildare, had entered into military conditions, and no force remained in the field but a very inconsiderable body in the mountains of Wicklow.

At this time, without any concert with those individuals who were afterwards employed to negotiate on behalf of the State prisoners, and even without their knowledge, a plan was set on foot for rescuing the country from the vindictive massacre of its defeated inhabitants. Persons not at all implicated in the insurrection had taken up the measure, and the old lord Charlemont was represented to the State prisoners as desirous of being useful in procuring a retreat from all persecution for the past. Though too infirm to be an active agent between them and the Government, he would undertake, it was alleged, to obtain a satisfactory guarantee of whatever terms might be settled. Accordingly, Mr. Francis Dobbs, one of the members in parliament for his borough, prompted as well by innate philanthropy as by the patriotic wishes of his noble friend, went round, with the permission of Government, accompanied by one of the high sheriffs, to the different prisoners, and obtained the assent of most of them to an agreement of a somewhat similar import with that which was afterwards concluded. In this visit he publicly assured his hearers that the scope and object of his mission was to procure a most important advantage for the country at large; to put a stop to further carnage, and to terminate, without the infliction of more calamity, an insurrection which had failed.

It became manifest to the State prisoners themselves that present success was hopeless, and that the United Irishmen could not then struggle through the surrounding defeats to the independence and prosperity of their native land. The Anglo-Irish Government had found a profligate informer, who, by false pretensions to principle, obtained the confidence of the gallant and unsuspicious lord Edward Fitzgerald. The ruffian, of the name of Reynolds, became acquainted with some of the executive and with the proceedings of the Leinster provincial committee, to which he had been elected through the influence of the friend and patron whom he afterwards betrayed, and whose family he reduced, through confiscations, to poverty. He thus enabled Government in the preceding March to arrest some of the persons then most efficient in the United Irish organization. There was an interruption of all system since those arrests, and no one had yet appeared sufficiently capable of filling the chasm which that misfortune left in the direction of the Union. The arrest and death of lord Edward himself in the month of May, had drawn after them a train of disastrous consequences, that were at that time perhaps irreparable. The loss subsequently sustained of other energetic patriots, who were prepared to second his exertions, occasioned the failure of his well-concerted plans. The Irish nation could not sustain a greater misfortune in the person of any one individual, than befell it in the loss of Fitzgerald at that critical moment. Even his enemies, and he had none but those of his country, allowed him to possess distinguished military talents. With these, with unquestioned intrepidity, republicanism, and devotion to Ireland, with popularity that gave him unbounded influence, and integrity that made him worthy of the highest trust—had he been present in the Irish camp to organize discipline, and give to the valour of his country a scientific direction, we should have seen the slaves of monarchy fly before the republicans of Ireland, as they did before the patriots of America. And if at last the tears of his countrymen had been constrained to lament his fate, they would have been received on the laurels of his tomb.

In the midst of these heart-rending misfortunes, the unresisted wreaking of implacable animosity, hitherto somewhat suspended through fear, began to rage in all the revengeful wantonness of security. The military, the orangemen, the magistrates, glutted their bigoted fury or personal hatred with the blood of United Irishmen, and still they seemed to be insatiable. The riding-house of Mr. Claudius Beresford daily witnessed the torture of flagellation, while that zealous supporter of British supremacy presided himself at the execution; and, as often as the instrument became too much clogged with the flesh of the sufferer, he was seen to pick the cords of the cat-o'-nine-tails, that they might lacerate with deeper loyalty. Even children were sometimes scourged, sometimes immersed to the lips in water, to extort information from them against their parents, and concealment was punished with death. The privacy of families was insecure; the delicacy of females was not respected. Everywhere you beheld a spectacle of atrocities or a melancholy gloom. Acquaintances and friends passed each other with averted eyes, and the stillness of terror was interrupted only by the march of military cut-throats, the processions of executions, and the savage orgies of orangemen, maddened with ebriety and fierce from bloodshed.

At the same time that the military tribunals were cutting down the most virtuous citizens in every quarter, the ordinary criminal courts were dooming to death, by the help of furious and malignant orange juries, those of the United Irishmen against whom the least evidence to go to a jury could be had. The vilest beings, informers and malefactors, were able, with a dreadful facility, to sacrifice in these courts, I will not say of justice, but at the bar of fanaticism and frenzy, the most upright men, who were led successively to certain death, passing through the forms of trial only to afford a more solemn festival to the enemies of Irish liberty. The blood that would be shed on the scaffold and in the field, it was now certain, could produce no other effect than displaying the determined valour and undeviating integrity of those who suffered for the common cause. If the Union were prevented from exhausting itself in such an unequal contest, it might still be formidable to its enemies; perhaps more formidable than ever, in consequence of the courage and fidelity it had manifested.

What, then, was the best service that remained for prudence or virtue to perform? To stop the ensuing horrors, to save the country from the cold-blooded slaughter of its best, its bravest, its most enlightened defenders; to prevent those calamities that are consequent on an unsuccessful civil contest, and that frequently render a future effort impracticable.

There was something even in the passing moment to incite to an attempt at such a compromise as would secure those benefits. Lord Cornwallis had just entered upon the government of Ireland, and declared himself inclined to justice and conciliation. He was violently opposed by the Orange faction in the cabinet; and from a motive which he did not then disclose, but which subsequent events have shown to be the projected Union of the two countries, he wished to make a merit with those who had suffered most from the British Government, by teaching them to throw the severity of their sufferings on their own villainous parliament and merciless countrymen. Good policy required from the United Irishmen that they should avail themselves of his avowed disposition. A faint, but in the end illusive hope, was conceived that as he was, in some measure, at war with their old oppressors, if a fair statement of the objects and motives of the United Irishmen were laid before him; if the precipice, on the brink of which his majesty's ministers had been madly walking, were pointed out to him—he would be convinced of what is truly the fact, that Ireland cannot be retained in the bonds of British connection without adopting comprehensive measures of reform and speedily removing the discontents that produced her alliance with France.

To such considerations was superadded a most anxious wish to preserve the lives of Michael William Byrne and Oliver Bond. They who knew those excellent men, will not say that the State prisoners violated the brotherhood of affection to which they had sworn, by an effort to restore them to their families and to society; especially when no return whatever was made for those manifold advantages, that it would be of the smallest importance, in that advanced season of the affairs of the Union, to withold even from its enemies. Alas! that effort was vain; a stroke of apoplexy snatched Bond from his friends, after they had rescued him, as they thought, from the grave. Against Byrne, the rancour of party and the thirst of blood prevailed. He was executed.

Mr. Byrne was of one of the first families of the country, and among his relatives had many friends, who, without his knowledge, exerted their interest to preserve his life. They were told that if he would express regret at being an United Irishman, and declare that he was seduced by Lord Edward Fitzgerald, he should be forgiven. When this proposal was made known to him, he spurned at it with abhorrence. He declared that he had no regret but that of not leaving his country free; that he was never seduced to be an United Irishman, and least of all by that hallowed character, whose memory they wished to traduce. Perhaps, said he, they intend to rob his children of his inheritance; but my existence shall never be disgraced by giving sanction to so base a design. This young man having a strong sense of religion, received its rites with a cheerful hope and an assured conscience—expressing the greatest consolation at quitting life in his perfect senses, with leisure for previous preparation, and in so virtuous a cause. His very adversaries were forced to admire and do homage to that cause which produced such martyrs. So complete was the self-possession and delicacy of his mind, that in passing to the scaffold by the window of Mr. Bond's apartment, where Mrs. Bond was then with her husband, he stooped so low as not to be seen by her, lest he should alarm the feelings of a wife and a mother at that moment trembling for all that she held dear.

If the repetition of things that are become familiar by use could astonish, the demeanour and fortitude of that young man, from his condemnation to his execution, might be truly called astonishing. He was not only undaunted and unmoved, but he was collected, cheerful and happy. He had hazarded his life in a good cause, and was determined, by publicly manifesting the enthusiasm with which he would die, to give resolution to the timid, and constancy to the brave. Fortified by the examples of those who mounted the scaffold before him, he went, perhaps, to the utmost bounds of magnanimity, and put it out of the power of those who followed to surpass him.

Mr. Bond, though an United Irishman, was certainly not one within the personal knowledge of his prosecutor, Reynolds, who, in almost everything he advanced respecting that gentleman, swore falsely. But Mr. Bond was highly beloved by the friends of Irish independence, and equally hateful to its enemies. He was one of the earliest in planning and promoting the union of Irishmen. He possessed a force of understanding, an elevation of soul, and an integrity of heart, that placed him in the first rank of patriots. His feelings were truly Irish, his principles, those of an enlightened republican. His character had fully established itself in the esteem of his countrymen, and will be honoured by them when the guilty triumph of his oppressors shall have passed away, or be remembered only to be abhorred.

The mode in which Byrne and his predecessors met their fate must have taught the Government that although they could immolate more victims, they would not thereby lessen the general indignation, exasperated by such losses, and strengthened by such examples. On this account, perhaps, Bond was respited from Friday, the 27th of July, until the Monday following; for Mr. Bond likewise had passed before the sitting commission of Oyer and Terminer, where the juries were infuriate Orangemen, and where such an extension was given to the law of treason as to embrace the population of the land.

In the interval Mr. Secretary Cooke had an interview with him and Mr. Neilson in the prison of Newgate, to know if, notwithstanding the execution of Mr. Byrne, the State prisoners would renew the negotiation. These again consented as far as they could; for notwithstanding the loss of one revered associate, it did not become them, they thought, to abandon many other valuable lives, and the safety of their brethren at large. In consequence of this second assent, Mr. Cooke visited the prisons. When he came to Kilmainham, Dr. Mac Neven, from a mistrust of the man, and of all the subordinate agents of Government, informed the secretary that until the terms were formally ratified by lord Cornwallis his lips should remain sealed. On Mr. Cooke's retiring, he consulted with his fellow-prisoners, Emmet and Sweetman, about the propriety of desiring a conference with the minister, lord Castlereagh. His friends agreeing with him in opinion, he wrote a note to Mr. Cooke to that effect.

Whether ministers found that what had been hitherto the basis of the treaty was not sufficiently extensive for their purpose, or from what other cause, is unknown; but Mr. Dobbs again visited the prisoners, with a letter which had been addressed to him by Mr. Cooke, stating that some mistake had taken place in the terms, without specifying what that mistake was, and containing a *new proposal* of giving up names, on a promise from Government that the persons so mentioned should not in any event be prosecuted capitally; and also that the prisoners should consent to emigrate to such country *as to his majesty should seem meet.* The letter likewise stated, that unless the information communicated by the prisoners should be important, Government would not consider itself bound by the agreement. These new terms were inadmissible, and were unanimously rejected. At the same time it was manifest that if anything could be effected, it must be done by directly treating with the head of the Government. For this purpose the prisoners, after some intercourse permitted and had between the different prisons, unanimously appointed as agents to negotiate on their behalf, Messrs. Emmet, O'Connor and Mac Neven. Lest there should be any indelicate appearance towards lord Castlereagh, Mr. Dobbs was requested to communicate to his lordship the wish of the prisoners, that their deputies should have liberty to wait on lord Cornwallis, or on him. The next morning, July the 29th, they were sent for to the

Castle of Dublin, where they had an interview with his lordship, the chancellor, lord Clare, and Mr. Secretary Cooke. The discussion between those ministers and the deputies turned on the following points:

First:—Lord Castlereagh revived to the deputies the proposal of disclosing the names of their associates; but would engage that they should be exempted from prosecution. It was observed to him that, if he meant to press this condition, it was needless to proceed, that there could be no treaty with such a clause; on which it was entirely dismissed.

The second point related to the confidence to be placed in each other's engagements. When the deputies expressed doubts as to the execution of the agreement on the side of the Government, since their part of it must be first performed: 'Gentlemen,' said the lord chancellor, 'it comes to this—ye must trust to us, or we must trust to you; but a Government that would break its faith with you could not stand, and ought not to be allowed to stand.'—The Government did afterwards break its faith, and incurred the chancellor's sentence. At last it was settled as a matter of sacred honour to act on both sides with good faith, and up to the spirit of the compact. Agreeably to the principles which led the deputies to negotiate, they insisted, in the next place, on a general amnesty for all that had been done on account of the Union. The ministers, on their part, would not consent to make this a specific article, lest, as they said, the people should thank the deputies of the United Irishmen for it, and not the administration. But as on this point principally turned the negotiation, they gave the deputies the most solemn assurance, that it was the intention of Government, if enabled so to do by its agreement with them, to let no more blood be shed, except in case of deliberate murder, or conspiracy to murder. It was answered, that there was no wish to stipulate for persons coming properly under that description, provided that in it were not included those who had killed others only in the field of battle. In this sense, and with only the exception of deliberate murderers, if any such there were, the article was concluded. As the deputies had now secured all that was essential, they were content to leave to the ministry the popularity of the measure, especially as that was an advantage which it seemed eager to appropriate to itself.

The fourth point of discussion was the equivalent to be given to Government. The deputies urged that the importance of their communications could only be judged of by the extent of what was already known; but that the State prisoners would not consent to place themselves in the power of Government, unless it were first well ascertained that on their acting with good faith, the objects they had so much at heart would be completely secured. They requested, therefore, to have explained to them what in this case was meant by importance. After some conversation, they were told that it would be considered of importance *to give their authority for the alliance of the United Irishmen with France, the details of which the king's ministers well knew, but from such sources as they must keep secret;* and that it would be important for them to be able to separate the true from the false of what they had already heard.

As to the prisoners going to such country as should be pointed out, this also was peremptorily refused. Upon which, Lord Castlereagh said his exception was against those countries alone that were at war with England, or under the influence of France; but both parties agreed upon the United States of America.

The ministers, in the strongest manner, pledged Lord Cornwallis's administration to the utmost liberality in carrying the terms of the agreement into effect, and an immediate compliance was so fully expected, that a promise was obtained of giving the prisoners sufficient time for settling their affairs, before they were required to leave the country.

When it was proposed to make a draught of these stipulations, lord Castlereagh laboured to produce a persuasion of its being superfluous, since everything was so well understood, and would be honourably construed. The deputies, however, thought it their duty to commit the substance, at least, to writing; and drew up a paper, which must be considered a memorandum, and not a detail of the agreement—but containing a plain reference to the most important article of the general amnesty, which, notwithstanding all the promises of the ministry, they could not suffer to remain altogether a secret one. The following is that paper:—

'That the undersigned State prisoners in the three prisons of Newgate, Kilmainham and Bridewell, engage to give every information in their power of the whole of the internal transactions of the United Irishmen; and that each of the prisoners shall give detailed information of every transaction that has passed between the United Irishmen and foreign States; but that the prisoners are not, by naming or describing, to implicate any person whatever; and that they are ready to emigrate to such country as shall be agreed on between them and the Government, and give security not to return to this country without the permission of Government, and not to pass into an enemy's country—if, on doing this, they are to be freed from prosecution, and also Mr. Oliver Bond be permitted to take the benefit of this proposal.

'The State prisoners also hope that the benefit of this proposal may be extended to such persons in custody, or not in custody, as may choose to benefit by it.'

The deputies made the first sketch of this paper, containing the matters they had previously discussed, as far as the ministers had consented to the same. The chancellor and lord Castlereagh revised the draft, Mr. Secretary Cooke transcribed it, after which he and the deputies interchanged copies. Finally, it was stated by the persons who negotiated, that as they were not actuated by personal motives, but were employed for the rest of their fellow-prisoners, they must communicate the agreement to them, and that if it was refused by others, they also would decline signing it. The agreement was accordingly submitted to all the State prisoners in custody in the metropolis—none of whom refused to ratify it.

The necessity of effecting a retreat from an unsuccessful insurrection, first led the United Irishmen to negotiate. The publicity of all their transactions, especially after the insurrection, induced them to accede to the conditions which have been related. There could be no objection against giving every information of the internal transactions and external relations of the Union, which could be detailed without naming or describing any person whatever, for this simple reason— Government was already in possession of it all. They had repeatedly seized United Irish constitutions, and copies of the most material orders the executive had issued. They had obtained very extensive intelligence from all parts of the country notwithstanding the unparalleled fidelity of the United Irish body, considering that it comprehended almost the active population of the whole nation. Their knowledge of the negotiations of the United Irishmen with foreign States was equally notorious, and at this time one of the deputies had personal evidence of its extent and accuracy. That knowledge was obtained from some person in the pay of England, and in the confidence of France.[1]

On the 12th of March preceding, after the arrests in Dublin, Mr. Cook told Dr. Mac Neven that Government was in possession of a copy of the memoir given by him to the French minister, and he removed, in this instance, all suspicion of his own veracity, by detailing a great part of its contents. The day following, Dr. Mac Neven was again questioned by the Anglo-Irish privy council concerning the same paper. Of this discovery, he found means to inform several of his friends; and at the period of the negotiation, he had the satisfaction of knowing that one of those persons was actually in France, and had, in all probability, already communicated the intelligence to the Directory.

Here it is just to quote the words of lord Clare, the envenomed traducer of the United Irishmen and of their country. In a debate in the English House of Lords on the martial-law bill, in March, 1801, he declared that the United Irishmen who negociated with the Irish Government in 1798, had disclosed nothing with which the king's ministers were not acquainted before.

What, then, it may be asked, did Government gain by its agreement?

---

[1] 'Mr. Reinhardt, the resident minister of the French republic at Hamburg, when applied to by Dr. Mac Neven for a passport to proceed to Paris, insisted on his orders not to deliver any without the permission of his Government, first obtained for every individual case. Though much pressed he was inflexible; but always offered to transmit a memoir which should detail the object of the mission. This was at last prepared, in despair of proceeding, and as Reinhardt knew the English language, and must at any rate translate the memoir into cipher, it was deemed unnecessary to compose it in French. Two days after it was delivered, Mr. Reinhardt's scruples vanished, and he granted the passport. Mac Neven afterwards saw the deciphered copy of this paper, in French, in Talleyrand's office, where it was kept under the particular key of the chief secretary. The original, in English, was withdrawn from Reinhardt, and never afterwards entrusted by Mac Neven into any hands but those of a friend upon whom suspicion could not attach; and independent of the security offered by his character, there is this strong circumstance, that the copy of the memoir which Dr. Mac Neven saw in the hands of lord Clare, was from the French, and not the English.'

It gained that which the ministers acknowledged was *of importance to them.* It gained the ability of concealing its real channels of intelligence, and of putting the deputies and their associates forward to vouch for what it wished to make known to the world, and could not otherwise venture to authenticate.

The perpetrators of so much tyranny, of house-burning, torture, arbitrary transportation, and licensed murder, thought that they should be able to escape from the infamy of these crimes, by proving against the United Irishmen the design, so often attributed to them, of effecting a separation from England, and establishing a republic—a design, which, in the view of the English Government and its partisans, would justify, it was known, the violation of every principle, and the infliction of every horror. But the United Irishmen knew they could demonstrate that the persecution of their enemies began in a deliberate hostility to the rights of the people, whose first claims were preferred even with great reserve, and that it was the despotism with which they were resisted, that in a manner compelled men to open their eyes to the indispensable necessity of political liberty, and to all the rapturous prospects of self-government.

The persons who negotiated were far from declining the opportunity of making every man in the nation meditate on separation, and a republic; and they deemed it an advantage, in the circumstances of the times, to be at liberty to give their country and the world at large an authentic account of their principles and objects—things which, after what had taken place, would be subjects of general inquiry, which the enemies of the Union would be industrious to calumniate, and of which United Irishmen alone would be competent to give a true relation.

The insurrection had precipitated the moment when the utmost publicity was not less favourable than secrecy had been before to the designs of the United Irishmen; and in availing themselves of the passing opportunity, it was not their fault if they did not secure other objects of essential importance. Had the conditions of their treaty been as religiously observed as they were solemnly ratified, the persons who carried it through, and these were, properly speaking, the whole of the prisoners, must be acknowledged to have performed for the Union a most useful service. Not a drop of blood was afterwards shed on the score of what had been done in the insurrection or the Union up to that period, but was shed in violation of the compact between them and the Government. If public faith or private honour were obligations felt by the Anglo-Irish ministry, vindictive power and lawless violence would, in consequence of that transaction, have been arrested in their career. Perfidiously as every English Government had ever acted towards the people of Ireland, it seemed an unwarrantable mistrust to suppose that in no change of times or individuals would this execrable policy be altered. Moreover, such is the dependence of social man on his fellow-creatures, that stipulations and compacts, though often violated, are again forced on us by the necessities of our nature, and every principle of justice revolts at ascribing before-hand to a set of new men the dishonour of their predecessors. Accordingly, when better prospects had vanished, and the United Irishmen found themselves under the necessity of treating for a general amnesty, they were induced to believe that the engagements which the Government thought fit to contract, it would have sufficient honour to perform. This confidence was countenanced by the immediate proceedings of lord Cornwallis, who authenticated the general object of the treaty by two public acts:— 1st. He sent Mr. Dobbs, accompanied by popular and influential United Irishmen, whom he furnished with passes and safe conduct, to the county of Wicklow, where there was still a remnant of insurrection, to make known there the compact, and give the insurgents an opportunity of adopting it. 2dly. General Nugent, commander of the northern district, set forth the agreement in a proclamation which he issued in the month of August, 1798, and called on all those in the north, who might choose to do so, to avail themselves of the conditions.

In performance of their part, a memoir was prepared by the deputies of the prisoners and delivered to the Government on the 4th of August. A couple of days after it had been presented, Mr. Cooke came to Messrs. Emmett and Mac Neven at Kilmainham, to say that lord Cornwallis had read but could not receive it, unless some passages were expunged, as it was a justification of the United Irishmen. He acknowledged, at the same time, that it was a fulfilment of their engagements—adding, however, that Government could not publish it, for if they did, they must hire a person to answer it, to whom, probably, there would be a reply, and thus an endless paper war would be introduced. He was frankly told that any true account of the proceedings of the United Irishmen would, in fact, be a justification, and that no alteration could be made in the memoir consistently with character or conscience. Although Mr. Cooke said lord Cornwallis could not receive the memoir, yet he carried it away.

Ministers, judging that their purposes would be better answered by parole examinations, which they might mutilate as they thought fit, and as the chancellor afterwards declared they would do,[1] summoned before the secret committee of both Houses some others of the prisoners, as well as the deputies.—The examinations of two of these will be found in the Appendix.[2] They committed them to writing each day on their return, adopting that precaution merely to guard against suppressions on the part of Government, but not suspecting at that time the possibility of wilful misstatement. They were anxious to preserve only such answers as they suspected the committees would avoid publishing. This will account for one or two omissions, which they might have supplied by the help of the appendices to the report of the lords and commons committee; but they prefer leaving their answers as they were written while fresh in their memories, because it is in the reader's power, by comparing them with those appendices, to ascertain all that was said, the spirit in which it was said, and the candour with which it has been detailed by both parties.

Thus, a number of persons, against whom nothing could have been proved, but who were highly obnoxious to the British Government, making common cause with others, who, in consequence of the failure of the insurrection, were defenceless and in danger, offered to remove out of the sphere of injuring that Government, provided the spilling of blood should universally cease. Cemented as they all were by political attachment and brotherly union, those who were beyond the reach of legal conviction devoted themselves to make terms for their country. They joined together the safety of some with the danger of others, by a common sacrifice to obtain a national good.

Several perverted accounts of this compact between the prisoners and the Government, and of the examinations of the deputies before the

---

[1] See examinations of W. J. Mac Neven, pp. 163-176. [2] *See* pp. 163-190.

committees of parliament, appeared immediately after in the ministerial newspapers. They contained many falsehoods, probably issuing from, and unquestionably not disagreeable to, those who would be ashamed to avow them. In the enslaved state of the Irish press, it was not probable that articles so important would be permitted to meet the public eye, without having been perused, if not written, by some of the confidential servants about the Castle. Truth and falsehood were artfully blended, because it was probably perceived that a newspaper misrepresentation could extend more widely than the correction of it in a separate volume.

One most injurious falsehood caused great uneasiness, namely, that the prisoners had disclosed the names of their associates. Very fortunately they obtained early intelligence of these calumnies, and found means at the same time to contradict them by the following advertisement, which appeared in two of the Dublin newspapers on the 27th of August:

'Having read in the different newspapers, publications pretending to be abstracts of the report of the secret committee of the House of Commons, and of our depositions before the committees of the lords and commons, we feel ourselves called upon to assure the public that they are gross, and to us astonishing misrepresentations, not only unsupported by, but, in many instances, directly contradictory to the facts we really stated on those occasions. We further assure our friends, that in no instance did the name of any individual escape from us; on the contrary, we always refused answering such questions as might tend to implicate any person whatever, conformably to the agreement entered into by the State prisoners with Government.—ARTHUR O'CONNOR, THOMAS ADDIS EMMET, WILLIAM JAMES MAC NEVEN.'

The sending forth of this advertisement from the body of a prison, and authenticated by the names of the parties, left no doubt of the truth of its allegations. A tempest of folly and fury was immediately excited in the House of Commons. Blinded by their rage, the members of that *honourable* assembly neglected the obvious distinction between the newspapers and their report. They took to themselves the falsehoods that had been repelled. Mr. M'Naghton, and two virulent barristers, Francis Hutchinson and Cunningham Plunket, were even clamorous for having the persons who signed the refutation disposed of by a summary execution. Plunket had been the bosom intimate of Emmet, the companion of his childhood, and the friend of his youth. Hutchinson afterwards acknowledged that he was instigated to what he did by the administration, which imitated in this proceeding the ancient policy of the English, in making Irishmen the executioners of one another. The conduct of both marks the inhumanity and meanness to which Irish gentlemen debased themselves at this period, the better to signalize their loyalty towards the rulers of wretched Ireland.

The prisoners were immediately remanded to the closest custody, and no friend or acquaintance was suffered to approach them. In the meantime, the committee proceeded formally in printing their report, and as the advertisement had contradicted, by anticipation, every falsehood common to that publication and to the newspapers, three of the State prisoners were again summoned before the secret committee of the House of Lords, in order to draw the line between what they admitted and what they rejected.

They readily confirmed what they had actually asserted before the secret committees of parliament, and only wished that the committees would state it all to the public. But the object ministers had most at heart was to prove the existence of a military organization, the design of separating Ireland from Great Britain, and the alliance formed for this purpose with France. It was no part of their plan to bring evidence of the acts of tyranny which forced the United Irishmen into such measures. To those three points, therefore, were the questions of the committee directed. But to show more pointedly the license taken by the ministerial newspapers, Dr. Mac Neven instanced that of names having been disclosed, which was a misrepresentation of fact not warranted by the report of either house of parliament. It was only in allusion to this misrepresentation, and a few others of less importance, that the expression was introduced into his deposition, 'which are not supported by the report of either house of parliament.'

When the secret committees drew up their reports, they were neither on their oaths nor on their honours; but they allowed themselves every possible latitude in general accusations against the whole body of United Irishmen, with the vain hope of justifying themselves while they aspersed others.

The annexed memoir and examinations [pp. 147-190] contain all that passed between the Anglo-Irish Government and Messrs. Emmet and Mac Neven. The committees of the lords and commons examined those gentlemen to what matters they pleased, and asked them what questions they liked. They have given their own edition of the examinations, which contain whatever they could substantiate to criminate those persons, or the Union, on their authority. Out of this record, then, nobody has a right to travel for objections against them, because that accuser to which they were most obnoxious and best known, can specify nothing beyond what is there. The supplementary malice of others may evince inveteracy of dislike, but cannot affect those two deputies. It is, above all things, absurd to assert that they acknowledged any political acts not to be found in those admissions. If they did, the Anglo-Irish Government would not be silent on the subject. The moment specific charges are preferred, they are reduced to the memoir and examinations; and yet it appears from them that Emmet and Mac Neven had not even the merit of being United Irishmen until 1796. That is, after the recall of lord Fitzwilliam, when the British cabinet sent over lord Camden to foster the Orange system, to continue the slavery of the Catholics, and to resist every measure of reform; when, indeed, there was no alternative but bondage or resistance.

From the beginning, the whole course of English government in Ireland was unjust, tyrannical and degrading. No sooner did the United Irishmen endeavour to procure a reform of this iniquitous system, than the partisans of England, interested in its continuance, flew to fresh acts of coercion and cruelty, and then pretended that these were wrung from them by necessity, without adverting to the old and prior wrongs of the country.

During the secret imprisonment of these deputies, which followed the publication of their advertisement, an act of parliament passed through nearly all its stages, teeming in its recitals with the most injurious falsehoods. On reading them in the London Courier, Mr. Samuel Neilson wrote a letter, which he designed to send to the editor of that paper, declaring that the State prisoners had retracted nothing; but that they had entered into a compact with Government, of which he enclosed him a copy, for stopping the effusion of blood.

It well merits the attention of those who lived out of the Irish metropolis at that period, that the first knowledge which any of the prisoners had of that statute was from an English newspaper. This circumstance affords a specimen of the general darkness of that tyranny and terror which were predominant, and of the peculiar obscurity in which this transaction was meant to be involved. It also further evinces the faithlessness of the Anglo-Irish administration.

Some time antecedent to the introduction of this law, lord Norbury, then attorney-general, mentioned to Mr. Emmet that it was intended to bring in a bill for carrying into effect the agreement entered into between the State prisoners and the Government. Mr. Emmet replied that he could see no necessity for any such bill; but if one were introduced, that the State prisoners, as peculiarly interested, ought first to receive copies of it. This the attorney-general promised should be done, and sufficient time given them to make any observations on it they might think fit. Notwithstanding such assurance, it was passed without their ever knowing its contents, except by the newspaper already mentioned, while many of them were detained in close custody, and excluded from all external communication.

Neilson, in order to leave no room for cavilling, inclosed a copy of his letter to the editor of the 'Courier,' in one to lord Castlereagh, together with the newspaper and offensive passages underscored. In a few hours after, Messrs. Cooke and Marsden came to Neilson's prison, asked him if he really meant to publish a contradiction to the act of parliament, and being answered in the affirmative, Mr. Cooke solemnly declared that if so, it was his excellency the lord lieutenant's determination to make void the compact, and cause civil and military executions to proceed as before. 'But, sir,' said Neilson, 'how can an act of mine subject others to punishment?' 'It will,' was the secretary's answer. 'If you publish a syllable on the subject, the consequence shall equally affect all.' The loss of one life was not thought a sufficient curb against the workings of honest indignation, and therefore it was threatened that a mass of fellow-creatures should be involved in the same destruction. Thus we have seen men who invoke order rend the ties of social security, and set up for themselves the ruffian law of force; men who invoke religion, address heaven to witness only the perfidy of their engagements; and those who declaim about humanity, become very copyists of the enormities they stigmatize in their enemies.

The message sent by Mr. Cooke was singularly characteristic of inhuman duplicity, of remorseless cruelty, of a shameful disregard of public faith, and together with the subsequent treatment of the prisoners, forms a counterpart of the former conduct of lord Cornwallis towards the citizens of Charleston.[1] Nevertheless, had the British Government not found an obsequious instrument in the American minister, Mr. Rufus King, they could not have consummated their design, without a degree of undisguised perfidy of which they seemed solicitous to avoid the appearance. It was that minister who furnished the pretext under which many of the Irish State prisoners lost four years of the prime of their lives in close captivity; twenty of them were immured in a remote fortress in a foreign land, where they could not hold intercourse with their friends or their country, unless through the medium of their enemies. They saw the duke of Portland's order concerning them, which was harsh and rigorous in the extreme; but in passing through the hands of lieutenant-governor the Hon. James Stuart, it received what mitigation his duty would permit, and the prisoners were sensible it would have received more, if he had had the option. But they do not complain of rigour; it has protected character which might have been blighted by the kindness of the court. It vindicates them from the calumnies of the British Government and its retainers. It demonstrates that they did not sacrifice their principles to any unworthy compromise, and that they continued to deserve the enmity of the oppressors of their country.

After this view of the stipulated rights, the motives and proceedings of the Irish State prisoners, and of the whole conduct of the Anglo-

---

[1] 'After the battle of Camden, the behaviour of lord Cornwallis to the American prisoners was a kind of rehearsal of the perfidiousness and cruelty which he practised so many years later against the defenceless Irish. Christopher Gadsden and the citizens of Charleston had entered into a regular capitulation with him for the surrender of that city; but no sooner did the English general find himself the stronger than he caused, in direct violation of the articles, the most conspicuous of them to be arrested and transported to St. Augustine, as he did the Irish prisoners to Fort George. In both instances, the sufferers were sent off without previous notice; in both instances a formal compact was violated; in both cases their private papers were seized. Though his sanguinary acts in Ireland are scarcely noticed, they fell so much short of the more infuriate atrocity of the Orangemen, yet the blood he shed there was immense, and in violation of his compact with the United Irishmen.'—'Vide Castlereagh's account of the number of executions—debates in the house of commons.'

Irish Government, what must any impartial man think of the miserable affection of branding them with a crime by styling them traitors? To submit from fear, where there is just ground for resistance, is pusillanimous; to oppose tyranny with arms, where peaceable redress has been refused, is heroic and virtuous. The United Irishmen endeavoured to make it likewise prudent, by allying themselves with a power able to second them, and, if it had judged wisely, deeply interested in their success.

Those who are accustomed to confound names with things, will see in the term traitor nothing but reproach: To the United Irishmen, provoked by so many wrongs, it is matter of boast and triumph. If by applying to them that appellation, no more be intended than technically to express that they broke the laws which are calculated to protect the existing Government, be it what it may, they adopt the epithet, and proudly avow themselves traitors to the tyrants of their country, and to the acts of power by which it is enslaved. They hazarded their lives in order to overthrow a system of government, and to destroy a connection which, after very mature reflection, they considered as the most baneful curses on their native land. But let it be observed that they never meditated the destruction even of that system of government, or of that connection, until they had tried and found vain every other effort for giving liberty and happiness to Ireland.

If by applying to them the term traitor, it be intended to express that they violated any duty which a citizen owes to the community of his fellow-citizens, they deny the accusation, and repel the charge of treason on the Irish parliament and the Anglo-Irish Government. These were the subverters of whatever little liberty Ireland enjoyed. They were the supporters of a connection which they have practically shown can never exist with Irish prosperity and freedom. Notwithstanding all the great physical and moral advantages which Ireland possesses, she is unknown, and almost always has been, as a nation, in consequence of that connection; she is bent down and prostrated by the incumbent pressure of her tyrant. To maintain the avarice and ambition of England, Irishmen are daily forced to shed their blood without glory or profit to their country. Victory itself rivets their chains the faster. In vain are they placed in the most advantageous position for unlimited commerce; in vain are they blessed with a fruitful soil, with inexhaustible mines, with navigable rivers, with the noblest harbours. All those-natural benefits are blasted by an imperious rival, before whose domination their strength is withered, their resources exhausted, their aptitudes sacrificed, and the spirit of emulation strangled in its birth. Ireland never has enjoyed a free constitution: even before the Union had annihilated her a nation, her Government was provincial, servile and corrupt; her people were represented nowhere. England bought her nominal representatives to betray her, and paid them with the money levied on herself. Of the three hundred seats of the Irish House of Commons, two hundred were the property of between thirty and forty individuals, who received for them a compensation of a million and a half sterling at the passing of the Union, and which sum, by the authority of those very men, was levied on the nation. The sanguinary and deluded Orangemen is also the legitimate growth of English policy, which has long fomented, and still perpetuates, the spirit of religious dissension; because that in the cordial union of Irishmen, England beholds the downfall of her usurpation, and the establishment of their liberties. Will any patriot, will any honest man, accuse the United Irishmen of having violated a duty towards their fellow-citizens, by labouring to destroy this horrible combination of flagitious fraud and systematic tyranny?

Look at the map of Europe. Place Ireland side by side with England: her climate is as auspicious, her soil as fertile, her people as intelligent, her situation more favourable. Why, then, has Ireland been sunk in poverty and wretchedness, while in East, West, and South, in Asia, Africa and America, the name of Britain is not more known and dreaded, even for the enormity of her crimes, than for the greatness of her dominion? Because from the first landing of Henry the Second, Ireland was a dependent province, and England an independent nation.

As to the charge of overturning the constitution, when it is preferred, let the question be also asked, what was meant by this anomalous thing, which the Government have since overturned by the Union, without substituting a better? Was it the sale of representation, an oligarchical monopoly of power, an exclusive enjoyment, by a few, of the universal rights of nature, the political tyranny of one thousandth part, and the political slavery of the residue of the community? And by whom are the United Irishmen accused? By those who, to palliate the corruption they must admit, allege, as Lord Castlereagh did to Mr. Emmet,[1] that a free House of Commons would be incompatible with, and destructive of, the other two estates. The Irish never had, nor indeed have even the English themselves ever had, what political philosophers, in their speculations, call the English constitution; an English minister says they never could by possibility have it—and then, under the insidious use of an equivocal expression, he accuses the United Irishmen of endeavouring to subvert a thing that did not, and, as he alleges, cannot exist.

But those persons whom their enemies style leaders of the United Irishmen, were actuated, it is said, by ambitious and unworthy motives. What are the proofs, and who are the accusers? The proofs are absolutely none; and let it be again observed, the accusers are men who, to apologize for their own vice, deny the reality of virtue. Those who have studied human nature only in the meanness of their hearts, and the depravity of Irish politics, may be expected, and perhaps permitted, to dispute the existence of disinterested patriotism; but the upright and moral man will not credit such foul calumnies without proof. With impartial minds, the purity of the object will be considered the best evidence of the purity of the motive.

Guarding the secret of those leading United Irishmen who have escaped persecution and suspicion, and particularizing only some of those whose names have acquired publicity, these imputations may be repelled by observing, that if Lord Edward Fitzgerald had been actuated in his political life by dishonourable ambition, he had only to cling to his great family connexions and parliamentary influence. They unquestionably would have advanced his fortunes and gratified his desires. The voluntary sacrifices he made, and the magnanimous manner in which he devoted himself for the independence of Ireland, are incontestable proofs of the generosity and purity of his soul. Mr. Henry Jackson, now happily in America, and Mr. John Sweetman, an emigrant in France, embarked very large fortunes, and the advantages of the highest commercial credit, in the same service; and, finally, they relinquished their country to redeem the blood of her children. Hampden Evans, than whom

---

[1] 'Vide [pp. 183-190] the examination of Mr. Emmet before the secret committee of the House of Commons.'

Ireland did not possess a more respected name, in the first line of connexion, affluent in fortune and temperate in every personal wish, what could induce him to set those advantages all at hazard, but the commanding sense of duty, the irresistible impulse of patriotic virtue?

The reputation which Mr. [Thomas Addis] Emmet inherited on his entrance into his profession, and the character he had acquired in it, were sufficient to flatter the most sanguine expectation. Had he chosen to yield to the solicitations of ambition, without regard to the means of elevation; had he entered the parliamentary career in the service of Government; had he adopted that line of conduct, by which very inferior abilities, provided there was still less integrity, were raised to eminence, he might, without much delay or any personal hazard, have arrived at the guilty honours of the Anglo-Irish court. It was only necessary to desert Irish interests for British domination, to support religious intolerance, to grasp at personal emolument, while the strength of Ireland was frittered, isolated and paralyzed; only requisite to resist that parliamentary reform which alone could correct abuses, and afford the nation a guarantee for its rights; simply to prefer the advantage of England in every competition; in fine, to signalize obedience and confirm loyalty, by selling the existence of an Irish parliament, and making war on the principles of liberty itself.

Integrity, indeed, forbade this course; but ambition has universally trodden it, in the way to fortune and to power.

When the United Irishmen are censured, it is not by those who think there is a moral obligation of doing all we can, and at every hazard, to maintain the independence and rights, to defend the honour and happiness of our country; to resist the attacks of despotism, whether in the shape of corruption or violence. No, it is by those creatures in whom the principle of action does not rise above the level of individual interest; by those corrupt minds that never expand to a love of country, a love of liberty, a sense of public prosperity. But the United Irishmen were taught by their principles, that the people alone are the fountain of all just power, and that to their freely chosen delegates belongs the right of exercising authority over the nation.

References to letters, documents, etc.

Abbreviations: MSS.:—Additional MSS., British Museum, Pelham Papers.—W. J. M.:—Papers by W. J. Mac Neven, New York: 1807.—G.:—MSS. in collection of the Editor.

Page	Head No.	MSS.	Page	Page	Head No.	MSS.	Page
91	1	33118	257	141	21	33105	437
99	2	33113	66	141	22	,,	441
101	3 i.	,,	76	142	23	,,	443
103	3 ii.	33104	179	143	24	33106	27
104	4	33119*	80	147	25	W. J. M.	174
117	5	33104	71	162	26	33106	186
117	6	,,	151	163	27	W. J. M.	194
118	7	,,	163	168	28	,,	202
119	8 i.	33105	307	176	29	,,	215
119	8 ii.	,,	311	183	30	,,	224
120	8 iii.	,,	313	190	31 i., ii.	G.	—
121	9	,,	327	191	32	33106	70
124	10	,,	368	192	33	,,	118
125	11	,,	372	193	34	,,	120
127	12	,,	386	194	35	,,	156
128	13	,,	388	195	36	,,	165
130	14	,,	396	197	37 i.	,,	178
132	15	,,	412	198	37 ii.	,,	182
133	16	,,	416	201	37 iii.	,,	186
135	17	,,	423	202	37 iv.	,,	190
135	18	,,	427	203	38	,,	196
137	19 i.	,,	431	205	39	,,	235
138	19 ii.	,,	433	207	40	33105	258
139	20	,,	439	208	41	W. J. M.	142

INDEX I.

ACCOUNT OF SECRET SERVICE MONEY.

P. 1—88.

Abbott, Mr., 64
Aberdeenshire Fencibles, 58
Address of loyalty, 1803, 81
Admiralty, 83
Alexander, colonel, 81, 82
Alexander, William, alderman, Dublin, 65, 73
Allen and Green, Dublin, 85
Altamont, earl of, 8, 16, 31, 32
Anglen, ——, Rev., 35
Annesley, A., 15
Annesley, earl, 78
Antrim, co., 61, 63, 66
Archer, 13, 40, 56
Ardee, 54
Armit, 13, 58, 79
Asgill, Charles, sir, 35, 52, 62
Athlone, 11, 12, 24, 69
Athy, 53, 62, 66, 68, 83
Atkins, T. J., 27
Atkinson, W., 8
Atkinson, lieutenant, 21
Atkinson, 65
Attorney-general, 29
Auditor-general, 29
Aylmer, prisoner, 19
Aylmer, colonel, 87

B., 31, 80
Baker, S., 40
Ball, 67
Ballina, 73, 82, 85
Ballinascorney, 79
Ballymore, 44, 82
Ballymore Eustace, 43
Baltinglass, 35, 53, 80
Barry, Michael, Rev. Middleton, 61
Barry, Thomas, Rev., Mallow, 57, 68, 75
Baynham, 9
Beckett, John, 66
Belfast, 8, 19, 21, 27, 34, 51, 79, 84
  ,, News-letter, 60
Bell, corporal, 40
Bell, J., 4, 59
Bell, justice, sheriff, 9, 10, 39
Bell, Mrs., 12
Beresford, J. C., 17, 69
Bergan, 30
Bergin, 17
Bermingham, 37
Bird, alias Johnston, 17
Blaquiere, 51
Blaquiere, John, sir, 26
Blessington, 8
Bond, Oliver, 11
Bordeaux, 73
Bourke, 9, 15, 25, 28, 45, 51
Bourke, M., 21
Boyce, J., 38
Boylan, 75, 76, 78, 81, 85
Boyle, 4, 35, 67, 72
Boyle, alias Burke, M., 65
Boyle, E., 44
Boyle, lord, 27
Bray, 19, 26
Bremer, 14

INDEX I.

Brennan, 10, 12, 15, 16
Brennan, James, 76, 77
Brewer, 15
Brien, Luke, 71, 73-77, 79, 80, 81-84, 86, 87
Brown, 28
Browne, Denis, 23, 28, 63
Brownlow, 14
Bruce, captain, 74, 83
Bruce, major, 14, 16
Burck, 35
Burke, 21, 22-24, 39, 43, 47, 49, 53, 56
Burke, Michael, 41, 58, 60, 61, 63-65, 67
Burnet, 78
Burns, 41
Butler, 33
Byrne, John, 78

Cahill, 13, 15-17, 19, 20-25, 28, 46
Cahill, James, 84
Cahill, Philip, 43
Callaghan, 82
Camble, Mary, 5
Campbell, 13, 27, 67, 72, 85
Campbell, Arthur, 40
Campbell, Colin, 79
Campbell, of Treasury, 64
Campsie, Richard, 64
Cappoquin, 73
Carden, John, sir, 28
Carey, Mrs., 30
Carhampton, earl, 6, 8, 9, 15, 20, 23, 31, 39, 43, 49, 56, 63, 70, 71, 76, 83
Carleton, Oliver, 13, 20, 23, 27
Carlow, 14, 52, 70
Carr, Denis, 66
Carrickfergus, 42, 48, 51, 58, 65-67, 69
Carroll, 73-76, 78, 79, 81, 85
Cartland, Shaw, 39
Cashel, 85
Cassidy, 66
Castlebar, 16
Castlereagh, viscount, 4, 11, 14, 16, 18, 20, 22, 23, 27, 30, 31, 42, 44, 48, 59, 70, 73
Caulfield, 15
Chambers, 22-28, 39, 41-44, 46-49, 51, 53
Chambers, John, 16, 20, 21
Chapman, 9-12, 28, 39, 41, 59, 75
Chapman, Richard, 75
Chapman, sergeant, 8, 11
Clare, militia of, 60
Clarke, general, 85

Clarke, James, 8
Clerk, 31
Clibborn, George, 50
Clonard, 5, 55
Cloney, 83
Clonmel, 19
Cochlan, John, 5
Cocks, Reginald, 75
Cody, H. B., W.B., 57, 66, 72, 74, 76, 79, 85
Colclough, 44, 45
Cole, captain, 85
Cole, H. St. George, 9, 12, 18, 26, 29, 33, 35, 37-39, 42, 45, 49, 52, 56, 60, 63, 66, 69
Coleman, 37, 38, 41, 43, 48, 49, 52, 53, 56, 60, 62, 64-67, 69
Colgan, 84, 85, 86, 87, 88
Coligan, Terence, 83
Collins, Thomas, 8, 18, 22, 25, 28, 31-33, 36, 41
Cologan, 84
Colton, 43
Commins, 29
Committee, secret, 20
Condon, 80, 85
Coulan, 37, 53, 64, 67, 69, 70-72
Conmee, —— Rev., 31
Connell, John, 8
Connellan, J., 16
Conolly, 19
Cooke, Edward, 2, 4, 5-7-17, 19, 20-22, 24-30-33, 36-39, 41, 42, 48, 49, 53-55, 59, 60, 62
Cope, 11
Corbett, W., 10, 60, 66, 74, 75, 77, 79, 81, 85
Cork, 11, 12, 14, 15, 20, 22, 27, 30, 43, 45, 52, 54, 56, 59, 62, 70, 75, 86
Cork, north, militia, 39
Cornwall, Leonard, 26
Cornwall, R., 29
Cornwallis, marquis, 61
Corran, James, 70
Cotter, James, sir, 76, 78
Coughlan, 12, 54
Coughlan, John, 55, 67
Coulson, captain, 8
Courtduff, Kildare, 70
Courtney, Thomas, 88
Courts-martial, 39, 54
Cox, 74, 83, 85
Cox, sergeant, 86

INDEX I.

Cranny, 62, 63-65
Cranny, John, 53, 66, 68
Crofton, 26
Crow, 87
Cullen, P., 86
Cummings, John, 12
Curran, James, 59
Cushmore, Waterford, 63
Cutting, major, 69

D., 75
Daly, sergeant, 26
D'Auvergne, 31
Dawes, 4, 5, 6, 10, 78, 79, 82
Dease, ———, Rev., 23, 33, 35, 40
Deering, 86
Dejune, John, 73
Dennis, 16
Derry, 6, 16, 23
Derry, bishop of. *See* Knox
Develin, Frederick, 67
D'Evelyn, 11
Dillon, 81, 86
Dillon, John, 87
Dive, colonel, 53
Dobson, 51
Dolan, Bridget, 54, 69, 76
Dominica, 41
Donnelly, 11
Donohoe, Patrick, 49
Doran, 13
Doran, C., Rev., 57, 66
Dorr, 84
Dowis, James, 20
Dowling, 6, 7
Down, 20, 34, 45, 58, 78
Downshire militia, 83
Doyle, 15, 79, 82, 84
Doyle, captain, 19
Dragoon guards, 10
Dresdon, 34
Drogheda, 19, 28, 39, 71, 81, 83
Drummond, general, 64
Drury, justice, 36, 38, 51, 65, 73, 80, 86
Dublin, 85
Dublin, barracks, 16, 21
Dublin, Bridewell, 5, 21, 28, 29, 31, 36
Dublin Castle, 6, 7, 9, 13, 14, 15, 20, 23, 25-29, 30-33, 37, 39, 40, 41, 43, 51, 61, 64, 66, 70-72-74, 76, 79, 80, 81, 83, 85, 87, 88

Dublin, Castle-street, 82
Dublin, Custom House, old, 17
Dublin, Exchange, 17, 25
Dublin, gaol, new, 36
Dublin, Hospital, Royal, 58
Dublin, Infirmary, Royal, 12, 19, 29, 33, 37, 43, 45, 52, 63
Dublin, James'-street, 6, 14, 18
Dublin, Merchants' cavalry, 16
Dublin, Smithfield, 16, 18, 24, 32, 81
Dublin, Town Clerks. *See* Allen
Dublin, Trinity-street, 30
Duff, James, sir, 48
Duignan, 13
Dumbarton, regiment, 19
Dundalk, 16, 54, 79
Dunlo, lord, 80
Dunn, 43, 66
Dunn, gaoler, 87
Dunn, sergeant, 6
Dunne, general, 79, 82
Dutton, 6, 9, 13, 16
Dutton, F., 22, 28, 30
Dwyer, 40, 48, 86

E., 78
Echlin, Henry, sir, 17
Edgar, W., 16
Edmonds, 25, 26
Edwards, Michael, 31
Eldon, Mary, 55
Ellis, 21
Ellis, Henry, 75
Emmet, Robert, 79
Ennis, 58
Enniskillen, 21, 61, 86
Enniskillen, Cole, earl of, 12, 18, 26, 29, 33
Erris, lord, 74
Erskine, 43, 45, 46, 52, 58, 59, 63
Esmonde, John, M.D., 17
Esmonde, Thomas, sir, 19
Eustace, general, 54
Eves, Benjamin, 8
Executions, 35

F., 55
Fagan, Michael, 44
'Fall of Underwald,' 38
Faris, W., captain, 40
Farrell, 78, 82-84
Farrell, James, 85; Patrick, 80

Feris, James, 8, 15, 23, 31, 39, 43, 49, 56, 63, 70, 71, 76, 83
Fermanagh, militia of, 28, 85
Ferrar, major, 81
Fifeshire Fencibles, 8
Finglas, 29, 67
Finlay, banker, 81
Finnerty, 82, 85
Finney, 81
Fitzgerald, captain, 48
Fitzgerald, colonel, 39
Fitzgerald, Edward, lord, 16, 17
Fitzgerald, Edward, of Newpark, Wexford, 15, 18, 19, 39, 61, 65
Flannagan, 27, 37
Flannagan, Joseph, 87
Flannery, ——, Rev., 73
Flattelly, 23
Flattery, 87
Fleming, 79, 82, 83, 85
Flint, 72, 78, 80, 82-84, 86
Foley, Catherine, 76
Foote, 81
Forde, Bryan, 32, 54-57, 63, 66, 78
Fort George, 82
French, F., 23
Frenchman, 71
French officers, 21
French prisoners, 14, 82
F——y, 7

G. M., 26
G. M. J., 29
Gahan, Philip, 11
Gallaher, 5
Galway, 58
Gardner, James, 58, 74, 83
Garnett, 17
Gavin, James, 30
Geraghty, informer, 19
Geraghty, Michael, 28
Gerraghty, 36
Gibbons, T., 76
Giffard, 75, 77, 78
Gilbert, William, publisher, 72
Ginoud, 53
Glasgow, 18
Gleeson, sergeant, 20
G. M., 26
G. M. I., 29, 30, 33
Godfrey, 12, 17
Godfrey, justice, 87

Godfrey, Philip, 23, 51
Gore, Daniel, 44
Gorges, 51
Goulding, G., 73
Graham, captain, 66
Grandy, Richard, 69, 73, 86
Grattan, Mrs., 32
Greenshields, W., 41, 42
Greenshiels, 58
Grey, 4-17, 19, 20-29, 30-39, 40-49, 51-59, 60, 83
Griffith, 86

Hacketstown, 42, 45
Haggarty, 21
Halpen, Halpin, 48, 83
Hamburg, 81
Hamilton, 6, 11, 86
Hamilton, Lodwick, 20
Hamilton, R., 4
Hamilton, Sackville, 2, 71
Handfield, colonel, 19
Hanlon, Anne, 79, 80, 81, 83-86-88
Hanlon, John, 8. 19, 37-39, 40-49, 50-59, 60-69, 70-79, 81, 84
Harberton, lord, 32, 54, 55, 66
Hardimens, 32
Harding, ——, M.D., 27, 30, 44
Harding, Robert, 22, 25
Hardy, E., 86
Harpur, 5, 32, 50
Harpur, R., 45
Hart, John W., 86
Harvey, W. D., 81
Hassett, Jeremiah, 4, 6, 8, 9, 11, 14
Hayden, 54, 76
Hayes, 5
Hayes, Edward, 66
Hearn, ——, M.D., 27
Hepenstall, captain, 80
Herbert, Richard, 19
Hermione, ship, 83
Heron, Isaac, 44, 45
Hide, prisoner, 60, 61
Higgins, Francis, 9, 16, 46
Higgins, Michael, 44
Highlanders, 53
Hill, Dudley, 52
Hill, George, sir, 4, 13, 35
Hill, James, 45-48, 70
Hill, John, 70
Hill, Mary, 70

INDEX I.

Hill, Philip, 46, 58, 60, 70
Hill, William, 46, 70
Hills, 22, 25, 27, 30, 43-48, 52-59, 60-69, 70
Holmes, 23, 83
Holyhead, 31
Horsley, 80
Hospital, co. Limerick, 84
Houston, 35
Howley, 80
Hughes, 53, 64, 67, 83
Hughes, John, 66
Hume, 77
Hume, W. H., 86
Hunt, apothecary, 15, 65, 88
Hutchinson, James, 18
Hutton, lieutenant, 24
Hyde, 15
H., F., 16
H., J. W., 10
H., W. A., 78

I., G. M., 29
Indies, West, 82
Information, 82
Informers, 41, 63, 75, 77, 80
Irish Office, 86

Jackson, colonel, 27
Jackson, Hugh, 19
Jackson, prisoner, 19
Jackson, Thomas, 67
Jacob, 81
James, William, alderman, 16, 21, 25, 77
Jenkinson, John, 61
Jennings, 16
Jennings, ——, Rev., 31
Jennings, Richard, 30
Johnston, alias Reid, 17
Johnston, alias Smith, 8
Jones, colonel, 43
Jones, J., 83
Jones, Richard, 81
Jordan, Richard, 63
Jordan, sergeant, 76, 87
Joyce, 9, 20
Joyce, Edward, 4, 15
Joyce, Patrick, 8
Joyces, 11, 12
J. W. *See* W. J.

K., 30, 59, 82
Kane, 5

Kane, Charles, 84
Karlan, 87
Kavanagh, 5
Kearney, John, 44, 66
Kearney, Thomas, 29
Keating, Mary, 29
Keevan, Connor, 81
Kelaher, 12
Kelly, 70
Kelly, John, 28, 29, 30-36, 39, 40-42, 44, 45, 48, 49, 51, 52, 55-59, 60, 62, 63-69, 70
Kellys, 29
Kennedy, 75
Keogh, 85
Keogh, J., 63
Kernan, 86
Kerr, 5
Kervan, John, 4
Kiernan, apothecary. *See* Hunt
Kiernan, Farrell, 77
Kilcullen, 15
Kildare, 51, 54-56, 70, 85
Kildare, militia of, 9
Kilkenny, 24, 75
Killala, dean of, 16
Killaloe, bishop of. *See* Knox
Killeshandra, cavalry of, 40
Kilmainham, county Dublin, 12, 13-15, 17, 23, 32, 33, 38, 45, 54, 69, 84, 87
Kilpatrick, 44, 48
King, colonel, 73, 82, 85
King, Thomas, 81
King's county, 87
Kinsley, 17
Kirwan, 6, 11
Knox, 75
Knox, William, bishop of Killaloe and Derry, 77, 82
Kohan, F., 79

L., 82
L., M., 78, 79
Lacy, 86
Lake, general, 39
Lambart, George, Rev., 25
Lardner, James, 19
La Roche, 21
Lauder, 87
Laverty, Henry, 48
Lawler, alias Wright, 15, 29, 43, 64, 72, 76
Leahy, 51

INDEX I.

Leake, William, surgeon, 17
Lee, John, 37; M., 43
Leech, 19
Lees, 11
Lees, J., 15, 16
Leitrim, militia of, 43
Leixlip, 18, 54, 84
Lenehan, 16
Lennan, Bryan, 11, 23, 44
Lennan, Edward, 60, 62
Lennan, Lennon, 12, 13, 38, 66
Lennon, Thomas, 25
Lewis, Anne, 49
Limerick, 20, 22, 39, 48, 56, 57, 60, 65, 72, 84
Lindsay, 7, 8, 12, 21-28
Lindsay, J., 32, 64
Lisbon, 32
Little, Thomas, 70
Liverpool, 81, 82
Logan, 11, 24
Logan, W., 75
Long, 82
Long, Francis, 73
London, 48
Londonderry, earl of, 74, 83
Londonderry, regiment of, 49
Longfield, colonel, 8
Longford, 79
Longueville, lord, 61
Lord lieutenant, 1798, 16 ; 1799, 37
Loughrea, 81
Louth, militia of, 21
Lowry, 4, 5, 7, 11, 13-15
Lowther, R., 69
Luttrell, Mr., 15

M., 75, 84
Mac Allaster, 13
Mac Anally, 13
Mac Cabe, 80, 83
Mac Cann, 5, 8, 10
Mac Carry, 6, 7
Mac Cartney, ——, M.D., 61
Mac Cawly, Denis, 9
Mac Cawly, sergeant, 20
Mac Clelland, Baron, 84
Mac Cue, 10
Mac Dermott, 5, 81, 83
Mac Donald, T., 17
Mac Donnell, Alexander, 44
Mac Donnell, colonel, 42

Mac Dowall, 42-44, 46-48
Mac Dowall, Hamilton, 42, 49
Mac Fillan, 16, 20, 35
Mac Gowan, Charles, 66
Mac Guckin, James, 34, 38, 41, 43, 51, 66, 73, 83
Mac G., 27, 44, 76, 79, 86
Mac Kay, sergeant, 82
Mac Kenzie, 14
Mac Kenzie, Alexander, 25
Mac Loughlin, Hugh, 32
Mac Manus, 30
Mac Naghten, 16
Mac Neven, W. J., 72
Mac Nevin, Andrew, 6, 42, 51
Magan, Francis, 46, 72, 74
Magin, J., 19
Magowan, 5
Magrath, 13
Mahaffy, 80
Mahon, Darcy, 4, 7, 12, 14, 30, 31
Mahon, John, 31
Mahon, Ross, 32
Mallow, 57, 68, 75
Mallow, James, 71, 75, 81
Man, isle of, 84
Man of War, co. Dublin, 17, 79
Manders, Joshua, 18
Manders, Richard, alderman, lord mayor, Dublin, 26, 27, 30, 36, 53, 67, 69
Mangan, William, informer, 36
Markey, 54
Marsden, Alexander, 20, 27, 32, 35, 41, 43-45, 47, 48, 57, 64, 70, 72-79, 81-83, 85-87
Marshall, Robert, 8, 9, 28, 30, 32, 38, 60
Martin, 19
Martin, Bell, 5
Martin, ——, Rev., 17
Mathew, lord, 62
Maynooth, 82
Mayo, sheriff of, 31
Mayrick, general, 58
Medlicott, 5, 15
Mernagh, 87
Merrett, 85
M., G., 26
Middleton, 61
Mitchell, 4-10, 11-19, 20-28, 39, 41-44, 46-49, 51-59, 60-65, 66
M., L., 78, 79
Mohill, Leitrim, 26

INDEX I.

Monaghan, 12, 86
Monasterevan, 57-66
Moncks, John, 14
Monk, 33
Monks, 11, 12, 28, 31
Montgomery Mills, 19
Moore, sergeant, 39
Moran, 27
Morgan. *See* Murray
Moroney, William, 62
Morris, Mrs., 6, 7, 9, 10
Mumford, Mumford, Lewis, 43, 52, 58, 59, 63
Murdock, 5, 6
Murdock, George, 11
Murphy, 35, 48, 82-86
Murphy, James, 44
Murray, ensign, 17
Murray or Morgan, J., 83
Murray, William, 86
Musgrave, Richard, sir, 41, 43, 45, 47, 49, 50, 53-56, 58, 60, 61, 63-65, 67

N., 26, 38, 42, 48, 49
Naas, 16, 17, 43, 78, 79, 80, 81, 83, 85, 87
Naughton, major, 34
Naul, 81
Needham, general, 20
Neil, John, 67
Neilson, A., 12
Neligan, ——, Rev., 74, 85
Nesbitt, captain, 49
Neville, 49
Newell, E. J., 4-6, 10
Newry, 21
Newtownards, 20
Newtownbarry, 76
Newtownmountkennedy, 42
Nicholls, 6, 14
Nicholson, 32, 78
Noble, 30
Norbury, lord, 67
Norman, Robert, 30
Nowlan, 29, 55
Nugent, 6, 17, 22, 23, 78, 81, 83
Nugent, Joseph, 8, 43, 45, 53

OBre, 10
O'Brien, James, 5, 7, 8, 18, 19, 20-29, 30-39, 40, 41, 42, 46, 54
O'Brien, Mrs., 67
O'Connor, Arthur, 13, 15
O'Hara, Henry, 66
O'Kean, 24, 26

Oliver, Silver, M.P., 72
O'Neill, 16, 17, 19, 20-28, 39, 41-44, 46, 47, 49, 50-51, 56-59, 63, 65, 68, 69, 71
O'Reilly, Bryan, 62
Ormsby, James, 20
Owen, 75

P., 74, 81
Page, Samuel, 79
Paine, 78, 79, 81
Parnell, John, sir, 29
Parrot, John, 81
Partland, 42
Patrickson, William, 7
Pelham, Thomas, 2, 8, 9, 11
Perrott, 80
Perry, captain, 35
Phaire, colonel, 76, 87
Phelan, 20, 21
Plunkett, William, 24
Pole, W. W., 38, 41
Police, 85
Pollen, W., 49
Pollock, John, 6, 7, 10, 14, 16, 18, 20, 21, 24-28, 30, 33, 38, 40, 44, 57-59, 60, 73, 75, 76, 78, 81, 85-87
Pope, Thomas, 56, 57
Portaferry, 48, 59, 70
Power, R., 63
Poyle, 11, 14
Prendergast, captain, 70
Prendergast, P., 61
'Press, beauties of,' 60
Price, 32
Price, Nicholas, 34, 58
Provost, F., 14

Queen's county, 30, 41
Quigley, 13, 75, 80

Rafferall, 61
Ram, 41
Rathdrum, 17, 61
Rawson, captain, 53, 66, 68
Rea, 6
Redfern, 57
Redmond, 80
Regiment, ninth, 87; seventy-ninth, 78
Reilly, John, 78
Reynolds, Thomas, 18, 21, 23, 25, 26, 31
Richardson, J., 12
Ringsend, Dublin, 22

1 H

Robson, Stephen, 13
Rochford, 14
Rochfort, Gustavus, 36
Rockbrook, Kilkenny, 75
Roscommon, 9, 12, 20
Ross, 37, 82
Ross, Charles, sir, 73
Rossmore, lord, 42
Rourke, 84
Rown, W., 88
Ruddle, 78
Russell, 82
Ryan, 80; D. F., 16

Saintfield, co. Down, 32
St. George, colonel, 54
St. John, William, 87
Sampson, 14
Sandys, William, major, 5, 13, 16, 18, 21
Scotch revenue cutter, 20, 21
Shaw, 5
Shane's castle, 47
Shannon, earl of, 57, 68
Shee, 27
Shepherd, 49
Sheares, trial of, 73
Simmons, lieutenant, 18
Sirr, Henry Charles, major, 5, 6, 10-13, 15, 17-19, 24, 26, 31, 32, 36-39, 41, 43-46, 48, 49, 54, 55, 64, 66, 67, 72-79, 80, 81, 83-86
Skeffington, C., 10
Sligo, 23
Sligo, marquis of, 76
Smart, Thomas, 77, 78
Smith, 4-9, 75, 78
Smith, alias Johnston, 8
Smith, ensign, 28
Smith, Guy, 77
Smyth, captain, 19, 21
Smyth, Ralph, 88
Sneyd, 77
Sproule, 15, 17, 18, 20, 21, 30
Stafford, 80
Sterling, captain, 4, 6, 11, 14, 18
Stewart, George, surgeon-general, 9, 17, 37, 51, 65, 72, 85
Stockdale, 60, 66
Stockdale, John, London, 73
Stuart, C., 6, 13, 15, 18, 19
Surgeon-general. *See* Stewart
Sutherland, adjutant, 78

Sutherland, captain, 82
Sutherland, lieutenant, 80
Swan, W. B., 7, 11, 13, 16, 25, 51, 71, 77
Sweeny, 12

Taaffe, 13
Taggart, 20
Talbot, Edward, 77
Tallant, 36
Tandy, Napper, 37
Taton, major, 80
Tay Fencibles, 58
Teeling, 21
Teeling, C., 81
Telegraph, 10, 74
Thackary, major, 23
Tiernay, Owen, 30
Tipperary, 43, 70
Tone, M., 40
Tone, Theobald Wolfe, 23
Toole, 81
Tottenham, Loftus, 73, 86
Townley, J., 34
Townley, Thomas, 58, 74, 83
Townsend, 15
Trainor, 14
Tralee, 88
Travers, 9, 10, 12, 13-23
Treasury, advances of money from, 3
Trench, Frederick, 17
Trevor, Edward, M.D., 11-13, 26, 29, 32, 33, 38, 45, 46, 57, 59, 60, 65, 69, 70, 72, 80, 85
Trim, Meath, 12, 54
Troy, 86
Tucker, 22
Turner, 41, 59, 75
Tuttle, sergeant, 41
T. W. *See*, W. T.
Tyler, Thomas, 12
Tyrawley, lord, 57, 66
Tyrrell, 5, 51

'Underwald, fall of,' 38
Uniacke, colonel, 35, 38, 39, 40, 42, 48, 54, 56
Usher, sergeant, 12

Vaughan, 14, 33
Verner, 5
Vignoles, ——, Rev., 11

Wainright, captain, 69, 76

INDEX I.

W., A. H., 78
Waldron, 33, 35
Wall, Joseph, 16, 18, 21, 24, 28, 32
Wallace, W., 34
Walsh, J., 12
Ward, John, alias Jenkinson, 61
Ward, Judith, alias Carr, 51
Warren, 10
Warren, B., 16
Warren, R., 31, 36
Waterford, 35, 39, 63, 67
Waterford, marquis of, 27, 67
Watkins, 5, 8, 11, 14, 16, 20, 22, 26, 27, 29, 31, 33, 35, 37, 40
Welsh, 12
Wexford, 20, 41, 42, 75
Wheatley, Hugh, 7-9, 43-49, 51, 52
Whelan, 62
Whitehaven, 14
Whitley. *See* Wheatley
Whitly, 54
Wickham, William, 71, 72, 78, 80, 83, 84, 85

Wicklow, 7, 12, 14, 28, 40, 49, 56, 69, 74, 76, 82
Wigelsworth, 19
Williams, captain, 23
Wilson, 12
Wilson, E. D., 41
Wilson, Edward, 85
Wingfield cavalry, 24
Wolfe, colonel, 76, 85
Wood, George, 81
Woodward, R., Rev., 75
Workington, 82
Workington, Alexander, 7, 14, 19, 24, 30, 35, 41, 46, 51, 60, 67, 71, 72, 80
Wright, William, alias Lawler, 15, 23, 29, 40, 51, 64, 72, 76
W., T., 26, 40, 44, 58, 74, 82

York, duke of, 53
York, regiment of, 17
Young, Charles, 58, 74, 83

INDEX II.

LETTERS, DOCUMENTS, ETC.

P. 89—232.

Abercromby, Ralph, sir, 126
Agar, Charles, archbishop of Cashel, 164-168, 178, 182
Alexander, Henry, M.P., 170, 184, 187, 197
Alexander, Joseph, 115
America, 166, 168, 178, 210, 212, 218
Amsterdam, 112
Antrim, 116, 131, 134, 135, 140
Ards, Ulster, 136, 139
Argyle fencibles, 117
Arklow, 125, 126, 131, 133, 136, 141
Armagh, 116, 128, 150, 156, 177
Arms, searches for, 154
Ascendancy, 147
Assassination, 151, 179
Attainder, bills of, 146
Attorney-general, John Toler, 145, 200

B., 144
Bacon, Thomas, 125
Balbriggan, 92, 96
Ballycotton, 98
Ballynahinch, 134, 136, 138, 139
Balscadden, 92
Baltinglass, 136
Bangor, 110
Bank-notes, 156
Bantry bay, 106, 115, 153, 158, 177, 183
Bar, Irish, 202
Barrett, 184
Bartera, Mayo, 190
Belfast, 98, 103, 104, 106, 108, 110, 111, 113, 131, 134, 139, 148, 184

Bell, 110, 112
Bellamont, lord, 200, 201
Belmore, lord, 200
Beresford, John, 172, 184, 189, 203, 212
Beresford, Marcus, 116
Berkley, 110
Blaris, 110, 117, 134
Bond, Oliver, 143, 144, 214, 215, 219
Borough interest, Ireland, 147, 148, 188
Boyd, 113
Bravery of Irish, 136
Bredalbane Fencibles, 117
Bremen, 121
Bristol, earl of. *See* Hervey
British connection with Ireland, 170
Bruce, 114
Bullock, co. Dublin, 92
Burke, corporal, 109, 113
Burn, Michael, 116
Burnside, 106, 184
Byrne, Edward, 114
Byrne, Patrick, 116
Byrne, William, 143, 144, 214, 215

Camden, America, battle at, 228
Camden, earl, lord lieutenant, Ireland, 102, 119, 133, 137, 140, 146, 195, 226
„   „   letters from, 128, 132, 137, 138, 141, 228
Campbell, general, 141
Canon, captain, 103
Carhampton, Luttrell, earl of, report by, 91

Carleton, Hugh, chief justice, 144, 190
,, ,, letter from, 201
Carlow, 117, 126, 131, 163, 180
Carnew, 127, 131, 133
Carnot, M., 209
Carrickburne, Wexford, 131
Carrickfergus, 99
Carysfort, lord, 201
Cashel, archbishop of. *See* Agar
Castlereagh, Robert Stewart, viscount, 136, 139, 144, 145, 146, 162, 163, 169, 170, 172, 174, 176, 183, 188-190, 197, 199, 203, 204, 206, 209, 216-219, 227, 231
,, letters from, 127, 130, 133, 185, 139
Catholic clergy, Ireland, 175
,, ,, proposed provision for, 195, 206, 207
Catholic committee, 175
Catholic emancipation, 167, 171, 181
Catholic prelates, 195, 206, 207
Catholics, Ireland, 106, 107, 113, 126, 147, 149, 150, 166, 192
Catholics, Ireland, representation of, 201
Cavan, lord, 103
Champagné, general, 131, 139
Charlemont, James, earl of, 121, 200, 211
Charleston, America, 228
Charost, colonel, 190, 191
Chatham, lord, 138, 140
Chetwynd, lord, 200
Chouannerie, 171
Church, established, Ireland, 173, 175, 182, 185, 186
Clanrickard, lord, 134
Clanwilliam, lord, 200
Clare, John Fitzgibbon, earl of, 127, 144, 163-168, 178, 179, 181, 182, 191, 192, 201, 209, 217, 219, 220
Clarke, 110, 111
Clergy, Ireland, 121
Clonfert, bishops of. *See* Hamilton; Young
Coals, supply of, Ireland, 178
Cockran, lieutenant, 115
Code, criminal, 185, 188
Cole, 202
Commander-in-Chief, Ireland, 138
Commerce, Ireland, 185, 188
Committees, secret, 104, 162-190, 223, 224
Commons, house of, Ireland, 224, 230
Confiscations, Ireland, 180, 184

Coningham, 110
Coningham, Lenox. 107
Connaught, 134, 167
Conolly, Louisa, 127
Conolly, Thomas, 197, 203
Constitution, English, 188, 189
Convention, Ireland, projected, 148
Cooke, Edward, 120, 125, 144, 163, 183, 216, 217, 219, 220, 222, 223, 227
,, ,, letters from, 119, 120, 135, 141, 142
Coote, general, 118
Cope, colonel, 127
Cork, 98, 99, 114
,, bishop of. *See* Moylan
,, gazette, 109
Cornwallis, marquis, lord lieutenant, Ireland, 129, 137, 141, 142, 145, 146, 191, 192, 202, 203, 213, 216, 218, 222, 223, 228
,, letter from. 192
Corry, Isaac, 169
'Courier,' London, 226, 227
Cove island, Cork, 103
Covenanters, 115
Crawford, 137
Creevy, 134
Cumber, 115
Cummings, 110
Cuthbert, 112, 113

Dalkey, Dublin, 92
Dalrymple, William, general, 102
,, ,, letter from, 103
,, ,, letter to, 118
Dalton, captain, 114
Danby, lord, 170
Defenders, 107-111, 114, 150, 157
Derry, 108, 115, 139
,, bishop of. *See* Hervey
Dickson, William, bishop of Down, 200
Dillon, lord, 167, 177, 179, 182
Directory, France, 144
Dissenting clergy, Ireland, 207
Dobbs, Francis, 210, 216, 222
Domingo, St., 145
Donaghadee, 110, 112
Donaldson, 110
Donegal, 108, 127
Down, 116, 134 136, 139, 140, 199

Down, bishop of. *See* Dickson
Dry, T., 104
Dublin, 91, 93, 101, 113, 114, 125, 128, 131, 132, 137, 140, 147, 148, 155, 180, 198, 218
 „ castle, 119, 124, 176, 217
 „ county, 130
Duff, general, 136
Duignan, 114
Duncannon, 133, 136
Dundas, general, 131, 133, 136
Dungannon, 113, 131
Dunleary, co. Dublin, 92
Dunsany, lord, 201

Edinburgh, 127
Education, national, Ireland, 182, 185, 187
Elliot, William, 132, 133, 139, 142
 „ letters from, 125, 143, 162
 „ letters to, 135, 137
Emmet, Thomas Addis, 147, 162, 216, 224, 226, 227, 231
 „ „ examinations before select committees, 176-190
England, constitution of, 183
 „ forces from, 128-130, 136, 140
 „ friends of, 114
 „ influence of, 147
 „ invasion of, 128, 148
Enniscorthy, 127, 131, 133
Enniskillen, Cole, earl of, 200
Europe, relation of Ireland to, 149
Eustace, general, 126
Excommunications, 208
Executions, military, 117, 180

Faris, 113
Farmers, Ireland, 114
Farnham, lord, 200, 201
Fawcit, general, 127
Finerty, Peter, 120
Fingal, lord, 126
Fitzgerald, Edward, lord, 116, 119, 120, 126, 127, 145, 163, 189, 211, 212, 214, 231
Fitzgerald, James, prime sergeant, 202
Fitzwilliam, lord, 149, 156, 171, 226
Fortescue, 202
Fort George, 228

Foster, John, speaker, House of Commons, Ireland, 119, 120, 144, 169-176, 183, 185, 187, 188, 198, 203
France and Ireland, 106, 107, 109, 111-113, 115, 121, 126, 128, 131, 135, 136, 144, 149, 153, 156, 158, 159, 160, 161, 164, 167, 168, 170, 174, 177, 179, 182, 183, 190, 210, 218, 220
 „ soldiers from, *See* Killala
French, Arthur, 189, 202
Funerals, engagements at, 114

Gadsden, Christopher, 228
Gallican clergy, 207
Galway, 134, 183
George III., 137, 191-193
Germany, 187
Glandore, lord, 201
Glentworth, lord, 182, 202
Godwin, William, 108
Gordon, 113
Gordon, Alexander, 104-107
Gordon, John, 104, 116
Gorey, 125, 127, 133
Government, English, provisional, 191
Graham, 114
Granard, earl of, 200
Grattan, Henry, 113, 120, 175
Green colours, 105
Green flag, 107
Greville, 117
Griffith, Richard, 140
 „ „ letter from, 198
Grinsted, east, 208
Grogan, 145
Guernsey, 112

Haislett, 114
Hamburg, 160, 220
Hamilton, Dr., 115
Hamilton, George, sir, 115
Hamilton, Hugh, bishop, 193
Hanover, 121
Harvey, Bagenal, 136, 145
Hay, captain, 136
Hervey, Frederick, earl of Bristol, bishop of Derry, letter from, 121
Hewett, John, major-general, 102
Hill, George, sir, 139
Holland, 178

INDEX II. 247

House-burnings, Ireland, 161, 180
Howth, 92, 96
Huson, James, 115
Humbert, 210
Hussey, Thomas, bishop of Waterford, 176

Imprisonments, arbitrary, Ireland, 161
Indemnity act, Ireland, 177
Independence, Irish, 178
Informers, 149
Insurrection, Ireland, 131-133, 180
    "   "   act, 150, 177
Ireland, commerce of, 178
    " condition of people, 187
    " geographical position of, 230
    " invasion of, 131, 156, 158
    " separation from England, 108, 147, 149, 155, 156, 161, 173, 178, 179, 183, 185, 209, 210
Irishmen in army and navy, 99
    " in foreign services, 155
    " United. *See* United Irishmen
Ivers, 163

Jackson, Henry, 231
Johnson, Henry, general, 126, 130, 131, 133, 136, 137
Jones, captain, 131

Kean, 139
Kelly, William, 194
Kenmare, lord, 175
Kennedy, Samuel, 108-111
Kerry, knight of, 199
Kesh, Kish, the, 93
Kilbeggan, 175
Kilcock, 142
Kildare, 114, 130, 131, 140, 180
Kilkenny, 114, 127, 131
Killala, bishop of. *See* Stock
Killala, French soldiery at, 190
Killiney, co. Dublin, 92, 93, 96
Kilmaine, lord, 200
Kilmainham, co. Dublin, 216, 218, 222
Kilwarden, Arthur Wolfe, lord, 144, 163, 165, 179, 182, 183
King, Rufus, 228
King's county, 124

Kinsale, 99
Knocktopher, 202
Knox, John, 190, 191
Knox, John, brigadier-general, 102, 131, 145

Lake, Gerard, general, 103, 110, 126, 129, 131, 136, 137, 140, 159
    "   " letter from, 117
Landlords, Ireland, 167, 187, 190
Langrishe, Hercules, sir, 203
La Touche, 169
Leinster, 155, 167, 181
    " duke of, 200
Leitrim, 125
Lifford, 108
Limerick, 109, 111
Lions, 115
Lisburn, 110, 116
Lisle, 160
Liverpool, 108
Loftus, William, general, 126, 127, 133, 136
Londonderry, 127
Lords, house of, Ireland, 163, 188, 200, 201
Lord Lieutenant, Ireland, 119, 138, 140
Louth, 111
Lowrie, Alexander, 116

Mac Cabe, 110, 113
Mac Cracken, 110, 111, 113
Mac Donald, Dr., 112
Mac Donald, sergeant, 114
Mac Murdoch, 112
Mac Naghten, Edward, 224
Mac Neven, William James. M.D., 119. 144, 147, 162, 209, 216, 220, 222, 224, 225
    "   " examinations before secret committees, 163-176
    "   " account of treaty with Government, 208-232
Maghera, 140
Maitland, Robert, 116
Marksmen, 175
Marsden, Alexander, 227
Marshall, Robert, 131, 162
    "   " letter from, 124
Martin, 108
Maynooth college, 195, 206
Meath, 127
Mémoire from Ireland to France, 164

Mid-Lothian, 127
Military, seduction of, 111
Militia, 111, 124, 134
Missionaries, political, 111
Moate, 175
Monaghan, 117
Monarchy, views on, 149
Money, public, 117
Moody, 108
Moore, John, general, 133, 136
Mountcashel, lord, 200
Mountnorris, lord, 200
Moylan, Francis, bishop of Cork, 207, 208
  ,,   ,, letters from, 194, 205
Munroe, general, 139
Munster, 134, 167

Needham, Francis, general, 131, 133, 136
Neilson, Samuel, 108-111, 113, 226
Newell, E. J., 104, 105, 107
Newspapers, governmental, 224, 225
Newtownards, 132, 134, 136, 139
Newtownbarry, Wexford, 131, 136, 139
Nicols, 114
'Northern Star,' newspaper, 108, 115
Norbury, John Toler, lord, 227
Nugent, George, major-general, 103, 131, 134, 135, 138, 139, 141, 222

Oaths, 108, 115, 134, 188
O'Beirne, Thomas L., bishop, 193
O'Connor, Arthur, 103, 119, 120, 143, 147, 162, 216, 224
O'Donnell, 198
'Olive Branch,' ship, 171
Omagh, 108
Orange associations, 125, 150, 157, 163, 177, 212, 228
Ormsby, captain, 124
Orr, 110
Orr, Mrs., Belfast, 105
Osborne, Rowley, 113
Ossory, bishop of. *See* O'Beirne

Pacification, Ireland, 135
Paine, Thomas, 104
Paris, 112, 160, 220
Parkgate, 108

Parliament Ireland, 1797, 118; 1798, 142
  ,,   ,, constitution of, 188
  ,,   ,, debates in, 1799, 197, 203
  ,, *See* also Reform
Parnell, John, sir, 169, 189, 173, 174, 719, 199, 203
Parsons, Laurence, sir, 197, 202
Peep of day boys, 151
Pelham, Thomas, 117
  ,,   ,, letters from, 99, 101, 118, 121, 124, 125, 127, 128, 130, 132, 133, 135, 138, 139, 141-143, 162, 191-194, 197, 198, 201-203, 205, 207
  ,,   ,, letters to, 103, 119, 120,
  ,,   ,, memoranda by, 1797, 104
Penal laws, Ireland, 161, 186, 188
Pensions and places, Ireland, 175
Pery, lord, 290
Philanthropic society, Dublin, 104
Pikes, 105, 174
Pitt, William, 129, 134, 137, 138, 140, 209
Plunkett, W. C., 108, 198, 200, 224, 225
Pollock, John, 119
Ponsonby, George, 171, 197-203
Poor in Ireland, state of, 185
Portland, duke of, 117, 129, 132, 133, 228
  ,,   ,, letters from, 191, 193, 207
Potts, 112
Powerscourt, lord, 200, 201
Presbyterians, Ireland, 107, 147, 192
'Press,' newspaper, 120
Priests, Catholic, Ireland, 186
Prisoners, State, Ireland, 143
Property, landed, Ireland, 114
Protestants, Ireland, 126, 147, 166
Publications, inflammatory, 115

Quarters, free, Ireland, 140, 180
Queen's county, 120
Quigly, James, Rev., 116
Quit-rents, 156

Randalstown, 131
Rathcoole, 124

Reform, parliamentary, Ireland, efforts for, 104, 113, 147, 148, 156, 167, 171, 172, 181, 185, 201
Reinhardt, M., 220
Religion, freedom of, 166
Rents of land, Ireland, 185, 187
Republic, Irish, projected, 106, 107, 148, 149, 175, 185
Revolutionists, England, 157, 170
„ Ireland, 180, 181, 184, 185
Reynolds, Thomas, 143, 211
Richardson, 111
Rinabelly, 99
Rochambeau, 168, 178
Roche, colonel, 126
Roche's bay 98
Rochfort, lord, 304
Roscommon, 202
Rose, George, 117
Ross, 127, 130, 131, 133, 136, 141, 211
Russell, captain, 113

S. J., 108
Saintfield, 134, 138
Sampson, William, 143
Sassanagh, term, 166
Schools, Ireland, 187
Scotland, 110-112, 114
Scrabo, 134
Secrecy, obligation of, 149
Secretary, chief, Ireland, 142
Servants, 114
Shannahan, 109-112
Sheares, John, 180, 189
Shee, George, sir, letter from, 202
Sheerness, mutiny at, 118
Simpson, 114
Sinclair, 113
Skeffington, 109, 110, 112
Smith, Edward, general, 102
Smith, William, 199, 200
Society, corresponding, London, 108
Somers, lord, 170
Songs, distribution of, 115
Spain, 160
„ loan from, 175
'Star, Northern,' 139
Stark, major, 127
Statute, mendacious, 226

Stewart, Henry, 115
Stewart, James, sir, 133-135
Stock, Joseph, bishop, 190
Stokes, 108
Strangford lough, 110, 132
Stuart, James, Fort George, 228
Sweetman, John, 216, 231
Swilly lough, 115

Taghmon, 131
Talleyrand, 220
Tallow, 186
Tandy, James, 119
Tandy, James Napper, 119
Teeling, 110
Texel, 161
Thellwall, 110
Tighe, 197
Tithes, Ireland, 121, 175, 182, 185, 186
Toasts, Irish, 109
Toler, John. *See* Attorney; Norbury
Toome, 131
Torture, use of, 161, 180, **212**
Treasury, London, 117
Trinidad, 194
Troops from England, 135
Troy, John T., archbishop of Dublin, 206
Turner, Samuel, 116
Tyrone, 107
Tyrone, lord, 199

Ulster, 111, 136, 138, 140, 142, 153, 177, 181, 184
Union with England, 145, 193, 195, 204, 206, 209, 213
„ debates on, 1799, 197
United Irishmen, 104, 105, 110, 147, 152-155, 163, 168, 180, 185, 190, 209, 229

Vendée, la, 171
Vesey, major, 130
Vicars, 120
Viceroyalty, Ireland, 141
Vincent, St., lord, 118
Vinegar hill, Wexford, 131, 211

Walker, Abraham, 116
Walpole, Lambert, Theodore, colonel, 127, 130
War office, Dublin, 146
Waterford, 127, 131, 133
Watson, 137
Wexford, 125-128, 130-133, 135, 136, 138, 140, 163, 166
Wicklow, 131, 148, 180, 222
Wiffen, 117
William III., 170
Willis, 114

W., I., 119

Yelverton, lord, 201
Yeomanry, Ireland, 116, 140
York, duke of, 129
  ,,   ,, letters to, 99, 101
  ,,   ,, report to, 91
Young, John, 110, 111
Young, Matthew, bishop of Clonfert, 192, 193, 198
  ,,   ,, letter from, 203

THE END.

CORRIGENDA.

Page 7, line 7, *for* Mr.,	*read* Mc
,, 10, ,, **14**, ,, O'Bren,	,, OBre
,, 16, ,, 31, ,, Fallen,	,, Fallin
,, 22, ,, 21, ,, Goaler,	,, Gaoler
,, 26, ,, 32, ,, R.	,, H.
,, 54, ,, 13, ,, Whitty,	,, Whitley
,, 70, ,, 33, ,, Coady,	,, Cody
,, 108, ,, 15, ,, April [*sic* in Ms.]	,, May
,, 110, ,, 33, ,, Berkley [*sic* in Ms.]	,, Berkley's

CATALOGUE:
HISTORIC LITERATURE OF IRELAND.
[SERIES OF WORKS PRINTED IN LIMITED NUMBER.]

In this series are printed original, contemporary writings, letters, and personal narratives in relation to Ireland and Irish affairs from authentic manuscripts in English, Irish and Continental archives. These documents supply important and interesting details not to be found in works hitherto published.

The volumes of the series are in the best style of typography, on fine, toned paper, in crown quarto size, illustrated with portraits and facsimiles.

The entire edition of any of the volumes of the series does not exceed two hundred copies; of some a much smaller number has been printed.

The following works have been completed and issued:—

HISTORY OF THE IRISH CONFEDERATION AND WAR IN IRELAND, 1641-1649. Seven Volumes.

CONTEMPORARY HISTORY OF AFFAIRS IN IRELAND, 1641-1652. Two parts and two volumes.

JACOBITE NARRATIVE OF WAR IN IRELAND, 1688-1691. One volume.

DOCUMENTS RELATING TO IRELAND, 1795-1804. One volume.

NARRATIVES OF THE DETENTION, LIBERATION, AND MARRIAGE OF MARIA CLEMENTINA STUART, STYLED QUEEN OF GREAT BRITAIN AND IRELAND. One volume.

"CREDE MIHI:" The Most Ancient Register of the Archbishops of Dublin before the Reformation. One volume.

In the Press: PAPERS CONNECTED WITH JACOBITES OF IRELAND.

From the London "ACADEMY."

"We know what the English had to say about the Irish, but we did not know what the Irish had to say about themselves. Any new light on Irish matters should be heartily welcomed on both sides of the channel which divides the two nations. To the Editor of these works, for his assistance in dispelling the darkness, are due the thanks of everyone interested in the affairs of the seventeenth century. Every student of English, as well as of Irish, History will turn with pleasure to these pages."

HISTORIC LITERATURE OF IRELAND.

Seven volumes, with portraits, plans, and facsimiles.

HISTORY OF THE IRISH CONFEDERATION AND THE WAR IN IRELAND, 1641—1649:

With Original Documents, Correspondence of the Confederation and of the Administrators of the English Government in Ireland, Contemporary Personal Statements, Memoirs, &c. Now for the first time printed from original manuscripts, edited by Sir John T. Gilbert, LL.D., F.S.A., M.R.I.A., late Secretary of the Public Record Office of Ireland; Author of a "History of the City of Dublin;" Editor of "Facsimiles of National MSS. of Ireland," published by command of Her Majesty, etc.

Hitherto no attempt had been made to collect or publish in their integrity such authentic original documents as still survive for the elucidation of the history of the Irish Confederation and its transactions in peace and war. To supply this want is the object of the present work, for which important materials, hitherto unprinted, have been obtained from archives in England, Ireland, and on the Continent.

Subscription, £10 for the seven volumes. Twenty-five copies of each volume are on extra large paper, similar to the Roxburghe Club books: Subscription, Three Guineas per volume.

A CONTEMPORARY HISTORY OF AFFAIRS IN IRELAND, FROM A.D. 1641 TO 1652.

An original Narrative, entitled "An Aphorismical Discovery of Treasonable Faction," including account of Oliver Cromwell's movements in Ireland. Now for the first time published. With numerous original letters and documents, hitherto unprinted, from the archives of the House of Lords, etc. Illustrated with portraits and facsimiles. Edited by Sir John T. Gilbert, LL.D.

In two parts and two volumes. Subscription, Four Guineas.

HISTORIC LITERATURE OF IRELAND.

A JACOBITE NARRATIVE OF THE WAR IN IRELAND, 1688—1691:

With illustrative letters and papers hitherto unpublished. Edited by Sir John T. Gilbert, LL.D.

This unique Jacobite Narrative, written soon after the events which form its subject, supplies information not elsewhere accessible on the affairs of Ireland, and in relation to many of the chief persons engaged in them at the period of the revolution of 1688. In the "Narrative" are also embodied expositions of the views and projects of the Irish adherents of the House of Stuart. The "Narrative," in its entirety, is now printed for the first time, and elucidated by the addition of contemporary diaries, letters and documents. Among these are the following:—Official List of the Jacobite Army in Ireland, with particulars of the regiments, names of officers, etc.; list of members and extracts from acts of the Parliament at Dublin in 1689; contemporary journals of the sieges of Limerick, 1690, 1691; plan of battle of Aughrim; articles of the treaty of Limerick; letters from James II., and Sarsfield, Earl of Lucan.

The illustrations comprise a reproduction of the rare portrait of Sarsfield, Commander-in-chief of the Jacobite forces in Ireland, with a facsimile of a letter from him; facsimiles from writings of the Jacobite Attorney-General, Sir Richard Nagle; Colonel William Wolseley; and the Duke de Lausun, Commander of French auxiliary troops in Ireland.

Complete in one volume: Subscription, £1 5s.

From the "ATHENÆUM."

"The 'Jacobite Narrative' is undoubtedly an acceptable contribution to the authentic materials for the history of Great Britain and Ireland at the period of the Revolution of 1688."

"An exceedingly interesting and valuable work."—"NOTES AND QUERIES."

From "THE ENGLISH HISTORICAL REVIEW."

"It is not merely for Irish history that these letters, diaries, state papers, and soforth are invaluable. In the years with which they are concerned English and Irish history continually influenced each other, and it, therefore, becomes almost imperative upon the English as upon the Irish historian of these troubled periods to consult these volumes."

HISTORIC LITERATURE OF IRELAND.

DOCUMENTS RELATING TO IRELAND, 1795-1804.

Official Account of Secret Service money in Ireland, from 1797 to 1804.—Governmental Correspondence and papers, from MSS. of Thomas Pelham, Earl of Chichester.—French soldiery at Killala.—Parliamentary debates on Legislative Union with Great Britain; etc. Edited by Sir John T. Gilbert, LL.D.

Illustrations: Portraits of Lord Edward Fitzgerald, Arthur O'Connor, Edward J. Newell, and passport from French soldiery at Killala, in 1798. In one volume: Subscription, £1 5s.

MARIA CLEMENTINA STUART, STYLED QUEEN OF GREAT BRITAIN AND IRELAND, 1719-1735:

Narratives of the detention, liberation and marriage of Princess Maria Clementina, mother of Prince Charles Edward Stuart, and of Henry Benedict Stuart, Cardinal of York. With documents hitherto unprinted. Illustrated with portrait and facsimiles. Edited by Sir John T. Gilbert, LL.D. Edition limited to one hundred and fifty copies. In one volume: Subscription, £1 5s.

"CREDE MIHI:" THE MOST ANCIENT REGISTER OF THE ARCHBISHOPS OF DUBLIN BEFORE THE REFORMATION:

Now for the first time printed. With illustrations. Edited by Sir J. T. Gilbert, LL.D. Edition limited to one hundred and twenty copies. In one volume: Subscription, £1 5s.

PAPERS CONNECTED WITH JACOBITES OF IRELAND.
In the Press.

Communications connected with the series to be addressed to the Secretary, Villa Nova, Blackrock, Dublin.

Subscriptions are to be remitted to the "Manager of the National Bank, College Green, Dublin," for the "Historic Publication Account."

www.ingramcontent.com/pod-product-compliance
Lightning Source LLC
Chambersburg PA
CBHW032055230426
43672CB00009B/1597